George Saintsbury, Archibald John Stuart-Wortley, H. A Macpherson

The Grouse

Natural History

George Saintsbury, Archibald John Stuart-Wortley, H. A Macpherson

The Grouse
Natural History

ISBN/EAN: 9783744704229

Printed in Europe, USA, Canada, Australia, Japan

Cover: Foto ©Thomas Meinert / pixelio.de

More available books at **www.hansebooks.com**

HOME LIFE.

THE GROUSE

NATURAL HISTORY
BY THE REV. H. A. MACPHERSON

SHOOTING
BY A. J. STUART-WORTLEY

COOKERY
BY GEORGE SAINTSBURY

WITH ILLUSTRATIONS BY A. J. STUART-WORTLEY AND A. THORBURN

LONDON
LONGMANS, GREEN, AND CO.
AND NEW YORK: 15 EAST 16th STREET
1894

PREFACE

THE design of the *Fur and Feather Series* is to present monographs, as complete as they can possibly be made, on the various English birds and beasts which are generally included under the head of Game.

Books on Natural History cover such a vast number of subjects that their writers necessarily find it impossible to deal with each in a really comprehensive manner ; and it is not within the scope of such works exhaustively to discuss the animals described, in the light of objects of sport. Books on sport, again, seldom treat at length of the Natural History of the furred and feathered creatures which are shot or otherwise taken ; and, so far as the Editor is aware, in no book hitherto published on Natural History or Sport has information been given as to the best methods of turning the contents of the bag to account.

Each volume of the present Series will, therefore, be devoted to a bird or beast, and will be divided into three parts. The Natural History of the species will first be given; it will then be considered from the point of view of sport; and the writer of the third division will assume that the creature has been carried to the larder, and will proceed to discuss it gastronomically. The origin of the animals will be traced, their birth and breeding described, every known method of circumventing and killing them—not omitting the methods employed by the poacher—will be explained with special regard to modern developments, and they will only be left when on the table in the most appetising forms which the delicate science of cookery has discovered.

It is intended to make the illustrations a prominent feature of the Series. The pictures in the present volume are after drawings by Mr. A. J. Stuart-Wortley and Mr. A. Thorburn. All of them, including the diagrams, have been designed under the supervision of the first-named.

ALFRED E. T. WATSON.

CONTENTS

NATURAL HISTORY OF THE GROUSE

By the Rev. H. A. Macpherson

SHOOTING THE GROUSE

By A. J. Stuart-Wortley

COOKERY OF THE GROUSE

By George Saintsbury

ILLUSTRATIONS

BY

A. J. STUART-WORTLEY AND A. THORBURN

(Reproduced by Messrs. André & Sleigh, Augerer & Göschl, Universal Process Company, and Walker & Boutall)

VARIOUS DIAGRAMS IN THE TEXT BY A. J. STUART-WORTLEY.

NATURAL HISTORY OF THE GROUSE

BY THE

REV. H. A. MACPHERSON

B

CHAPTER I

IN PRAISE OF THE GROUSE

It is hardly too much to say that the Red Grouse
enjoys a unique position among the members of the
feathered community. Certainly no other bird exacts
a similar amount of homage from its admirers, or
affords as large a share of enjoyment to sportsmen.
In these days of increasing taxation, it would go hard
with many of us Highland lairds if we had no grouse
moors from which to draw the rates which go to
support school boards and other luxuries exacted by
the oppressive democracy. Scotland is pre-eminently
the home of this splendid bird—a fact to which she
owes a very large portion of her material prosperity.
It was a happy hour when the Sassenach discovered
the pleasure to be gained from renting a Northern
grouse moor.

Until then the bird had existed only on sufferance,
persecuted by many enemies and little cared for by
anyone. It is true that its value as food was always

recognised ; but that circumstance only led to its increased pursuit in the days when Englishmen killed the 'pootes' as well as the parent bird in the nesting season. Happily those evil days have well-nigh passed into oblivion. For us moderns the name of grouse has a fragrance of its own. Its bare mention suffices to set us dreaming of the fresh, breezy hillside, with its varied animal life and endless expanse of purple heather. Considering how widely the term grouse circulates, there is a certain quaintness in the fact that the word is not a British one at all, but only an addition to our language and of doubtful origin. Our forefathers borrowed the word from abroad, apparently from an old French adjective *griesche*, signifying grey or speckled. From this originated a plural word *grice*, printed thus in 1611 by Cotgrave, who used it to denote the 'moor-henne,' the female, as he tells us, of the 'mooregame.' The grouse was originally the moor-fowl, moor-game, moor-cock, or muir-fowl, and preserves these titles at the present day in many districts of both England and Scotland. Willughby called it the red game, and very properly. But the plural word *grice* was early modified into the singular *grows*. Professor Newton has shown that this title was first applied to the blackcock, notably in an ordinance for the household of Henry VIII., dated

from Eltham in the year 1531. Similarly, Charleton
tells us that two species of the heath-cock or grouss
are indigenous to Great Britain respectively entitled
the black game and the grey game. In course of time
the name grouse, very variously spelt, has, curiously
enough, come to be applied to the red grouse
almost exclusively. It may be well to mention that
some scholars have sought a derivation of grouse in
the Celtic terms grug=heather and -iar=a hen ; but
the suggestion has not met with favour. If the origin
of grouse, however, be somewhat perplexing—and I
for one should be very thankful for further light upon
the subject—it must be allowed that the origin of another name of the species is still more mysterious. I
allude to the name gor-cock, which appears to have
latterly dropped out of use, but which was formerly
much in vogue both south and north of the Border.
Professor Newton assures me that he has no clue to
the etymology of this term, though he thinks it may
have some connection with the harsh cry of the bird.
My own belief is that it signifies red-cock, like the
Gaelic ‘Coilleach Ruadh,’ referring to the reddish
plumage of the typical bird. This view has not
obtained the support of scholars ; but it is borne out
by the fact that it was current in the seventeenth
century. Thus Ray writes : ‘The Red Game, *Lagopus*

altera Plinii, an Attagen Aldrov. In the north of
England it is called the *Gor-cock* and *Moor-cock*, the
hen the *More-hen*, the *brood Gorfowl.* *Heath-cock* is
also a name common to this with the precedent.
Turner's More-hen is the female of the precedent or
Blackcock. Gor in the north of England signifies red,
so the *Gor-Cock* is the red cock, &c. For the understanding and exact distinctions of these names we
are beholden to Mr. Johnson, of Brignal, in Yorke-
shire.'[1]

The prefix 'gor' has been applied to some other
birds, notably to the great black-backed gull and to
the carrion crow. The fishermen of the Solway Firth
often speak of the great black-backed gull as the 'gor
maw.' In Oxfordshire, as Mr. O. V. Aplin tells us,
the carrion crow is still recognised as a 'gor-crow.'
The syllable 'gor' seems in these two instances to be
identical with the Saxon gor (carrion, or refuse), and
to refer to the fact that both the black-backed gull and
carrion crow feed upon carrion. Of the appropriateness of the prefix in these cases there can be no
question. The gull preys habitually upon such fowl
as escape wounded from the wildfowler, and often
attacks a sickly lamb. The carrion crow is equally a
foul feeder. But with regard to grouse, I think that

[1] *The Ornithology of Francis Willughby,* p. 23.

'gor' must refer to the red plumage of the bird, when-soever it may have been imported.

Macgillivray was fond of coining new names for English birds, and he thought the grouse should be designated the red ptarmigan. The Gaelic names usually applied to this species are Coilleach Fraoich= the heather-cock, and Cearc Fhraoich=the heather-hen. It is also called Ian Fraoich=the heather-bird. The term most employed, at any rate in Skye, is the Cearc Fhraoich.

The red grouse is not limited in its distribution to the mainland of Scotland. Wherever the common ling or heather grows most rapidly and richly, there grouse naturally most abound. The islands of Scotland are generally inferior to the mainland as regards their properties for growing heather in the dense profusion which the grouse loves to find. In Skye, for instance, the birds are scattered over a wider area than on a good Perthshire moor ; in other words, they have to range more widely in search of food. Of course, we can assist nature considerably by infus-ing fresh blood into our insular races. I have not tried turning down birds in Skye for more than two seasons, and cannot, therefore, speak of, with certainty, local results ; but I am assured that the introduction of Yorkshire grouse into Rum has greatly increased

the bags obtained on that magnificent island. Messrs.
Harvie Brown and Buckley describe the grouse of the
Lews as deteriorating in size, and as tending to die
out, for which they specially blame in-breeding, an
evil easily remedied, if desired. I believe, myself, that
the fault lies in the want of zeal of the proprietors,
who allow enormous numbers of hooded crows to
exist and to plunder their moors. In Skye we persistently trap and poison these arch robbers, but we
cannot get entirely rid of them, because a fresh
supply is always forthcoming from the Long Island.
Farther north, there are plenty of grouse in the
Orkneys, not upon all the islands of the group, but
upon the majority—viz. on the mainland, Hoy, Burray,
Flotta, Fara, Risa Little, Cava, Eday and Rousay.
Stragglers occasionally visit the other islands in the
autumn and winter months. But there are no grouse
in the Shetlands. There never were any there until
they were introduced. Their first introduction must
date back two hundred years, since Brand tells us, in
1701, that grouse had previously been introduced into
Shetland, but could not live there. They were
numerous even then in Orkney, and the Fair Island
peregrines used to visit Orkney to procure the moor-fowl
as food for their young. Of late years, several efforts
have been made to naturalise grouse in Shetland ; but

the experiments appear to have been conducted carelessly, and have, so far, proved useless. It was about
the year 1870 that Mr. D. D. Black, of Kergord,
endeavoured to establish grouse at the head of
Weisdale Voe. A quantity of trees were planted at
the same time to afford shelter to the birds ; but the
situation did not suit the Norway firs, and they consequently perished. At last one pair of grouse nested,
however, because three young birds were caught upon
Sandness Hill by a woman who carried them to Dr.
Scott, of Melmby. In 1882, Mr. John Harrison of
Windhouse, in Yell, procured upwards of forty grouse
from Scotland for the purpose of turning down ; but,
unhappily, almost all the consignment perished on
the way, and only a single pair of birds was set free at
their destination. These birds nested, and were joined
in 1885 by five additional pairs. They lingered for some
time on Yell, and tenanted the island in 1890. In Unst
a female grouse nested in 1886, but the eggs proved
unfertile, and the species became locally extinct. Mr.
Harold Raeburn, to whom I am indebted for my present
information, considers that there is no reason why
grouse should not become perfectly well established
in Shetland, if sufficient trouble were bestowed upon
the experiment. The birds would have to face some
drawbacks here as elsewhere ; e.g. the dense popula-

tion, the wet and stormy springs, and the sinful custom of burning heather all over instead of in suitable strips. Another difficulty in Shetland, as in very many places, is the great abundance of the hooded crow and other vermin. Mr. Raeburn thinks that the peninsula of Röness on the mainland would suit grouse particularly well. What is required, if grouse are to become naturalised in Shetland, is the united effort of the various proprietors, who should join together in extirpating vermin, and turn down some hundreds of grouse for two or three successive seasons. I have no great faith, myself, in the virtue of experiments carried out on a small scale ; because introduced grouse would have, in the first instance, to fight stoutly for existence.

On the other hand, a well-considered scheme, accompanied by remedial measures for the protection of heather, would probably result in material benefit to the Northern Isles. Upon the Scottish mainland the grouse enjoys a general distribution, ranging freely over elevated moorlands as well as those situated in low-lying districts. A wonderful region of Scotland is that which lies between the high mountains and the western seas, bathed in a flood of thin mist or decorated with a variety of soft and soothing tints, marvellous reds and browns and greys mingling to-

gether in glorious harmony. To lie upon an open
shelf of rock, from which the sun has newly drawn
the early dew, to listen silently, and drink in at leisure,
all unnoticed, the cries of the wild population that
hold their own among the pathless hills, this for the
naturalist is a feast of intellect. Now it is an old male
capercailzie whose fine bold form appears suddenly
upon the scene, as he speeds through the top of a
cluster of Scotch firs, having been rudely startled from
his favourite perch by some passer-by. Anon, a restless
curlew sweeps into the field of the binoculars, and proceeds to wheel in agitation above the rushy ground in
which her progeny are skulking, quaint little downy
morsels with their curious, straightened bills. A wary old
blackcock comes speeding along the hill in full view
of us, and a skein of wild duck appear circling overhead, wheeling round and round at a vast height from
the earth. If we lingered a few minutes longer, we
should surely be visited by a blue merlin, or, perhaps,
a tercel might favour us with a morning call. Much
of the charm with which the hills are invested is due
to the delicious uncertainty as to what we may or may
not meet with among the rocks and heather of the
lonelier glens ; and I, for one, am obliged to confess
that our national scenery exercises a stronger spell
over my imagination than the beauties of Switzerland

or the gloomy grandeur of the fiords of Western Norway. The grouse is pre-eminently bound up with our happiest memories of home scenery. Of course, the wealthy men among us can go to Spitzbergen and enjoy good sport with a form of ptarmigan which Mr. Abel Chapman considers to be almost identical with the red grouse ; or they may visit Northern Europe and kill willow grouse to their heart's content ; but the grouse holds a unique position in the affections of most British sportsmen ; all the more, perhaps, since it is essentially an insular production, and cannot be met with out of Great Britain and Ireland, except, indeed, under certain artificial conditions.

I do not know anything of Irish moors at first hand, never having visited Ireland ; but the north of England affords as fine a race of grouse as can be found anywhere in the Northern kingdom. The Pennine range, especially, with its infinite number of outlying spurs, affords an enormous area for grouse to range over, and possesses the advantage of being near to the metropolis. Many quiet nooks of exquisite beauty are to be found among the grouse moors of Yorkshire and of Westmoreland. Farther south, the grouse manages to exist in close proximity to some of the grimy manufacturing towns of Lancashire. The account of the habits of the red grouse furnished by Mr. Seebohm to Dresser's 'Birds of Europe' was based upon his study of the species in Derbyshire. Farther south than this it seems useless to look for grouse, unless we turn aside into little Wales, which is not famous for the quality of bags obtained upon the Twelfth, though the species appears to exist in most suitable places in the Principality. It would be a mistake, however, to suppose that the grouse cannot thrive at a distance from the great lonely moorlands which constitute its natural home. I believe that the species could be naturalised in any part of Britain, provided the conditions of life proved suitable. The experiments that have been made in Norfolk, although carried out on a small scale, are full of encouragement. Mr. J. H. Gurney tells me that Mr. J. Hardcastle turned some grouse out on Holt Heath nearly twenty years ago, but that they have long since vanished. Better results have been obtained at Sandringham. 'Some fourteen years ago,' writes Mr. Jackson, the head keeper, 'thirty brace were turned down, and the following year another thirty brace. The experiment was not made with a view to add to the shooting, but for the pleasure of hearing and seeing the birds on the estate. I found that they nested and reared their young quite satisfactorily, but that they decreased in number between the breeding seasons—a fact which was doubtless due to their straying off our ground. They have an area of about 1,200 or 1,500 acres of heather, which is for the most part surrounded by grazing land. The stock is now reduced to about eight or ten brace.' It must be the wish of all good sportsmen to see such experiments as that just described meet with an enlarged success. We do not take as much pains to improve our sport at home as we might. I wonder, for example, that landowners do not unite to turn down gadwall and other fowl all over the country, and thus convert our ponds and rivers into a national preserve of wildfowl. There are thousands of places that would hold a brace of teal or a few pairs of pintail, if only they were planted with large beds of rushes and well preserved. As for the grouse, its good qualities have begun to attract attention among our Continental neighbours. The pioneer was Baron Dickson, who established red grouse in Sweden between twenty and thirty years ago. It is now reported that the Belgian Government intends to people the sandy heaths of that country with drafts of red grouse.

Already the example of Baron Dickson has been emulated by Count Kniphausen, who owns a property in East Friesland, and has given the following account of his experiment : 'In the autumn of 1891 I ordered

from a game dealer in England five pairs of live grouse
for my game preserves near Wittmund in East Friesland, as an experiment in the way of naturalising this
foreign game bird with us. My prospects regarding
this attempt did not appear to me unpromising, as I
could offer the birds on my sporting domain freedom
from disturbance, plenty of water, heather, and various
berry-bearing plants, and patches of buckwheat, to
all of which these birds are said to be partial. The
grouse were transported across the North Sea in
November. They were sent from Scotland *viâ* London
and Flushing, the consequence of which was that, by
reason of the long railway journeys, the birds suffered
very much, and succumbed, chiefly, I fear, from want
of water—at any rate, I only received one pair alive
on their arrival at their destination. I had taken pains
beforehand to erect for them, in a thicket, an aviary
of wire netting, with canvas overhead, provided plentifully with water and buckwheat, and with the wire
netting stuck full of sprigs of heather, partly so that
they might feel themselves more hidden, but chiefly
because I understand that heather tops are their chief
source of nourishment. After a few days' rest I had
one of the sides of the inclosure raised, so that the
grouse might go out of their own accord. In the
spring of 1893 I was rewarded by coming across the

cock grouse in the company of a blackcock on my
preserve, and had the pleasure of listening to his call.
It also came to my knowledge that the hen was alive,
and that she had incubated for about fourteen days,
though too late in the year, for it was during the
harvesting of the buckwheat that she was disturbed
by the mowers. The cock and hen both flew away,
and the hen, alas ! never sought her nest again. The
eggs, fourteen in number, I have preserved. This
delightful discovery, that a pair of grouse had lived
all but two years on my property, and had even made
a good attempt to rear a brood, made me resolve to
go on with my experiments. The dealer to whom I
addressed myself undertook, for twenty marks the
pair, to deliver ten brace of grouse to me ; and we
came to an understanding that he should send them
at my cost from Hull to Bremen, that he should
undertake their being carefully secured in boxes made
expressly for the purpose, and that he should not be
bound to make good any losses that might occur.
Messrs. Weltmann, in Hull, who forward goods for
the North German Lloyd's Company, kindly undertook the delivery of them, and promised to see that
they did not want for food or water on their thirty
hours' sea voyage; and thus, to my joy, my gamekeeper,
whom I had sent to Bremen to fetch the birds, was

enabled to deliver to me the whole lot of seven brace (more were not to be had at the time).

'The birds this time flew strongly when let out in their inclosure, but did not hurt themselves, owing to the canvas spread over the top. My sporting neighbours all belong to the Prussian and Oldenburg Forest and Moor Game Preservation Societies, to both of which I successfully applied, and they have, as before on the introduction of black-game, promised that for some years to come the protection of these grouse shall be looked upon by them as a strict duty. So it is to be hoped that this attempt to naturalise them in the plains of North-West Germany may succeed, as it did with the black-game, which had for many a long year been extinct there.'

And here I may remark that, as the red grouse is systematically netted in large numbers in the north of England, it should be easy enough for any of our Continental neighbours to repeat the experiment just described on a larger scale. Any such endeavour to naturalise the red grouse abroad should be extended over several seasons, and care should be taken to supply an adequate number of female birds. The latter are rather less hardy than the opposite sex, and are consequently more liable to perish on the journey than their male companions.

c

It has been suggested that the eggs of the grouse could be exported to other countries. No doubt Count Kniphausen might very well have tried the experiment of introducing grouse eggs into the nests of greyhens. The eggs could be obtained in Yorkshire, and carried by water to their destination without incurring much risk. But very few sportsmen would allow eggs to be lifted on their moors, and any trafficking in the eggs of game birds gives an unfortunate stimulus to poaching practices. On the other hand, live grouse might safely be sent very long distances if packed in roomy cages and not overcrowded. The tops of the cages should be lined with canvas, so that the birds could not injure their heads by flying upwards. I remember a charming sand grouse which became extremely domesticated and familiar with the members of the household to which it belonged. It was fearful, however, of strangers, and when alarmed the poor bird almost always started upwards and struck the wooden roof of the cage. I mention this practical point, because I have found by experience that, obvious as it seems to be, it is in fact generally disregarded by those persons who send live grouse about the country. I feel sure that its recognition would materially reduce the risks of travelling.

CHAPTER II

THE MANNERS OF THE GROUSE

THE anxious time for those of us who happen to
possess moors, or even to have leased those of others,
arrives in the spring of the year, when the grouse, that
have long since paired off with their respective mates,
begin to occupy their stations for the summer and to
go to nest. Without wishing to dogmatise too nicely,
it is fair to say that almost every bird upon the moor
occupies its peculiar station for many successive
years, unless, of course, interfered with by human
agency. It has been said, for example, that if an
ornithologist wishes to explore any district in Lap-
land in search of the eggs of the rarer species, he
should spend the time of a preliminary expedition in
marking down the precise situations which each pair
of any one species choose to occupy. We can all of
us see the force of this remark even at home. Season
after season witnesses to the faithfulness with which
the curlew and its mate return to a long and desolate

strip of broken moorland lying under the shadow of
the Coolin Hills; the eggs are almost always laid
about the same spot, and generation after generation
of downy chicks enter into existence on the same
patch of heather and rough grass. It is the same
with the ptarmigan that nestles up in the lonely
corrie above Sligachan. I have seen the nests of
two seasons placed side by side on a slope of green
turf, screened from observation by the same convenient boulders of rock. Indeed, I could tell you
where to find the nest of the greenshank and many
another rare bird, knowing from long intimacy with
their haunts precisely the positions that these birds
are likely to occupy in successive seasons. This
principle applies as truly to the red grouse as to
other birds, making allowance for the destruction of
old females in the shooting season. On my own
ground, at any rate, I have a very good idea where
to look for grouse nests, although I never search for
them intentionally, but only stumble upon them inci-
dentally. No good sportsman would wish to organise
a hunt for grouse nests. The grouse is a very particular bird, and often deserts her eggs if suddenly
startled from her charge. Of course, there are many
hen grouse which would rather allow themselves to be
trodden upon than leave their eggs, and their faithful-

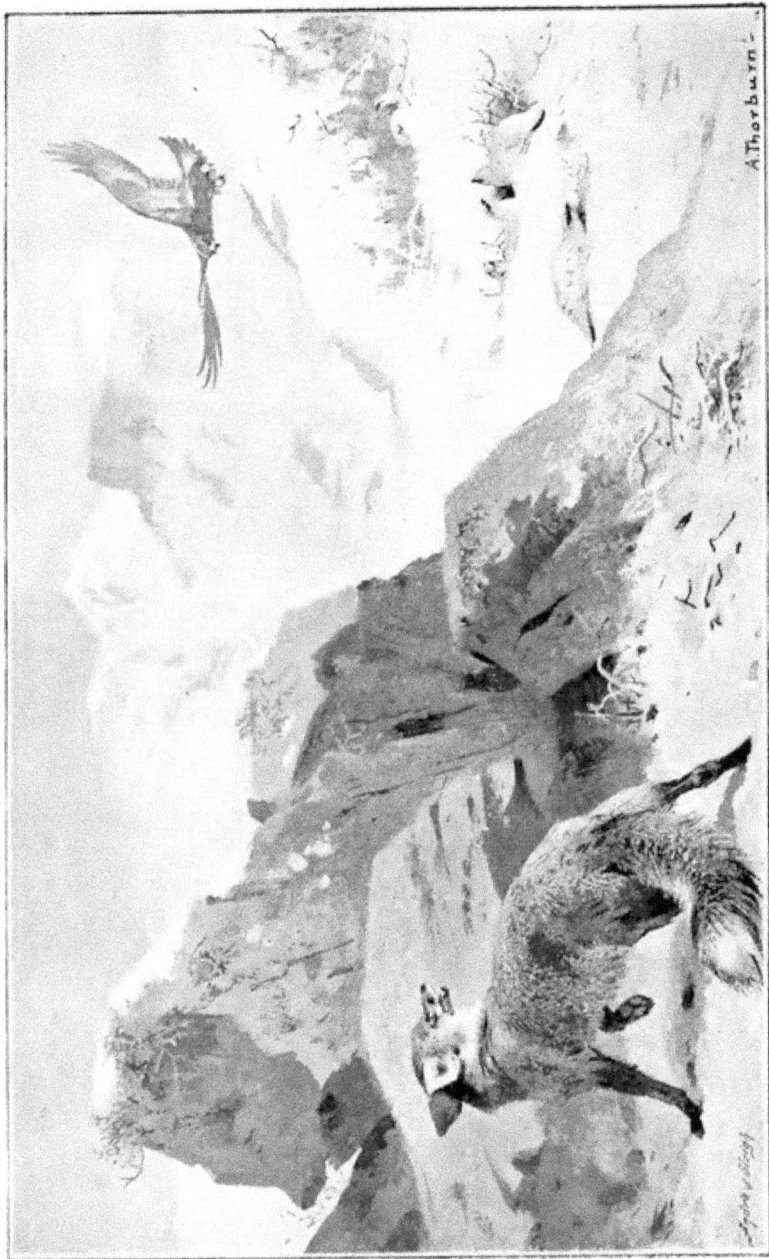

BETWEEN TWO FIRES.

A.Thorburn.

ness to maternal duties is touching in its way. But
the grouse is naturally a shy, timid creature, and will
not willingly brook much interference. A grouse
moor can hardly be kept too quiet in the breeding
season. That is the reason why proprietors object so
strongly to the intrusion of parties of tourists being
forced upon them by any Radical legislation. Strangers
do not, of course, intend the least in the world to do
us any harm, but in point of fact they are pretty certain to scare some birds badly, and thus to diminish
the supply of chicks hatched out. Some people may
suggest that grouse breed so very early that the young
are hatched long before the tourist season. The
grouse is an early breeding bird in the north of
England, and often begins to lay eggs during the
month of March if the season happens to be warm
and genial. In the north of Scotland incubation is
much later. In the island of Skye, April 24 is a decidedly early date for a full clutch of grouse eggs.

May and June are the two months in which the
majority of grouse hens go to nest. Although most
of us have accustomed ourselves to speak of grouse
nests, the expression is hardly exact, for the eggs are
deposited in a mere scratching, scantily lined with a
few dry stems of grass or twigs of heather. Some of
the text-books, it is true, speak of feathers being used

to line the nests of grouse, but I believe that any
feathers found in a grouse's nest have been accidentally dropped by the old bird. The nest is very often
placed near a little burn, generally under the shelter
of a tuft of heather. I have occasionally seen perfectly open nests, but they are very liable to be
flooded. The grouse is one of the hardiest birds in
existence, and frequently continues to sit upon her eggs
after the nest has filled with water ; but the eggs are
delicate, and are generally addled by such unfortunate
immersion, notwithstanding the devotion exhibited
by the old hen. It is a fallacy to suppose that grouse
like to nest in *very* old heather. As a matter of fact
they prefer younger plants as cover, choosing to avail
themselves of the shelter of well-grown but not really
old ling.

As to the number of eggs usually laid by grouse,
my belief is that seven and eight are the numbers
which occur most frequently Five is the smallest
number that I have seen incubated, nor have I ever
seen more than a dozen eggs in one nest. Indeed, to
find more than ten eggs in a nest is quite an exceptional event, although probably most sportsmen have
at one time or another come across large coveys of
young birds. It often happens, however, that one or
more eggs prove unfertile. There are records of as

many as seventeen eggs being found in a single grouse nest, but I imagine that two hen birds had laid together. Mr. Henry Seebohm is perhaps as high an authority upon the eggs of British birds as any member of the B.O.U. He says that he has not found much variation in the size of eggs of the grouse. 'The ground-colour of the eggs of the grouse is usually a pale olive, spotted and blotched all over with dark red-brown. The spots are frequently so confluent as almost to conceal the ground-colour. In fresh-laid eggs the brown is often very red, in some instances almost approaching crimson. It appears to darken as it thoroughly dries, and sometimes almost approaches black. When fresh laid the colour is not very fast, and before the eggs are hatched the beauty of the original colouring is generally very much lessened by large spots coming off altogether, no doubt from the friction of the feathers when the bird is sitting. If the weather is wet when the bird begins to sit this is much more the case. When the colour has once become thoroughly dry it will bear washing in water without injury. The colour of the eggs is admirably adapted for the purpose of concealment from the prying eyes of rooks, crows, and birds of prey, being very much like the mixture of moss, lichens, and peat where they are laid. Most of the eggs laid come to maturity. I once asked a gamekeeper to watch half a dozen nests which were near his house. He told me that out of forty-nine eggs, he counted forty-seven chicken grouse. As soon as the young are hatched, especially in dry seasons, the hen takes her brood down to the more swampy parts of the moor.' It will be obvious to most people that the proportion of eggs that hatch out depends very much on the rainfall. Still more does this affect the tiny grouse during the first few days of their existence. If the weather is dry and sunny, the little fellows grow rapidly and soon become fairly independent, learning to peck at small caterpillars, flies, and other insects. If heavy showers of rain arrive at the critical time the number of young grouse that perish is often very considerable, for, hardy as they eventually become, they are extremely tender during the first days of their existence. Gradually the cheepers grow stronger, and learn to forage on their own account. They do best in fairly dry seasons, provided always that they have a good supply of water easily accessible. Should this be scarce, the chicks are sadly liable to seek to satisfy their thirst in deep ditches and drains, out of which they cannot easily make their escape.

Of course it is impossible to guard against such misfortunes. Happily the hen grouse is a careful parent ; indeed, both the male and female birds take every care of their young broods.

The grouse depends chiefly upon heather for its subsistence, feeding on the common ling (*Calluna vulgaris*) and also on the fine-leaved heath (*Erica cinerea*), breaking off the fresh tips of the twigs, which are reduced to pulp by the action of the gizzard, assisted by fine fragments of quartz and pebbles introduced for the purpose of aiding the action of the latter in comminuting the food. Grouse are partial to the berries of both the bilberry and cranberry. Clover leaves have also an attraction for them. Occasionally they eat the polypody, of which the pheasant is also fond. In severe weather grouse find that even hips help to support existence. Joseph Walton of Garrigill tells me that very small grouse feed eagerly on caterpillars, a fact which he has verified by dissection.

In the fall of the year grouse often shift their quarters from the tops of the hills, in order to feast upon the stooks of oats upon the shepherd's croft or the minister's glebe. Some birds take very kindly to the stubble. In some parts of Perthshire it is quite a common event to find a covey of grouse haunting a favourite field for many successive weeks, and the birds grow heavy upon the diet they thus obtain, though they are considered rather to deteriorate in flavour. It is this readiness to feed upon grain which makes it possible to keep grouse in confinement, or at any rate in a state of semi-captivity. Some few years ago, when the sand grouse were visiting England, I was told one day that a sand grouse in the possession of a neighbour had nested and laid some eggs. On inquiry we found that the bird, which had nested in the house of its owner, was a tame red grouse, which had voluntarily begun to incubate. No instance of the grouse rearing its young in captivity has come under my notice hitherto, although some half-dozen records of the fact appear to be authenticated. The late Mr. Osborne, for example, kept a number of grouse in confinement for several years, and on one occasion a pair bred and hatched out five healthy chicks. Their owner used to walk many miles from Wick to fetch the tender heather shoots for the old and young grouse which had hatched out within his walls in the town.[1]

It is remarkable that so shy and retiring a bird as the red grouse should become extremely bold and adventurous under artificial conditions, yet of this there can be no possible doubt. Mr. W. Oxenden Hammond tells us of a red grouse which was taken to

[1] *Fauna of Sutherland and Caithness*, p. 205.

Kent from a Yorkshire moor, and lived for several years in a cage in the hall of a country house. 'This was an old cock bird, and its constant call in the morning used to echo through the house.' [1]   A pleasing description of the tameness of a covey of grouse was contributed to the ' Field ' of February 5, 1887, by a correspondent who signed his article with the letter ' X.' 'Now the history of these tame birds is as follows : A friend of mine—one who delights in all matters relating to the habits of wild birds, and, what is more, is thoroughly versed in the subject—had a nest of grouse eggs hatched out under a hen—this on the same ground where his young pheasants were being reared. When first out of the egg the young grouse showed a disposition to stray somewhat too far from the maternal coop ; but this little difficulty was easily overcome by the intelligent keeper. At some distance a wire netting was placed round the coop. In a very short time this was removed ; but to show the result of habit and training on birds, it was found that the young ones circled round much about the place where the wire netting had stood.

'Time went on, and they soon settled into the habits of their pheasant companions. Some six or

[1] *Zoologist*, 1885, p. 183.

seven grew up, and about October the cock birds seem
to have made advances to the hens, and their overtures
doubtless being taken by the latter as inopportune—out
of season—they modestly levanted. There remained
three cocks, all in splendid plumage and condition,
feeding, be it remembered, entirely on pheasants' food
and what they could pick up about the house. One of
the birds remained in the corner of the field where
the coop had stood, taking possession of it for himself.
Here at all times he was to be seen ready to dispute
his ground with anyone passing near it. Usually he
challenged with a call, and then, if approached, he
was ready either for a fight or to be fed, or both—anything that suited the whim of the intruder. One day,
when I was giving some maize to my friend, the keeper
came up, and going on all fours, began throwing grass
in the face of the bird. At once the grouse responded
to the challenge by flying at him, coming up sideways,
and using his spurs. The bird allowed itself repeatedly
to be caught, and the moment he was liberated returned again and again to the unequal combat. More
than once have I seen this same bird fly across from
his corner and join us when shooting on the opposite
woodland bank, this being some 600 or 700 yards
across a narrow neck of sea at the head of a loch.
My friend's dogs—retrievers and spaniels—knew the

bird well, and paid no attention to him, nor did he to
the shots that were fired close to him. But not so my
retriever. He began by thinking it was his manifest
duty to bring the bird to me ; but, on being duly
warned, and on seeing the grouse trying to get to close
quarters to ram him, so to speak, with his spurs, a
feeling of alarm, droll to see, came over the dog.
Evidently he concluded he had to deal with something quite new to him, possibly a demented grouse.
Another day I fell in with my friend a mile from this
spot, and having two dogs with me, it was as much as
I could do to beat a hasty retreat into a thick wood,
so anxious was he to have a sparring match with one
or other of the dogs.

' This bird has now taken up his quarters close to a
house, a mile from the place he was reared, remaining
just as tame, and coming regularly for his breakfast.
The two others remain about the lodge, in the court-
yard, in the garden, and frequently come in at the
servants' dinner-time to pick up anything that may be
thrown to them. They have induced one wild bird
to come down off the moor, and this bird is now
fairly tame—that is to say, he will let one get within a
few yards of him. When, by the way, it pleased
Master Grouse to join us out shooting, if by chance a
spaniel came suddenly upon him, he was not in the

least degree disconcerted—he would simply fly on to a rock, and begin crowing at the dog.'

While the willow grouse is well known to be fond of perching in trees, its British congener rarely alights even on a bush except when forced by hunger to feed on hips in snowy weather. Mr. J. G. Millais gives a charming account of a Westmoreland grouse which was hatched and reared by a little bantam. 'Every evening the bantam used to repair to a large beech tree near the house, in which she was in the habit of roosting when unencumbered by family cares. So when she was allowed to remain out for the night her first thought was to make for her old perch, to which she considered the youngster was perfectly capable of following, as he could now fly well. The latter, after many ineffectual attempts to keep on his legs, was forced to sleep on the ground at the foot of the tree, for though he managed to get up to the perch, his efforts to keep there were quite useless, as he always fell off again, either backwards or forwards. However, in the course of time practice made perfect, and he acquired such a liking for sitting on the trees that he was often afterwards seen in the daytime flying from branch to branch, appearing to be perfectly at home.' Mr. Millais adds that this grouse 'had a particular affection for the lawn-tennis court, and when-

ever any of the members of my friend's family began
to play, Mr. Grouse would always put in an appearance, seeming to enjoy the fact that he was an
obstructionist, and refusing to clear off unless forcibly
removed and shut up in his pen. If taken to the
other end of the grounds he would almost immediately return to the tennis court. Such was the soci-
ability of his disposition that he had absolutely no
sense of fear at the report of firearms; in fact, he
would frequently follow the shooters out to a distance
of several fields from the house before he would
return home, satisfied that they had taken their
departure for the whole day, so that it would be of
no use accompanying them. Every night, before
retiring to roost in his beech tree, he would take long
flights round and round the house and village, which
was close by; and in the course of one of his evening
rambles he espied an old man digging, from whom
he very naturally expected he would obtain some
delicacy, as everyone was in the habit of giving him
something to eat; but this old scoundrel was a
stranger, and barbarously despatched the confiding
bird with his spade.'[1] Mr. Millais mentions another
tame grouse, which lived for a long time at Guisachan,
Lord Tweedmouth's place in Ross-shire. 'After

[1] *Game Birds and Shooting Sketches*, p. 50.

being kept for several years, he departed as usual in spring to the hills, where he annually assisted in the increase of the stock, but did not return to the house, as was his wont, during the following winter. He feared neither man nor beast, and became great friends with a certain dog in the house, on whose back he used often to ride. The following instance of his plucky disposition was related to me on separate occasions by each of the two guns who were present when the affair occurred. A shooting party were beating the hillside near the house, when a pointer that was working stood to birds, which eventually rose, and some were killed ; but as the dog still held, they correctly inferred that there was probably another bird left, which proved to be the case. This happened to be the tame grouse, whose presence was quite unexpected, and who considered being pointed such an insult that when the unfortunate dog approached near enough to be disagreeable, he flew up and attacked it so blindly that he was with difficulty rescued from its jaws.'

Cock grouse, in spite of their general shyness, are very pugnacious birds, and the old males especially show great intolerance of any strangers that venture to intrude upon what they consider their own proper domain. A Perthshire keeper tells me that he saw

two male grouse engaged in combat ; so completely
blinded with fury were the birds that they dashed
against the wall of a stone building, one of them killing himself with the impetuosity of his flight.

Individuals of the male sex appear to predominate
in most birds, and I have no doubt myself as to the
desirability of sportsmen endeavouring to shoot the
male birds hard.   Not only do more male birds reach
maturity, but the females are exposed to additional
risks in the breeding season.   Mr. D. J. Lamb states
that, out of 130 grouse killed near Pitlochry in four
days in 1893, as many as 120 were cock birds.[1]
This, of course, is an exceptional incident, but it
points the moral that cock birds should not be
allowed to live unpaired.   Otherwise they disturb
the breeding couples, and become a nuisance to
the grouse moor.   Of course, birds behave very
diversely in different parts of the country.   With
us in Skye the family parties live together in peace
and tranquillity until November, and rarely pack
before the end of that month.   If they pack in
November it is generally in consequence of bad
weather.   On the other hand, the grouse of the
north of England pack, as a general rule, early in
the season, and the sexes usually separate.   Every

[1] *Field*, September 19, 1893.

D

sportsman knows that the old cock birds often lie out singly in the heather on the tops of the hills, while the females and younger males are shifting in flocks about the lower ground.

I have gradually been led to the opinion that the custom of driving the moors has altered the habits of grouse enormously, and led to their becoming far more gregarious than they used to be. The mention of grouse driving always reminds me of a remark which was made in my presence some few years ago. A certain man was descanting rather loudly on the excellence of his shooting, when Sir Reginald Cathcart inquired whether the drives were good. The reply was somewhat unexpected : ‘Well, the fact is, we have not any drives yet, but I am—having them laid out.’ Our grouse in Skye never become *very* wild. Their tameness in December is often more openly expressed than in the breeding season. Of course, nesting grouse will allow you to tread upon them in the heather rather than rise from their place of concealment, and it is necessary to take a dog to the hill if you wish to form an estimate of the number of birds upon the moor in the month of May. A hen that is nesting in an open situation will generally dash away in trepidation if she thinks herself detected ; but most birds nest in cover, and greatly prefer to watch your movements while resting snugly concealed than to court your notice by any hasty action that might betray the safety of their treasures. Their habits become modified, however, when the young have hatched out. For example, if you happen to cross a bit of mossy ground on a July day you are sure to flush an old hen grouse, which sings out lustily as she rises from the heather. The dog makes a point, and lo! a newly feathered youngster is crouching at your feet, watching all your movements with a keen glance of its bright dark eyes. You pause for a moment to admire the little fellow's yellow freckled garb; it harmonises nicely with the rough cover in which the creature is nestling. The instinct with which it accepts an impassive position, as offering the best hope of safety, is truly marvellous. The old hen will not leave her young; another step forward, and you flush four or five more young birds, which start up with their plaintive cheeping cry, to fly a few paces across the moor before they drop back into cover. The anxiety of the old birds is often touching in its disinterestedness, especially if the young are newly hatched, in which case the mother birds worm this way and that way along the ground, trailing themselves through the heather with half-open wings, hoping by this transparent device to lead you away

D 2

from their tender charge. Grouse are good parents, full of solicitude for their young, and will endure any danger rather than allow their chicks to be injured. Sometimes they succeed even in beating off the attack of the hooded crow, or that rascally marauder the female sparrow hawk.

Grouse seem to me to thrive best upon moors of moderate elevation. The low-lying grounds suit them very well in winter, when snow and sleet have driven them down from the hills, and they will then fly long distances. It is not at all unusual for red grouse to cross the Solway Firth at a point where the estuary measures two miles in breadth, and I have known them fly longer distances. They often cross the valley of the Tees, flying about a mile from one hillside to another. Mr. Millais observes that 'the usual length of a grouse's flight ranges from a quarter to three-quarters of a mile, depending entirely, of course, on the nature of the ground over which they are passing, being as a rule much shorter on heather flats, where they have numerous and agreeable resting places, than on broken ground and rocky hill places. In a discussion which took place in the " Field " I noticed that most sportsmen were of opinion that grouse were incapable of flying four miles ; but I have twice seen grouse on the wing when they were crossing the " Bring," a wide

channel which separates the islands of Hoy and
Pomona, Orkneys.   The fishermen told me this
distance, at the point where I was sailing, was quite
four miles across, and the birds must have come at
least another mile on the Pomona side from the point
where they left the moor.'

Mr. J. A. Harvie Brown states that in December
1879 a pack of grouse was seen flying south over
the Moray Firth, making for the Banff coast. Their
journey must have been very considerable.   It is not
easy, in fact, to say how far the grouse is migratory,
but that individual birds wander far and wide in
autumn and winter there can be no doubt.   The Rev.
M. A. Mathew records that a solitary red grouse
was shot by Mr. C. Edwards on the Mendips, near
Wrington, Somerset, in September 1885, and this, he
suggests, must have crossed over the Bristol Channel,
migrating from Breconshire.   Very likely the bird was
pursued by a peregrine, and the chase carried it far
out of its usual latitude.   Similarly, the red grouse
included in Mr. Miller Christy's ' Birds of Essex ' had
no doubt strayed from Sandringham, or from some
other centre of introduction in Eastern England   In
1879 Mr. W. Stamper observed a pair of grouse in a
turnip field on his farm near Oswaldkirk, Yorks, early
in February.   The birds had strayed at least ten miles

from the nearest grouse moor.   Severe weather often affects the interests of the grouse bred on high ground. Thus, Mr. James Carter writes that in January 1886 the neighbourhood of Masham, Yorkshire, was covered to a considerable depth with snow, which, owing to sudden changes from thaw to frost, with frequent fresh falls of snow, became a very solid mass.   The depth above the heather on the moors was considerably more than a foot, and large drifts formed on a very extensive scale.   'The grouse suffered severely, being quite unable to penetrate the frozen mass for food, and in consequence they left the moors for the lower cultivated land to an extent never previously observed.   The nearest point of moor to Masham is three miles distant, but the open moors are considerably farther away.   Walking near this ground, great packs of grouse would sweep overhead and pass right down the valley over the town.   A field of turnips was swarming with the starving birds, which vainly attempted, with numerous partridges, to scratch down for food.   The grouse were perched on the fences, feeding on the berries like so many fieldfares, and on several occasions they alighted amongst the branches of trees.   They were feeding in the hedgerows about Durton House and close to the outskirts of the town, and even on the heaps of manure close to buildings

where persons were working all day. As far as one
could see they had abandoned the moors, and were
feeding miles away in the cultivated districts on anything they could get in the way of food. A large
farmer, whose land lies three miles still farther away
from their usual haunts, states that immense flocks of
grouse were feeding in his turnip fields. Gangs of
men were being employed to clear away the snow from
patches of heather, but their efforts did very little
towards providing feeding ground for the vast number
of starving birds.'[1] The Editor of the 'Zoologist'
appended to the communication just cited a note that,
' About the time mentioned there was an extraordinary
exodus of grouse from the moors in the neighbourhood
of Ilkley, in consequence of the very inclement
weather. The birds in many cases left the moorland
altogether, and large packs were seen in the fields
about Arthington and Weedon. . . . During a severe
winter some years ago we remember to have heard
that in Caithness the grouse were all down *on the sea-
shore*, and hardly a bird was to be found on the
moors.' A large amount of similar evidence might
be cited if it could serve any useful purpose, but the
foregoing will suffice to show that not only do single
pairs of grouse stray occasionally on to arable farms,

[1] *Zoologist*, 1886, p. 107.

but that under certain conditions the majority of English grouse desert their favourite moors for a short period in order to satisfy the pangs of hunger. The question whether grouse are liable to migrate in the early spring, when food is apparently plentiful, suggests a more difficult problem. There *are* good sportsmen, at any rate, and careful field naturalists who incline to believe that the grouse, like its distant relative Pallas's sand grouse, is occasionally seized by paroxysms of migratory fever, under the influence of which the birds travel for many miles from their home moor. But positive proof that this is so is still wanting, and the question can only be settled by means of marked birds.

CHAPTER III

THE GROUSE AND ITS ENEMIES

THE most important factor in grouse preserving is a judicious treatment of the heather which clothes the slopes of our northern hills. Of course many other points have to be considered. If we allow the moors to become overstocked, we increase the susceptibility of the game to the various forms of disease which have been so cleverly exploited by Dr. Klein and other scientific workers. But the vital question in the management of a grouse moor is the maintenance of a proper *food supply*. Grouse are hardy fowl, and can face wet seasons, not indeed with impunity, yet without seriously losing ground. They are well accustomed to meet the vicissitudes of our stormy and changeable climate. In droughty seasons they vary their diet with an additional share of blaeberries. Does the snow fall swiftly and thickly on the brae?— the grouse have long since learnt full well by experience of hard times how to find the gullies where the

snow will drift in eddies before the gusts of wind that
drive with such precipitancy, and are sure to assemble
in the places where they can get the best supply of
food.   If necessary, they can scratch off the snow that
shrouds the food plant from their vision.   But how if
we neglect the culture of the food plant?   In that
case our grouse must fail.   Shepherds have done
much to change the appearance of our Highland glens,
and to bring about a complete metamorphosis in the
conditions under which grouse live in many districts.
An enormous increase in the number of sheep kept
in Great Britain has destroyed, and is still destroying,
a vast quantity of heather.   This is all right up to a
certain point.   Vermin like old heather, but grouse
do not.   Young heather is very acceptable to grouse
as a variety.   But the practice of burning great
stretches of heather, instead of firing the ling in carefully selected strips, is much to be regretted.   Of
course accidents will occur from time to time.   No
amount of care will prevent a few sparks from a passing
locomotive firing a dry moss in a rainless season, any
more than it would prevent our grouse being felled
by a wire fence or by the telegraph wires newly erected
upon some spot where grouse often cross the hill.
But pains can be taken to see that heather is burnt
by the shepherds in such a way as to meet the require-

ments of each hursel of sheep, while respecting the rights and interests of the prince of game birds. Shepherds, however good and reasonable they may be in other respects, like to delay the burning of heather until the latest legal date. They have their reasons for their choice. They do not care to fire the heather until it is very dry, for this reason, that if the stems of the heather are green they will not burn well, but will become hard and sharp, and the sheep will not willingly feed among it. The drawback to postponing the burning of the heather is the fact that the grouse is an early breeder, and that late fires are likely to disturb breeding birds, and to drive them away from their nests. So the first point in keeping up a good supply of grouse is to secure a clever and thoughtful management of the heather.

The next point is to supplement a good supply of food for the grouse by waging war against its four-footed and winged persecutors. The modern game preserver has often a genuine sympathy for the wild creatures that are roughly classed together as 'vermin.' It would be a grievous sin, undoubtedly, to extirpate even 'vermin' altogether. People who have no game of their own to preserve are sometimes tempted to say hard things of those who have, because they kill out hawks and other high-spirited creatures. Nevertheless, there is a *mean* to be attained in game preserving as in all other things. Landowners exercise good sense and decency if they tolerate a little 'vermin,' both to gratify their own taste and to satisfy the requirements of an interested public. But if they allow their lands to swarm with 'vermin' entirely un-checked, they injure their neighbours and show a want of propriety.

'Vermin' should not be extirpated root and branch, but common sense requires that they should be kept within reasonable numerical limits. In the British Islands the birds of prey have become sadly reduced in numbers of late years. Collectors of blown egg shells—a very undesirable class of men— offer fancy prices for the eggs of the honey buzzard and hobby ; so that, if these species try to nest in their old haunts, say in the New Forest, they are ruthlessly pillaged and plundered without mercy. A love of daring induces a good many young fellows to storm the nests of the peregrines that nestle on the most precipitous portions of our coasts. The eggs are so handsome that they really constitute a pleasant memento of a hazardous venture, while the young are charming pets, and can be trained for the noble sport of falconry.

In many parts of Scotland, and, alas ! everywhere

in England, the man who manages to slay an unfortunate eagle of either species is sure to find his doughty deed duly advertised by the production of a spicy article which goes the round of the papers, usually converting a sea eagle from Northern Europe into a magnificent golden eagle from the wilds of Sutherland. The most amusing instance of the kind that has come directly under my notice related to the supposed capture of a great eagle-owl in Cumberland. A local newspaper gave a high-flown account of how the huge bird was winged by a keeper on a moor near Cockermouth, and was brought to bay by the intrepid exertions of a large retriever dog. I journeyed some sixty odd miles to pay my respects to the bird of wisdom, and was not a little entertained to find *Bubo maximus* resolve itself into a forlorn and miserable specimen of the short-eared owl. In this case there was no doubt as to where the blame of floating a *canard* lay. The editor of a local paper, Mr. Blank of Blankington, had seen the bird himself at the keeper's house, and the identification of the specimen as an eagle-owl was a flight of his own unassisted genius. Of course this brilliant hit was copied by many of his brethren all over England, and occupied a prominent position in some of the more foolish journals.

In point of fact, the golden eagle does prey to some extent on grouse. It likes blue hares better than any other diet. Rabbits are acceptable ; so also is venison, or hill mutton for the matter of that. But it kills a few grouse occasionally. Golden eagles have always been respected on our own ground. I am too pleased to see them about to grudge them a few grouse ; but they prefer the blue hare, which can be spared more conveniently.

A former tenant of Rum assured me that a pair of eagles which nested on a certain precipice in that island killed a good many grouse, in the absence of the blue hares and rabbits which they would have chosen. Happening to be a gentleman, he respected the safety of the birds, which belonged to the golden species. An outsider might have proved less magnanimous. The sea eagle has become so rare in Britain that it would be little less than a crime for anyone to raid its eyry or to slay a member of its race. Alas ! that the hand of the destroyer was stayed so late. I could say a good deal about the way in which the sea eagles of Skye were exterminated, on a proper opportunity.

The sea eagle has no objection to grouse, and is sure to pick off a winged bird. A neighbour of ours at one time kept a pair of sea eagles. They enjoyed

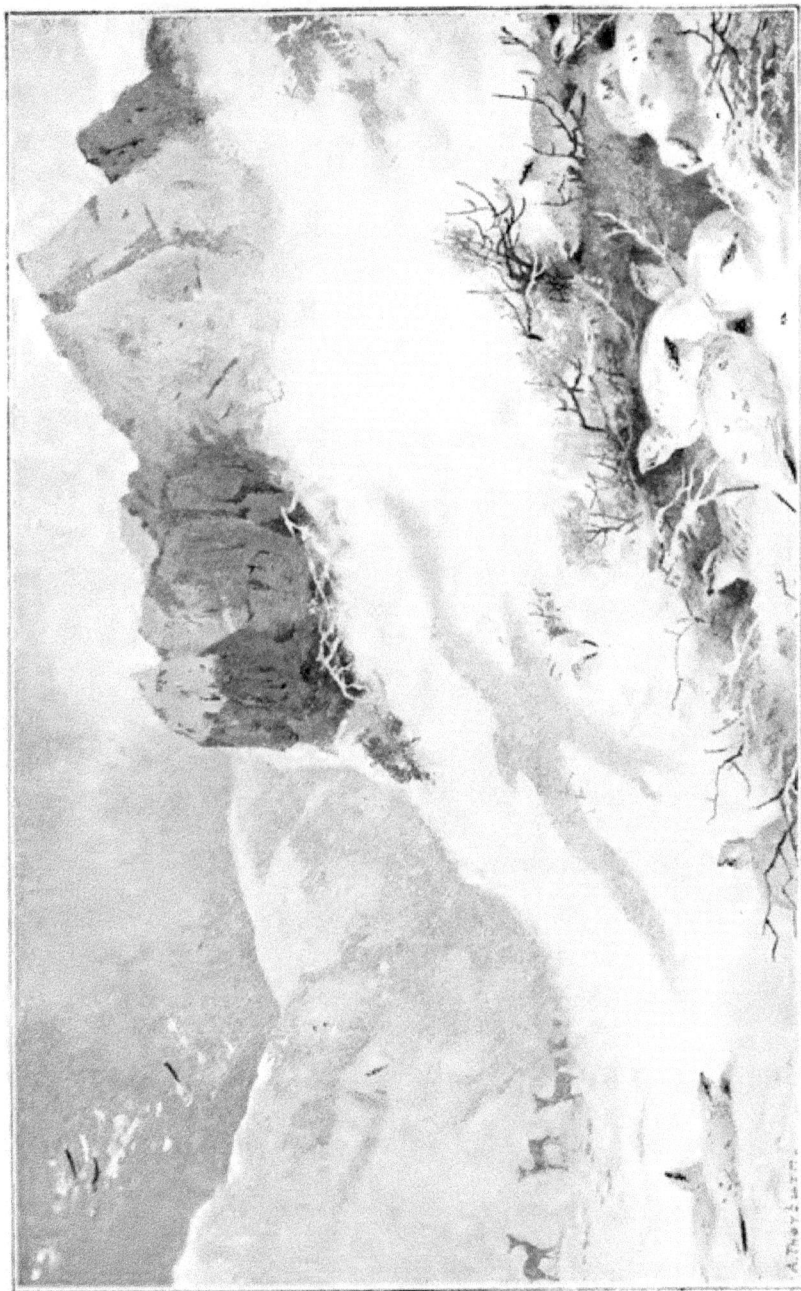

THE SHADOW OF DEATH.

their liberty, and used to love to accompany their master when he went to the hill, swooping down upon the birds he shot with great rapidity and unerring accuracy of aim. The kite, like the sea eagle, has almost been 'improved away' from our midst. I for one am heartily sorry that it has become rare. Those that I studied in Spain appeared to live chiefly on offal and small reptiles. But I do not believe the kite is constant to any one diet. In this district the common buzzard feeds upon field voles, because they abound and other prey is scarce. In another district, not twenty miles away from the first, the buzzards live chiefly upon wall lizards. If you open them, you find their stomachs crammed with these reptiles, which you would have fancied were too swift and agile to be captured by so clumsy a round-winged hawk as the common buzzard. It is the same with the kite. In Germany I have seen it trying to annex tiny partridges. In some parts of Scotland, grouse found an inveterate foe in the beautiful, high-circling glede or red kite. The term 'glede,' by the way, is often applied to the buzzard and hen-harrier. But let that pass. The late Mr. E. T. Booth was a singularly impartial and truth-loving investigator. He studied the habits of the kite to good purpose in a remote part of Perthshire. The result of his researches proved that the kites under observation fed upon squirrels and rabbits, as well as upon peewits, and the young of curlew, wild duck, and pigeons ; but he decided that grouse 'seemed to be their favourite food.' One kite's nest, in particular, was visited on several occasions, and each time 'the young bird had a fresh-killed grouse on the nest.' Further, he goes on to state that he counted the remains of over thirty grouse under the branches of a large fir. 'Some were only bleached and weather-beaten skeletons, and probably had lain for many months.' He considered that all the birds in question had been destroyed by a single pair of kites at the beginning of the season. I fancy that the offenders would have preferred more ignoble prey if it had been forthcoming. Sorry should I be to do any injury to a British kite. But our personal feelings must not be allowed to overpower our better judgment, and the preservation of rapacious birds, however desirable from a scientific or philosophical standpoint, possesses some distinct drawbacks for game-preservers. The male hen-harrier is a lovely bird in his delicate blue garb, and I know no more beautiful sight in nature than a hen-harrier quartering a moor, as I have seen it do in North Uist and other places. But there cannot be any doubt that both male and female harriers are both extremely destructive to grouse, and relentless in their pursuit. I do not justify the extermination which is so rapidly overtaking this bird, in consequence of its nesting on the ground, and being easily trapped beside its young, for it is a devoted parent. I do not go so far as to say that it feeds principally on grouse ; but I have no doubt that the presence of this charming harrier is highly inimical to the interests of both grouse and partridges. The peregrine falcon kills a good many grouse on some inland moors, but a long study of its habits has convinced me that it feeds on many other birds in a larger degree. I believe it prefers puffins and other sea fowl to grouse. Of course I admit also that this falcon kills grouse at every period of the year. Every sportsman knows the truth of this remark. It is not as well known that the peregrine feeds also on small birds. Young 'red' falcons are very destructive to young grouse, but they are not very discriminating, and live largely on thrushes and other small birds. I once crept within a yard or two of a beautiful peregrine, as he was perching on a crag of rock a thousand feet above the boiling waters of the Minch. He was so busily engaged in dissecting a fresh-killed skylark that he never observed my stealthy approach to his stronghold. It has often been said

E

that the peregrine picks off the weakliest bird of a covey. The statement is not, however, supported by my experience, neither is it in keeping with what we know of the peregrine's character. The fact is, that a high-couraged bird like the falcon disdains to strike an unworthy quarry. She prefers a good chase. A Highland deer-stalker expressed the true view of the case with the naïve remark, that 'the falcon is a *real* sportsman!' So she certainly is, and as such she has no stomach for flying sickly grouse. It is my belief that the peregrine, if she selects at all, selects the gamest bird in a covey, and the better the flight afforded by her victim, the keener is the falcon's enjoyment of the sport.

I am no advocate for exterminating peregrines. On the contrary, I have taken some trouble to afford them protection in the breeding season ; but we can-not expect everybody to see the falcon in a favourable light. One of my friends dissected six peregrines in a spring, all old birds. Five of them had been feeding on grouse, the sixth had eaten a wild duck. Of course this did not prove much. The birds were quite as likely to have contained rock doves or puffins. But the grouse has a strong and vigilant enemy in the falcon, and all that can reasonably be expected of the owners of grouse moors is that they will tolerate the peregrine without allowing it to increase locally. The trapping of peregrines is easily accomplished when the falcons nest in the face of the sea cliff. Such birds as breed in high rocks in the interior of the country have a better chance of defying the exertions of keepers. Whether the buzzard ever kills grouse, I cannot say. I incline to think that it would readily kill a weakly or 'pricked' bird ; but I do not think a buzzard cares much about grouse if field mice and carrion are plentiful. The rough-legged buzzard is a finer bird, and more likely to kill grouse. I have known of two gerfalcons that were in pursuit of grouse when killed. They share the fancy of the peregrine for the flesh of that persecuted bird the Cornish chough.

The sparrow hawk is common in many of the wooded parts of Scotland adjacent to grouse moors, and does some mischief in spite of its small size. A female sparrow hawk occasionally cuts down a full-grown grouse ; while the male, light as he is, has sufficient audacity to seize a winged grouse. Neither the kestrel nor the bonnie little merlin causes the grouse much sorrow. They may carry off the chicks when a day or two old, but only, I fancy, in very rare instances. I have preserved our breeding merlins for a dozen years, finding that they rear their brood

E 2

almost exclusively upon wheatears, meadow pipits, and other unimportant little birds. Once only in all my experience did I find the foot of a grouse chick in the nest of a merlin. I wish that the poor hen-harrier could be held equally blameless.

To summarise my own experience of birds of prey, I venture to say that, so far as they act merely as 'nature's police,' their presence on the grouse moor has at least its redeeming features. Our grouse are all the stronger and hardier for having to struggle hard to maintain their existence. The thoughtless persecution of birds of prey, or of any other feathered fowl, is culpable in the extreme. But the interests of the sportsman and of the naturalist are closely allied, and the one ought to help the other in the wise management of the grouse moor.

Proceeding now to speak of the less noble enemies which thin the ranks of our coveys directly or indirectly, I own to a considerable distrust of the raven. Certainly he feeds chiefly on carrion, but I am afraid he is fond of grouse eggs, and sucks their contents whenever a chance presents itself. So my endeavour is to keep the numbers of the raven down, without, however, threatening their local extinction. The worst, because most cunning, foes of the grouse are the carrion and hooded crows. They are the worst of

'vermin ;' there can be no two opinions about that.
In Norway, I know, the hooded crow is pretty omni-
vorous. So he is in Scotland, out of the breeding
time. In winter he will eat corn, or kill field voles,
or gorge himself on stinking fish on the seashores
But the black and hooded crows are dire enemies of
sitting grouse. They carry the eggs away to the rock
near their nest, and the amount of mischief they do is
incalculable. An acquaintance of mine saw three
'hoodies' attack a young grouse. He was a fine
bird, and could fly a little, but he could not withstand
the attack of three of the black rascals. A few sharp
blows upon the back of the head soon disabled him,
and placed him at the disposal of his cowardly assail-
ants. There is no worse pest in Scotland than the
hooded crow. The carrion crow is as mischievous,
but its visits to the grouse's home are more irregular.
Much as I dislike the use of poison, I think it should
be employed in the extermination of hooded crows,
provided only that the eggs which have been
'doctored' with strychnine be placed in a forked
branch, or in a crag of the rocks to which no four-
footed animal is likely to penetrate. The careless use
of poison almost amounts to criminality. Only a few
years ago, a fine golden eagle was killed by poison in
a curious way. A neighbouring keeper had prepared

some rats with strychnine and put them out on the hill as a bait for hooded crows. Unhappily, the male of a pair of golden eagles, then breeding in the locality, chanced to swallow one of the defunct rats, and perished miserably, to our eternal regret.

Some individual rooks are most persistent in harrying grouse nests, and owners of rookeries ought in my opinion to be held legally bound to shoot their rookeries every season ; for these voracious birds are long-lived, and if too numerous in a district, they do harm in a variety of ways that the general public never dream of.

Whether jackdaws are generally mischievous on a moor I cannot say, but I know that in a dry season they rob many grouse nests, and I think they should be treated as vermin, and shot if possible at sight whenever they appear on the hill. Richardson's skuas are sometimes shot as destructive to grouse. They would no doubt bolt a tiny grouse if they felt hungry, and a chance offered itself ; but that is not a contingency which happens frequently. The black-backed gulls are very destructive to young birds of every kind, especially the lesser variety. I do not think the great black-backed gull troubles much about grouse. He cares more for fish and for carrion. But the lesser black-backed gull is a shame-

less gourmand, and does a great amount of mischief.
He likes the young wild ducks better than the tiny
grouse, but nothing seems to come amiss to his
hungry maw. It occasionally happens that an old
herring gull takes to felonious practices. They suck
poisoned eggs eagerly, and I have seen individual
birds beating the hill day after day searching for
grouse nests. I have also known the herring gull to
carry off young chickens from a cottage door. But
the grouse suffers more from hooded crows than from
gulls or any other of its natural enemies. Cats that
have run wild, collies that are badly fed, these, with
foxes and stoats, are the worst furred foes that the
grouse has to dread. In the Highlands we kill out
the foxes, at least so far as is possible. It is very
necessary to keep them down, for they would com-
mit sad havoc among the lambs if allowed to become
numerous.

It may be said in conclusion that the grouse has
fewer enemies to fear than formerly. The marten
cat and wild cat anciently took their toll of moor-
fowl, but their presence has been banished from most
of the haunts of the red grouse.

CHAPTER IV

THE PLUMAGE OF THE GROUSE

CONSIDERABLE interest attaches to the plumage of the grouse, and most sportsmen have had occasion to remark upon the great variability of both sexes. This would not apply to the chicks, which are at first clothed in fine down, greyish yellow in ground colour, prettily variegated with chestnut and dark-brown markings. Nor does it apply either to the birds in first feather. 'At first the upper parts are brownish black, each feather edged and barred with yellow,' says Macgillivray, and a young bird in my hand agrees with this description, though some of the edgings to the feathers are pale chestnut rather than yellow, and the extremities of the feathers of the interscapular region are spotted with buffy white; the lower parts are yellowish grey barred with pale reddish yellow. From this condition the birds pass gradually into the chief stages of adult plumage, which have been very cleverly worked out by Mr. J. G. Millais, who possesses a

large number of skins of the Scotch grouse. Both
male and female grouse are liable to leucotism, or, in
other words, to exhibit a tendency to assume white or
light-coloured plumage. The male grouse have two
dominant types of plumage, the red and the black.
The females have three principal plumages : the black,
the spotted and the yellow. The red is found, according to Mr. Millais, principally in Ireland and the
Outer Hebrides. He finds little difference in Irish
birds whether they be killed on the swampy ground
of the north and south or upon the high mountains
of Mayo, Connemara and Donegal.

The black form ' is the most unusual of the three
types, and one which is very rarely developed to any
degree of purity. It is more often to be found mixed
with the red or the white type, but most commonly
with both. When combined with these two forms, it
is the one most commonly met with by the sportsman
during winter, and five old cocks out of six, shot
at that season, will be found to be of this type.'

As for the females, Mr. Millais decides that the
red type is the rarest, and the spotted and breeding
dress birds are the most beautiful. 'The females of
the red Irish bird are yellow, and not red, as would
be supposed ; they are, however, quite different from
what are generally known among Yorkshiremen as

" yellow hens," which latter are finer in the markings of the feathers, and lack the boldness of the lines found in the Irish bird.' Mr. Millais points out that grouse will be found in full moult in April, August and October, but they change plumage gradually all through the year. From the month of May the plumage of both sexes passes through all the changes mentioned in the case of the ptarmigan, and every fresh month brings its alteration of feathers, either by moulting, discoloration, or both, till by November the bird stands clothed in its winter dress, that shows the type completed in one form or another. Young birds of the year are easily distinguished till the month of September, but by November it is impossible to see any difference between them and the old birds. Many men who have spent the best part of their lives on the moors will assure you that grouse vary in colour according to the ground they frequent, just as others feel convinced that they find certain types of colour in certain counties. Thus they hold that what they call 'stone-bred grouse' are reared in rocky places, and that their plumage is barred rather than spotted, and of a generally greyer tone of colour than is elsewhere met with. I cannot say that I personally place much faith in such assertions, believing that birds vary almost indefinitely even on moors in a single county. As regards the white type, though Mr. Millais distinguishes it as a separate phase, I do not see how it is to be separated from leucotism. Albinism—i.e. the correlation of white plumage and pink irides—is another question altogether. Albino birds have often been obtained, but I have never yet come across an albino grouse, though I have heard of several white ones. But the white type of plumage seems to be akin to leucotism, and I hardly see how we can separate the two things. Many grouse have the lower parts beautifully frosted with white in winter. Sometimes white feathers appear among those of the back. Not rarely do white feathers crop out on the throat and breast. Birds which have the flight feathers of the wings partially or entirely white are obtained both in England and Scotland from time to time.[1] More decided varieties occur in which the ground colour of the plumage is buffish or greyish-white or pale silvery, varied with the usual characteristic markings in a subdued form. Such birds have been obtained in Ireland, England and Scotland. Mr. Millais considers that they are

---

[1] I should feel very grateful to any reader who would send us a white variety of the grouse for the Carlisle Museum at any future time. Such a gift would, of course, be cased with the donor's name attached to it, and should be addressed to myself, or to The Curator, The Museum, Carlisle.

most liable to occur at a high altitude in the north of
Scotland. It may very well be so. Most of those
that I have heard of myself were killed in the north
of England at a very moderate elevation above sea-
level. That such varieties are rare there can be no
doubt, but they are not always preserved, even when
procured. These pied and so-called white grouse are
often bred from ordinary parents. On the other hand,
when the sport has once cropped up, it is liable to be
perpetuated, if the first pied or light-coloured birds
are spared. Last season (1893) a hen grouse was
shot near Alston in curious plumage. The wings were
cream-coloured, and the body feathers were of a dirty
white. Three of her young birds were pied with
white ; the other four birds of the covey were ordinary
grouse. A few springs ago a Skiddaw shepherd sent
me word that a white grouse was sitting on eggs upon
the farm at which he worked. Unfortunately I was
not able to go and see the bird. I have often thought
of introducing the willow grouse to my own moor, in
the hope that it might interbreed with the red grouse.
These two species appear to be descended from one
common ancestor. The young of the willow grouse
bears a close resemblance to the young red grouse in
first feather. The willow grouse has an enormously
wide range ; it is, in fact, almost circumpolar, being

found in the northern parts of both the old and the
new worlds. Its flight and note are those of the red
grouse; but, in addition to having acquired a permanent
plumage of the white type, it has learnt also to perch
in trees, an accomplishment to which the red grouse
has not yet taken kindly. Possibly the red grouse is
an insular form of the willow grouse, which still puts
on many white feathers in some parts of its Western
home. This knotty point, unfortunately, we cannot
decide satisfactorily. The red grouse is monogamous
and consorts only with its own kind. There are
nevertheless a few well-authenticated specimens of the
wild cross between the red grouse and black-game,
as there are also perfectly black examples of the red
grouse. As long ago as 1836, Mr. Macgillivray
examined and dissected a hybrid of this cross.
Altogether he examined three specimens which showed
the characters of both the species from which they
were derived, and furnished the following description
of a male specimen : 'In form and proportion it is
similar to a female black grouse. The bill is of the
same form as in that bird. The supraocular mem-
brane resembles that of the red grouse, having a thin
free fringed margin, which is not the case with that of
the blackcock. The feathers are generally oblong,
broadly rounded, and have a large tufty tumule. The

tail is complete, slightly forked as in the female black grouse, but of only *sixteen* feathers, as in the red grouse. The quills are twenty-six. The tarsi are feathered all round, without a bare space behind. The toes are also feathered a third down, as are the interdigital membranes, and the plumage of these parts is as bushy as in the red grouse. They are margined with pectiniform scales, as in the black grouse. The claws are very long, arched, with thin parallel edges, like those of the red grouse and grey ptarmigan.' [1]

The bird just described, which we may consider the type of this variety of hybrid, had the upper parts generally minutely undulated with brownish black and brownish red, with very narrow terminal bands of white. The upper part of the head was minutely mottled with brownish red, brownish black, and grey, but the rest of the neck was black, with a tinge of reddish purple. The primaries were greyish brown. The tail was black, the eight middle feathers narrowly tipped with white. On the lower parts the feathers were black, tipped with white, those of the sides being banded with red. The only hybrid between the red grouse and black-game that has hitherto been obtained in England is a fine male preserved

---

[1] *British Birds*, i. 162.

in the collection of T. H. Horrocks, Esq., of Eden
Brows, Carlisle. Several specimens have been met
with in Scotland, and a single hybrid of this kind has
lately been obtained in Wales. I have heard of two
other birds referred to this species, but in neither instance was the bird preserved, the reason being that
they were hard shot. This is a misfortune, for the two
species interbreed so very rarely that all specimens of
their hybrid offspring possess great interest for naturalists. There is reason to think that a more extraordinary hybrid than that just named occasionally
occurs, viz. the offspring of the red grouse and partridge
Mr. Howard Saunders has devoted the following remarks to an accredited hybrid : 'Hybrids between
the partridge and any other species are uncommon,
but Mr. F. Bond has a bird shot on Blubber-house
Moor, near Harrogate, in August 1866, by the present
Lord Walsingham, which appears to be the result of
a cross with the red grouse, the bill being strong and
grouse-like, the tarsi and feet partially feathered, the
breast and body mottled with pale reddish-brown with
a sprinkling of grey, the quill feathers dirty white, with
lavender-grey outer webs. The brown colour of the
upper parts is not very significant, but the feathering
of the tarsi and feet seems tolerably conclusive.' [1]

[1] Yarrell, *British Birds*, iii. 114.

The feathering of the tarsi does not satisfy my mind about the bird ; for this reason, that I have grounds for believing that common partridges are liable to be 'feather-legged.' A Crossfell keeper assured me that he had shot partridges with feathered legs, and referred me to a shepherd whom we met on Crossfell. When I asked that worthy whether he had seen any 'fell partridges,' he asked at once, 'Do you mean the *rough-legged* ones?' adding that he knew them well.   Mr. J. G. Millais states that two hybrids between the red grouse and partridge have been obtained in Scotland, but he has not been able to describe these interesting specimens.   It seems perfectly possible that the red grouse may interbreed with its ally the ptarmigan, but upon this point no conclusive evidence is at present available.   One other point at least remains to be noticed, and that is the weight of grouse. The cock birds not infrequently weigh 28 or $28\frac{1}{2}$ ounces in the North of England, when in first-rate condition in every respect.   Anything over 30 ounces is noteworthy, but a weight of 32 ounces is not unprecedented.

CHAPTER V

GROUSE-BECKING

THE capture of wild birds has always exercised the resources of human ingenuity from time immemorial. The ancient Egyptians were masters of the art of fowling, and some of their methods still survive. I shall presently speak of certain methods of poaching red grouse ; but I propose to treat first of the dubious but not necessarily illegal pastime known throughout the breadth of the North of England as grouse-becking, or becking for grouse. Those writers who have hitherto essayed to write about the natural history of grouse seem to ignore one important feature in their habits. Exception must be made of Mr. H. E. Dresser, who published the following note by Mr. Alston in the ' Birds of Europe ' : ' Early on frosty mornings, the cocks are fond of perching on a "know" or hillock, and uttering their clear-ringing " *Er—eck—kek—kek !* *wuk, wuk wuk.*" At such times they may often be seen to rise perpendicularly

F

in the air to a height of several feet, and then drop
again on the same spot.' This brief remark supplies
the key to the sport of 'becking.' When grouse go
to roost late on in the afternoon, they do not huddle
together like partridges, but scatter over the ground
on which they intend to sleep, at the same time taking
care to keep but a little distance apart. When the
old male wakes in the morning, his first thought is to
find his mate and sport with her during the early
hours that precede the rising of the sun. Accordingly,
rising on the wing, the male grouse begins to indulge in short, playful flights towards the object of
his attentions. Rising quietly off the ground, the bird
flies up to a height of fifteen or twenty feet above the
ground. He then commences to drop again, and
simultaneously utters his cry, '*err—beck, beck, beck,
beck, goback, goback, goback,*' the latter portion of his
cry being concluded as he alights upon a tussock of
heather or some other natural prominence. The
female responds to the overtures of her mate, and he
continues to repeat his amorous performance until the
arrival of daylight suspends his erotic demonstrations.
The North-countryman who desires to go 'becking'
takes the trouble to ascertain in advance where the
birds are most likely to be met with in his neighbourhood. He rises from his bed in the dead of the

night, fills his pockets or belt with cartridges, and
sallies forth through the darkness to the spot in which
he intends to obtain sport. Arrived at the right place,
which is generally quite in the centre of the bleak
moorlands, and often miles from any human habitation, the fowler takes up his position behind the best
screen that offers itself. The angle of two stone walls
often serves as a temporary shelter, or he may hide
himself beside a pile of peats that are drying in the
wind. He has to remain perfectly still and silent, no
matter how cold the job may be, for any demonstra-
tion of impatience would surely spoil his chances of
success. As soon as ever he hears a cock grouse start
to call, his own business begins. His task in the first
instance is simply to reproduce as nearly as he can
the call of the hen grouse, which is not easy to in-
scribe upon paper, but may perhaps be rendered '*yap,
yap, yap, yap,*' or '*youe, youe, youe.*'

The cry of the hen is reproduced in several ways. I
know a Cumbrian peasant who despises the assistance of
any instrument in 'becking.' He contrives to imitate
the cry of the female grouse by compressing the
nostrils with one hand and drawing in his breath, which
is then emitted in deep gasps. This he has practised
for years, and he can call male grouse up to his cottage
door most successfully. Some men use a metal bird-

call, others a bramble stem which has been hollowed
out with a red-hot wire. The majority of those who
go out ' becking' carry with them the stem of a clay
pipe, and use this as their call. It does not matter,
in fact, how the sound is reproduced, provided it be
communicated in a soft key and bear a close resemblance to the cry of the bird. Long and unwearied
practice in calling is the chief requisite for successful
grouse-becking, coupled with a quick and accurate ear
for sound. I have met with one or two men who can call
hen grouse almost as easily as cocks, but no one cares
to shoot the female birds. The strategy of the fowler,
then, is very simple. He has to call the cock grouse
up to him as to a supposed female. The bird that has
begun to answer him flies up and alights upon a tussock
of moss or other prominence in order to take his
bearings of the female companion which he wishes to
join ; the fowler calls the grouse at short intervals until
the bird arrives within shot. He then shoots him, if
he can, in the dim uncertain light which precedes the
arrival of the dawn. When the day breaks the grouse
cease to ' beck' and begin to look for an early breakfast. It is not a sport for a neophyte, but an old hand
often manages to bag several grouse in the course of
an outing. It must not oe supposed that this is
necessarily regarded as poaching. In Yorkshire, in

Cumberland, and Westmoreland, if not in other counties, 'becking' for grouse is or was recognised as a highly entertaining sport, and frequently put into exercise, though it has latterly fallen into disuse. Still no old-fashioned keeper in Lakeland or on the Border thinks anything of getting a brace or two of grouse for his master's larder by 'becking.' Lots of stirring stories about this sport are told by the reserved dalesmen ; but they are shy of favouring strangers with their confidences, and any irregularities that they happen to allude to, are sure to have happened to some acquaintance, for they are too sharp to willingly compromise themselves.

One of the most successful of latter-day fowlers was a 'proper poacher,' who chiefly resided in Durham and Northumberland, working at his trade as a miner. Cumberland was his native county, and he came home occasionally in order to indulge in a spell of poaching on his favourite preserves, the keeper in charge being his particular enemy. One fine morning late in autumn, when a sharp frost had just set in, the 'proper poacher' rose betimes and shook himself, after which he strolled off to the hill, a moor near Crossfell, to call grouse. The weather was so specially propitious that he felt certain of some exciting sport, nor was he disappointed. He had no sooner arrived at his hiding place, and 'got

set,' than he began to call. To his satisfaction he
was very soon answered by a grouse, which alighted
on a knoll within shot of his position. He took a
very careful aim with his old muzzle-loader, and his
finger was already touching the trigger, when, to his
astonishment, another gun 'went off and shot t' bird.'
Recognising the sportsman who had spoilt his shot,
he deemed it prudent to slip home unnoticed and
return to bed. A few hours later the keeper, who had
evidently expected to meet him on the moor, called
at his lodgings and proceeded to chaff the poacher
whose practices troubled him, with the homely inquiry,
'What's matter thou isn't out this morning?' The
old hand could not conceal his annoyance any longer,
and he blurted out the fact which he had tried to
conceal : 'If thou'd been half a minute langer, lad,
thou'd have seen whether I was out or not !'

Frosty weather suits the pastime of 'becking' best
—dry frost, that is to say, unaccompanied by any
serious fall of the temperature. It must be understood that 'becking' is not always successful even on
days that appear highly favourable. There are days
when the birds 'beck' freely and others when they
will hardly 'beck' at all, though no reason for their
acting differently on these occasions can be fairly
assigned. The champion 'becker' of a certain fell-

side village is the local shoemaker, who loves to narrate his experiences. It so fell out, he says, that upon a certain day he started soon after midnight for a favourite spot, distant about six miles from his cottage, and situated in the very heart of a 'smittle' place for grouse. The track was ill defined, and he seemed to be a long time in arriving at his destination. When at length he reached the scene of his intended operations, he sat down in the moss and waited for the approach of the grey twilight. After long suspense at last his ears were gladdened with the much-desired challenge of an old cock grouse. He called in answer, and the bird responded and flew nearer and nearer, until the exciting moment arrived when he saw the moorfowl 'sit up' upon a prominent tuft of heather. Taking a careful aim, as he thought, with his heavy fowling-piece, he pulled the trigger, and, as he thought, killed his bird. However, he was too old a hand to show himself prematurely, and as his gun was only a single muzzle-loader, he thought it best to reload before he jumped up. But no sooner had he rammed a fresh charge home than he looked up and spied the bird sitting on the tuft of heather as before. He concluded that he must have missed it after all, and he took a second shot at it with a similar result. To cut the story short, our hero fired nine successive shots, as he declares, without ever leaving his hiding place, at a grouse which seemed to lead a charmed life, as it always reappeared. He fired a tenth shot ; no bird could be then seen. He therefore jumped up, and ran to the knoll of heather, where he found no fewer than ten dead grouse disposed around the spot that had proved so fatal. His explanation was this : that he had fallen in with a company of birds which were running close together, and that each time that he fired and knocked over a bird, another bird in the company ascended the point of danger to make a fresh reconnaissance. It is not at all unusual for an old hand to get a brace of birds at one spot in the half light of approaching day. If a bird offers a chance to the gunner, but is missed and flies away, its companion is pretty certain to follow it. On the other hand, if one bird is shot dead, and drops still upon the heather, its companion will probably remain waiting for it to rise, and perhaps afford a second shot. Grouse can be shot in this way at any time between August and March, but the last months of the year are held in most esteem.

In March the male grouse are very restless, and fly from one knoll to another, frequently alighting. They still 'beck,' but their cry has become slightly altered since the autumn ; they now seem to say

'churrr—*goback, goback.*' It would be interesting to
know whether the custom of 'becking' was practised
by our forefathers when they shot with crossbows.
I am inclined to fancy that in those days their larders
were often supplied with *snared* grouse, which had
been captured upon the 'stooks' of corn. Probably
the methods of setting snares for grouse are various,
as indeed I know they are. That which appears to
be most extensively practised, at any rate in the north
of Scotland, is to prepare a number of snares of fine
wire and attach them to a stout cord, which is then
stretched across a 'stook' of oats, the ends of the
string being securely attached to two stakes which
have been driven into the ground on either side of
the 'stook.' Another plan is to set a great number
of snares in the runs which the grouse make through
the heather when feeding. These snares are generally
made of fine copper wire, bent in the form of a loop
of from five to six inches in diameter. The free end
of the wire is doubled, and attached to a tuft of ling
by a piece of string. The loop of wire is often held
in the proper position by a small cleft piece of wood.
Some men take grouse in drag-nets, when the birds
are roosting in rough grass and young heather ; but I
fancy that this method of poaching grouse is less
practised than formerly. Sportsmen cannot be too

careful to enlist the interest of herds and shepherds in
the preservation of grouse. The goodwill of the small
farmers and tenants of allotments abutting on the
moors should be courted sedulously, and their for-
bearance rewarded. I say so, as indicating a practical
policy, for these men have many temptations to acquire
birds dishonestly, or, as a working man expressed it,
'There can be no bigger poachers if they take it that
way.' Some individuals allow their dogs to snap sitting grouse. Colley bitches are often apt pupils in
such nefarious practices. The story goes that a coun-
tryman was known on a certain occasion to have
prematurely exhausted his credit at the bar of the
'pub' he patronised, for he was thirsty still. He
then inquired of a friend if the 'laal bitch' was at
home. Being answered in the affirmative, he called
for the sheepdog, and having taken her to the hill, he
soon returned with a brace of 'snapped' grouse, which
renewed his credit. On another occasion—the sheep
were being gathered—a small farmer who had volun-
teered to assist the shepherds was observed to be
carrying his short coat over his arm with more than
usual carefulness. On inquiry being made, it turned
out that this rascal had allowed his cur-dog to snap
a whole covey of little grouse. The dog's master
willingly joined in the illegality ; to quote his own

words, ' He thought he would have a pie when he got home.' But how was the game to be stowed away? He had tied the sleeves of his jacket, so that they were converted into bags, in which the birds were nicely concealed. He then turned the coat inside out, in order that the sleeves might not be seen, and congratulated himself upon his cleverness in smuggling stolen grouse. Mr. J. G. Millais unearthed an old Highland poacher, who explained an ingenious method of capturing both grouse and ptarmigan which is often adopted in Ross-shire and Sutherland when the snow is deep. ' The poacher discovers a place on the hill where the birds are in the habit of sitting when snow has fallen. To this spot he repairs when the down-fall has ceased, and before night if possible, so that the snow may be still soft and not frozen. He is armed with nothing but a bag of oats or corn, and a beer or, still better, champagne bottle. Thus, having nothing of a suspicious nature in his possession, he would be allowed to pass, even though searched. Arrived on his ground, he proceeds to make a number of indentations in the snow with his bottle, and the bottom of the cavity, just within reach of the birds, he fills up with grain, and, scattering the rest of the contents of the bag near the holes on the surface, he departs, to return next morning and collect his plunder. Unless a frost occurs the trick must necessarily be a failure, but if the cavity becomes properly hardened, and the birds find the food, success is almost a certainty. A grouse or ptarmigan finding what to them is a great delicacy, immediately imparts the knowledge of its presence to others in the neighbourhood. They at once greedily devour all the grain that is lying around, and then turn their attention to obtaining the stores lying in the holes. Probably by straining their necks to the uttermost they may be able to reach a few grains, but this only serves to whet their appetites, and they must have more. Consequently they go on reaching till they eventually topple over into the hole, which just comfortably corresponds to their own size, and in which the more they struggle to extricate themselves the more firmly do they become wedged. When a bird is forced into a hole, even should the sides be smooth, it is not easily withdrawn, as the feathers resist being pulled backwards ; but when the sides are rough the retention is doubly great, and the feeble strugglings of the unfortunate bird in its cramped position are not sufficient to enable it to escape.'

Of late years much vexation has been occasioned to sportsmen in the north of England by the deadly practice of netting grouse with fixed engines. These consist of nets made of very fine twine, netted to a three-inch mesh, which are suspended from poles placed ten yards apart, at such a height as permits the fellside sheep to pass under them. Each net in a series is independently suspended on a cord stretched across the poles, and can be hung tight or loose, as desired. They are easily put up—at least, I am assured that two men can fix up a thousand yards of nets in an hour. The nets are shifted according to the direction of the wind. Grouse have generally a favourite line of flight, but they do not always adhere to the same course. When the birds are flying, there is sure to be a leader in the company. This one strikes the net almost to a certainty, and down it instantly falls. The way in which these nets are worked is very simple. Of course they could not be tolerated on any gentleman's moor, but certain outsiders hire small farms and allotments on the edge of grouse moors, with a view to annexing their neighbours' grouse. The birds themselves assist inadvertently in their own capture. Their principal time for shifting about is in the evening, after feeding, and again after 'becking' in the morning. But they are particularly restless on many moors about the end of September and in October, especially the female birds, and the first strong gale brings many of them off the hill-tops, looking for more sheltered and genial situations. Naturally, many of them seek the edges of the moors, and are caught in the nets set upon such allotments as abut upon them. This method of netting grouse is very disastrous. The mischief of capturing the birds is only part of the evil. The worst feature about it is that the hens are caught in such numbers as seriously to interfere with the breeding stock. It is true that birds of both sexes will fly a long distance to a patch of black heather during a prevalence of severe frost and heavy snow, but earlier in the season the number of hens caught generally outnumbers the cocks very seriously. The reason for this seems to be twofold. The hens shift about in packs more irregularly than their male companions, and they are less partial to the high grounds, but seek the lower portions of the moor, and such as are most screened from the east winds. Fine open weather, however, suits the grouse-netters best, and they say that the birds fly very long distances when shifting about the hills. The old cocks keep their own 'heaf,' or station, on the hill with more constancy than their female companions. In the morning the birds 'start to feed' soon after they cease 'becking,' but they do not feed so heavily in the forenoon as later in the day, an hour or two before dusk especially, when their crops become distended with food. In the morning hours they like to sun themselves in dry moss or on an open slab of rock, each bird resting with one wing expanded like a fowl. As for the ways of disposing of poached grouse, they are manifold. Sometimes they are hawked about the country by persons selling peat. Often they are taken to market with other produce. The railways and parcel post both offer excellent facilities for furthering the distribution of the birds. Personally, I was once favoured with a fine red grouse in rather an unexpected fashion. Our keeper happened to shoot an Iceland gull, and wrote to inform me that he despatched the bird to me by that day's parcel post. His letter came, but no gull appeared, and I therefore begged the Post Office authorities to make a search for the lost bird. The gull arrived eventually by rail. Meantime the postal authorities had taken counsel, and finding that a grouse without a label had come into their possession, they forwarded to me the moor-fowl, plucked and roasted as it was, with a polite intimation that they conjectured that this, being evidently a bird of some description, might probably prove to be the Iceland gull that had gone astray.

SHOOTING THE GROUSE

BY

A. J. STUART-WORTLEY

G

CHAPTER I

'THE SCOTCH MAIL'

THE lamps are being lit in Bloomsbury. Long ago
they have begun to twinkle in the small bird shops of
the 'Dials,' and to flare in the gin palaces of the
avenues. As the dull brown haze of a London
August evening settles down the streets become
thicker with people, and every tenement in this part
of the town pours forth its quota to the stream upon
the pavement, there to strut or loaf, or drink away
its short hour of ease, until bed, straw, and plank
receive once more the weary bones of the toilers of
the city.

As your cab rattles along towards Euston or
King's Cross the wheels spatter black mud—legacy
of the leaden drizzle of the afternoon—upon the pale
faces and ragged clothing of the denizens of the
cellar and the garret : men, women, and children in
crowds, to whom gas serves for air, garbage for food,
and vitriol for drink ; who have never trod a hillside

G 2

or leapt a stream, and to whom heather and rock, bracken and pine are as unknown as the *Ovis Poli* to an Islington butcher.

Bound as you are for the land where these gifts of Nature, added to the charms of stag, salmon, and grouse, await you in plenty, the contrast between your happy state of mind and the cheerless, airless lives of these people is brought vividly before you, and you must give a glance of sincere pity to the groups of pallid faces—whiter and thinner, it seems to you, than usual —huddled together in dark doorways, or peering hungrily from cellar gratings.

But you and I were not ' born to set it right '— here is the great railway station looming dark but welcome through the fog, the narrow shave of an upset as you drive in at the tall narrow gates, the line of flashing lamps and eager porters, and as you leap 'o the ground and hand your minor baggage to the old man with a face like a winter apple, and well-worn patches of grey on the familiar green corduroy, the squalor of the Dials passes from your mind, and cheerfully you set your face towards the North.

Tickets are taken, luggage stowed, dogs bundled in, rod, gun, rifle, and cartridge cases carefully seen to, book selected, sleeping berth inspected, and ere you have quite finished the final instructions to the trusty servant who remains in town, suddenly, with no more warning than a short blast from the pea-whistle of the smart guard, the great train begins to glide slowly and smoothly away. As you pull up the window, a shout of 'Good-bye!' from some less fortunate person, seeing off a dear friend, rings along the platform, and turning back into the well-lit carriage you realise, as the train plunges into the dark tunnel under Hampstead with a quickening pace and an increasing rattle, that you are fairly off.

But you are very tired ; the last day's business has been heavy and anxious, and you haven't yet shaken off the clinging meshes of your work-a-day life. Wearily you lean back in your seat, and as the hoarse roar of the tunnels and the flying flashes of the station lamps tell of the terrific pace at which the train is now travelling, you sink, the end of your cigar glowing fiercer in the dim light, into a lethargy variously tinged with care and hope. Presently you rouse yourself to make arrangements for the night, hand your tickets to the civil 'conductor,' with instructions to wake you half an hour before Perth, dispose your bed and wraps, and before darkening the light pull down the window for a moment to sniff an air that blows fresher and sweeter than St. Stephen's,

Capel Court, Lincoln's Inn, **or Pall Mall**, and to become aware that you are **tearing** over the borders of
Hertfordshire at fifty-five miles an hour, on a magnificent starlight night.   The great oaks and elms of old
England fleet by you like streams of cardboard trees,
the long, low landscape fades into the blue-black of
the sky, **and** so steady is the going that the distance
seems like **a** slow dioramic procession of woods and
hills, while **you** alone are motionless, and the nearer
objects—houses, fences, telegraph poles, parapets, or
platforms—but so many formless phantoms, rushing
with roar, scream, and rattle back to the South.

Then comes sleep, in which the monotonous vibra-
tion of the train reiterates itself persistently, and intrudes
upon your dreams ; your clients, patients, colleagues,
or opponents whispering vague things **to** you **to the**
eternal accompaniment **of the noise of the** wheels,
their words and your replies always twisted to fit in
with the exact beats of the pulse **of the engine** or the
clicking of the coupling irons.   A slackening, a hissing,
and a cessation of the throbs give you a moment of
conscious sanity at Rugby.   This has no concern for
you: **you gather** your rugs, always slipping off on to
the **floor, more** tightly round, **and** as the porters, like
far-off ghosts **shouting to each other** in a huge cavern,
repeat the **well-known name, all you** can think of is

that Dickens wrote something wonderful about Rugby Junction, and that you once knew a man who kept horses there and hunted from London—very inconvenient, but—— you are asleep again.

This time fairly and placidly, with hardly a pause in a vivid but pleasantly long dream, while you are whirled unconscious past the flaming cities and lurid wastes of the Black Country, to the open pure country, and suddenly, for no reason, you are broad awake ; a cold grey daylight is slanting through the cracks of the blinds, and the sight of your bundle of fishing rods in the corner reminds you that you have left London and business, and are going to the moors.

Ah, but it was the cold that woke you, for you are chilly, and drag down your cape—the old cape that has sheltered you from so many driving showers and cutting winds, that has been so often stained with blood and peat, oil and sea water, tea and travel—fold yourself in it up to your chin, and lie there in the grey dawn, thinking, listening to the occasional whistle of the engine, wondering whereabouts you are and what time it is, but supremely happy.

Your whole nature seems to have undergone some change. A purer air is filling your lungs, and though you have a very slight sore throat, and are, generally speaking, dirty, unkempt, and chippy, a wondrous calm

has come over your whole being. No longer do the
cares or dilemmas of yesterday assail your peace ;
the House of Commons and the City—how small
and far off they appear, as a little gleam of pale
sunlight illumines the details around you, and a
smothered rumbling tells that you are crossing a
bridge over a river. You *must* look out ; up goes
the blind ; and there, there are the everlasting hills.
Great grey-green slopes of Cumberland fells, patched
and scored with heaps and rifts of slaty stone, black
in the shadow and white and wet in the light ; veils
and wreaths of misty shower, like puffs from a colossal
steam-engine, travelling across the face of rock or
grass ; far up, a little slender white thread of a waterfall—you can almost hear the trickle and splash of
the water on the stones, or trace the sound of its
gurgling rush down through the beds of granite,
fringed with greener bracken, to the valley.

Black cattle grazing unconcerned along the lower,
white sheep on the higher slopes ; straggling stone walls
of any age dividing the huge pastures ; deep dens
down which the foaming becks are pouring, where the
mist clings longer and blacker until the early flight of
chattering rooks and jackdaws crossing to their feed
is relieved in deeper notes of black against it.

Now comes the sun, slanting along the hill, gilding

the knolls and silvering the wet stones ; the puffs of curling mist seem to draw themselves higher up, grow whiter and more palpable in his rays, and become absorbed in the solid gold-white mass of cumulus cloud floating against the blue of this glorious summer morning.

The hills, too, seem to have grown farther off, the landscape is lower, rich crops and waving corn appear, the silver stream of Eden reflects red bridges and black-green woods, and in a few more minutes a vision of red stone and brick, of old grey wall and clustering chimney, of filmy smoke against the luminous air, and — 'Carr-lisle' rings in a clear northern voice along the platform ; the train is still once more.

It is yet very early, and feeling warmer and more restful, though you peep out to look along the train (why ?), you do not care to rise. The northern dialect of the porters, contrasted with the accent of your London guard, arrests your ear for a moment ; you have time to note a few types, shepherds and nondescripts, loafing into the station as the light brightens, to catch some local train or receive some unsavoury package, and you are away again.

Soon appear the flat marshes that fringe the Solway Firth, the broad stretch of still water outside the reeds reflecting the white wings of the gulls or the strings of fowl rising seaward, the fainter, longer lines of the estuary, and far off, flecked with little diamond flashes of white in the sun, the great grey sea itself. Lines of black posts, of which you wonder the use and meaning, stretch through the reeds from the shore, as though seedlings from the black timbers of the long low bridge that carries you across the marsh. Little cottages nestling under sycamore and birch come in sight ; the great wreaths of steam from the engine float and fade away over the landscape, and as they whisk across a little village of white houses, brush over the slate roofs, and dance away into the fields beyond, a long wooden platform rattles past you, and the magic word 'Gretna,' in white letters on a blue board, tells that you are fairly over the Border, and fills your mind with thoughts of the comedies and tragedies which many such a glorious morning has witnessed around the blacksmith-parson's cot on the historic green.

What a contrast ! The whizz of your train, 'speed forty-five miles an hour,' with its living freight of a hundred persons, tearing past the little station, and the swaying, rolling post-chaise, with its steaming horses and sweating postboys, bearing the blushing girl-bride, the gallant bridegroom in laced cocked hat and coat, still in his hand the pistol with which he shot the leader of the pursuing chaise some ten miles back, clattering over the rudely paved main street and pulling up at the blacksmith's door !

Ah ! times are changed ; now no one stops at Gretna except by creeping trains to which in Bradshaw the ominous syllable ' Gov.' is tacked, and you yourself, sailing along in your sleeping car, to which a king's litter of a past age is for cost and cunning workmanship but a cheap and tawdry conveyance, are already among the rolling moors of Dumfries, and were you not so sleepy would be craning your neck at the window to catch sight of a brood of grouse rising lazily off the stone wall by the railway, and settling down again upon the nearest heathery knoll, crowing to the sun.

A second sleep comes over you, veiling your thoughts with delicious visions. Little you reck of the sweating toilers pausing by the great furnaces and glowing cinder heaps of Motherwell to stare as you roll by ; little of the clankings and shoutings, the shuntings and bumpings of inevitable Larbert ; little of the rush through station and town, past castle and cottage, manse and moor ; the rattle of wheels, the clanking of the iron, and the regular pant of the piston-rod have become your lullaby ; and you are enjoying a foretaste of the rest that we are promised in heaven.

The Dials wake to their dirt, Bloomsbury to its
business, and the slums to their squalor ; the lamps
are out again now, and the sickly rays of morning
rouses the pallid city folk to another day of struggling
toil.   The shiverings and fevers, vices and terrors,
miseries or murders of the London night are even
now being turned out naked to its bitter glare ; the
thundering din of traffic, the bawling of commerce,
and the shrieking of machinery drown in their deafen-
ing chorus the weeping of the weak, the moans of
the sick and dying, the cries of all their victims.
Only the strong, the clever, and the hopeful awake to
live in the stream that can no more be stemmed than
the tide of the ocean—the overwhelming civilisation of
a great city.

But you speed on in peaceful oblivion of all this,
in which at other times you bear your part, while you
are carried over hills and valleys clad with purple
heather, under a sky of boundless blue flecked with
shining white clouds, swaying gently round the
shoulders of great hills, gliding across deep ravines
and in and out of peaceful glens, threading through
thriving towns or lazy villages.   But now some
curious change in the music of the train noises
first puzzles, then half rouses you, and then, two
feet from your ear, one piercing cry of ' Scotsman,'

uttered in the shrill nasal twang of a Lowland newsboy, brings you straight up on your seat, and you are broad awake to find yourself at Perth. Hastily you get over a doubtful toilet, and feeling now as fresh as a lark, embark upon the sea of confusion which the great platform presents. Breakfast, rapid and hearty, refreshes you, and as you superintend the change of your baggage into another train—for you are bound still farther north—you have time to cast greetings to many an old friend, a bow or a smile to some fair ladies, and an oath or a caress to a brace of handsome setters who, coupled together and panting with excitement, have run between your legs and nearly upset you.

This is a shorter though slower run, and you feel yourself growing nearer and nearer to the magnet that is drawing you northward. Leisurely you mark the bloom on the heather, the emerald of the moss on the walls, the bright brown colour of the river, and the rings of the trout where he rises in the still, deep pool ; and as a greyhen sails out of the scrub and into a pine wood, you reflect with satisfaction on your new Purdeys, with the ejectors, and on the ' first-rate consignment' of Schultze powder with which your cartridges are loaded.

But here you are—arrived ! The sun shines brightly,

the breeze blows freshly, and there is no emperor or
sultan that may not envy your feelings as you cover
the short mile from the little station to the lodge in a
useful brown dog-cart with a fast-trotting pony in the
shafts.

A warm welcome from your host, and you are not
long in slipping into your shooting things, and ere the
clock has struck eleven are bowling along with a cheery
party to the moor. As you step on to the heather,
and feel the true moorland breeze in your face, your eye
is as keen and clear as the lens of a microscope, and
crossing the plank bridge over the river you pause to
mark in the brown waters flecked with snowy foam the
swirl where the big fish rose only yesterday, after the
great spate, which has left streamers of sodden hay,
dead logs, and leafy twigs clinging to the timbers of
the bridge and the overhanging birches at the side,
twelve feet above the present placid level of the
stream.

Can there be such a thing as toil or business, as
the turmoil of party strife or the grasping greed of
gain, in musty chambers, fœtid alleys, and paved courts?
It would be difficult to believe in their existence as
you survey the heavenly prospect before you after
climbing—somewhat laboriously, it must be confessed
—the first rounded knoll above the river, and paus-

ing to watch the dogs uncoupled and to give a first
eager and searching glance over your ground.

In the foreground the trim figures in grey home-
spun of your companions and the keepers, their keen
and healthy faces relieved against the peat or heather,
the polished gun-barrels glistening in the sun, the
liver and the white dog taking their first scamper, the
sturdy custodian of the ponies and the lunch, the
kilted boy with the other couple of dogs, the seedling
birches and feathery young larches of the moor edge
flickering in the golden light of the August noon, to
the sound of the steady roar of the great fall of waters
at the tail of the pool behind you.

Beyond, the colouring is gorgeous—away for
miles the slopes and shoulders, the knowes and
hollows of purple and pink heather stretch to where
the glassy loch lies shimmering under the solemn
precipices of a mighty peak with an historic name.
Supporting him on either side are ranged the rugged
forms of his giant brethren—a study in faint grey and
blue, with here and there a patch of dwindling snow
to tell of the bitterness of the recent storm. In this
glorious amphitheatre you attack your sport. The
white dog comes to a dead point on your side of a
knoll, and is beautifully backed by the liver-coloured
bitch, who halts on a great piece of flat rock some

seventy yards away, a motionless and perfect picture.
Three grouse rise, you kill with your first, and, your
host courteously waiting to let you deal with your first
right and left alone, strike the second hard but underneath, while he neatly drops the third bird—a beautiful
long cross-shot.

Exactly sixteen hours from the time you were
driving through Bloomsbury you have killed a right
and left of Perthshire grouse, on a spot which fifty
years ago would have taken eight days to reach, if
even in those days there had been anyone to try it.

The details of your day's sport, so well known in
their incidents, we will not follow. After a glorious
day, very weary, but, having acquitted yourself well,
supremely contented, what more delicious than the
long drive home down the glen, the moor darkling
on either side, the shadow deepening to blackness
as you wind through the big pine wood and are
shown against the western sky the capercailzie in
their accustomed place on the giant larch that over-
hangs the road, or the spot where the greyhen killed
herself against the carriage? Turning out of the
wood you come upon all the glory of the yellow
moon, just rising over the eastern hill, and glittering in
the waters of the loch ; the horses quicken their pace,
lights twinkle in the distance, and now as you swing

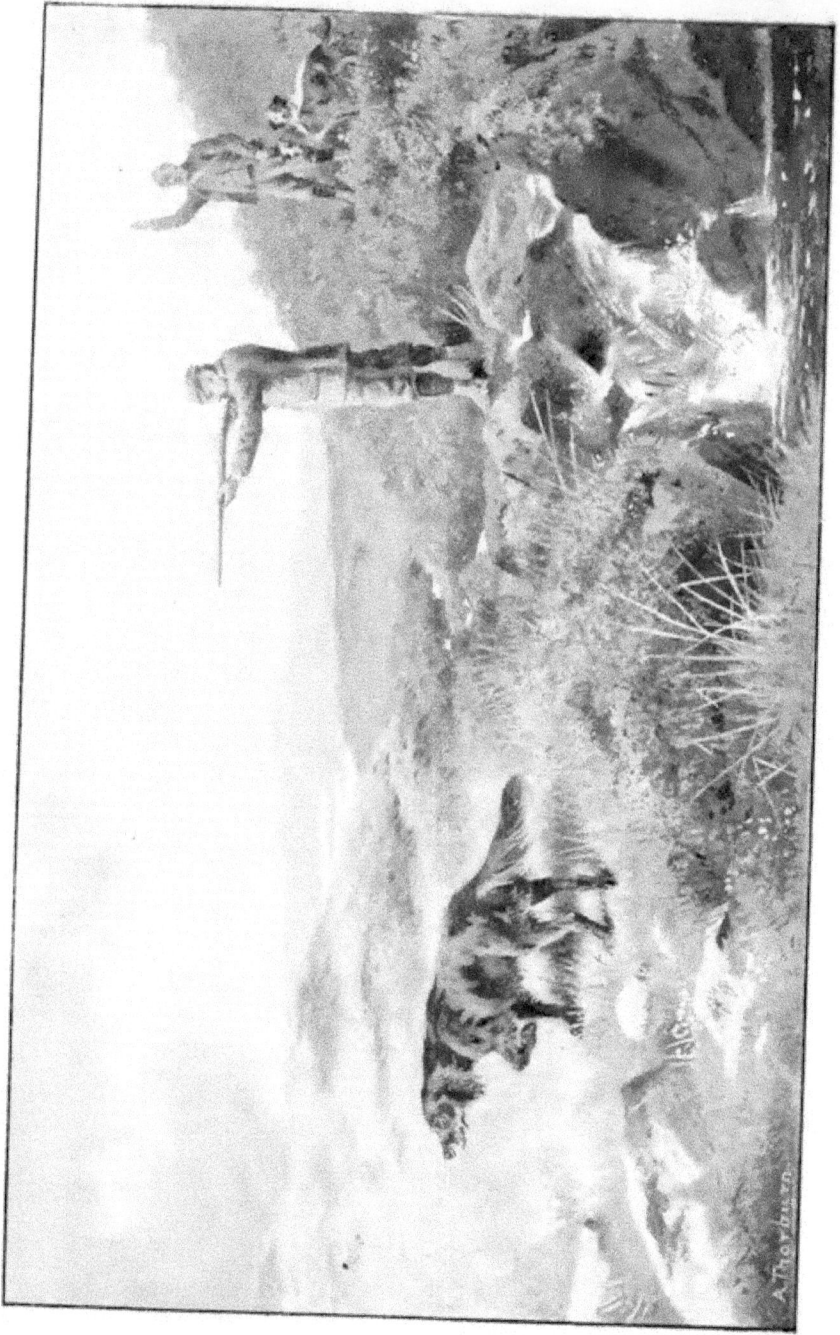

A.Thorburn.

in at the gate of the lodge grounds a savoury whiff
courts your nostrils from the shining kitchen window,
while as you turn the corner to the door the first
skirl of the pipes warns you that it is already half-
past eight, the ladies are waiting, and you must be
quick down to dinner.

A journey such as I have tried to describe is only
one of the many combinations which English brains
and love of sport have rendered not only possible but
usual. Truly the red grouse is responsible for many
things in these days, and, let envious or ignorant
persons sneer as they may, will continue to be so for
many years to come—until, in short, some one cleverer
than the rest of the world invents a means of driving
a plough through a peat bog, or dragging a harrow
across the rocky glens of Scotland and the north of
England.

The grouse has his influence over politics, as
we are constantly reminded ; over trade and railway
enterprise ; and last, but not least, over the well-being
and prosperity of a large proportion of our population.
The moors are to an Englishman what ' les eaux ' are
to the Frenchman, or the Alps to an Italian. Even
the wealthy Frenchman and the Italian are, with the
millionaire American or Austrian prince, to be found
pouring their gold into the pockets of the Highlander,

H

in pursuit of the hardy and succulent race of birds which will soon represent the only British monopoly in the world, and which are known as grouse.

Observe the scientific knowledge, the inventive power, the practical resource, and the financial enterprise which go to make up every detail of the marvellous journey from the south to the north of Great Britain. Short as it may seem to the man from New York or Chicago, it is still in moral and material detail the most remarkable piece of travelling in the world. And what has produced this? Not all the beauties of Edinburgh nor all the factories and furnaces of Glasgow; not the enterprise of Dundee nor the fisheries of Aberdeen ; nay, neither the Trossachs nor the Pass of Killiecrankie, the snows of Ben Nevis nor the depths of Loch Lomond, but grouse, grouse and nothing else !

It would be idle to attempt to forecast the political condition of these crowded islands in the next century, but of this I think we may be tolerably certain—that so long as the everlasting hills remain as they are, until, in short, some unthought-of metal, some unexpected industry arises to people their glens, tunnel their heights, and crush their rocks, so long will grouse remain a potent factor in the internal economy of the northern portion of our race.

It is notoriously difficult to get a straight answer
from a Scotchman, but this year, in conversation with
a very intelligent specimen of the Highlander, who
was, by the way, an enthusiastic supporter of Mr.
Gladstone, the replies that I elicited to my very direct
questions were so emphatic in favour of the existing
state of things, founded on his own intimate knowledge, that I wished some of those narrow city dwellers,
feeble in body and spiteful and envious in mind, who
so far as they dare attack everything in the nature of
sport and amusement, could have heard him on this
well-worn subject.

He would have none of the small crofter, who
starves himself and his family for a false sentiment
which ties him to the barren rock or spongy morass
which never can support them ; he was all in favour
of the large grazing farm of many thousand acres, and
of the wealthy sporting tenant from the South, who
comes to distribute his guineas and to repeople the
once famine-stricken glen. The men, he urged with
vehement sincerity and actual knowledge, who clamour
for the small holdings, have not the means to stock
them, nor those who encourage them the knowledge
to show them how to do it. How could these people
divide and pasture a hill, command a market for their
stock, or live in any fashion upon their allotted piece

of ground?   Pointing eloquently to the ruins of
many cottages of a bygone age, high up the glen near
the burn-side, he discoursed of the evils of the starving, hopeless life these little squatters led, and truly
observed that no men of to-day with any self-respect
would live huddled together in the filth and smoke,
and half-nourished on the snatches of meagre food
which were their normal conditions.

Fewer people, he said, there might be in the glen,
but there would after the first abortive trial be fewer
still were the rich graziers and the sporting tenants,
who between them employ so many hands and feed
so many mouths, to be chased away, and their places
taken by a lot of tag-rag and bob-tail with whom
discontent passes for independence, and insolvency
for liberty.   'Long live the grouse !' he cried ; 'they
do not interfere with sheep, and nothing else, save
eagles and foxes, hawks and stoats, could live up here.'

I have dwelt at some length in another volume of
this series [1] on the important question of the relations
between the owner or sporting tenant with the humbler
folk who become his neighbours or dependants ; on
the supreme importance, both to his sport and to the
well-being of the district, of goodwill and liberality on
his part and co-operation on theirs ; and I was rash

[1] *Partridge*, p. 239.

enough to appear as an optimist on the Game-law question. What I said of English, I might repeat more securely of Scotch sport. The value of game to the country in general—materially, from a commercial point of view; morally, from the interests and sympathies it tends to create or maintain between members of different classes—is enormous, and since it introduces civilisation and material prosperity to the most remote districts, it is especially so in the case of grouse.

The Scotch mail, running at lightning speed along its well-laid track, with all its luxuries and scientific appliances, its sleeping or dining cars, its heating apparatus and lavatories, its air-brakes and electric bells, its magnificent locomotives and trusty servants, its priceless freights and distinguished occupants, is the most intrinsically valuable expression of this state of things.

Long may it continue to run; long may the healthy attractions of the most picturesque and beautiful of British sports continue to fill its compartments, and help the dwellers of the far North to share the hard-earned gold of England's wealthier citizens!

CHAPTER II

'OVER DOGS'

To the average owner or tenant of a Scotch moor,
grouse shooting means 'over dogs' and nothing else.
A few years ago such was the onslaught made upon
driving and its partisans, that it became necessary to
take up the cudgels in its defence.   But now that all
Yorkshire, Derbyshire, and Durham have adopted it
exclusively, and that many persons in Scotland have
followed the example of these counties, the press and
the public recognise that it is useless to abuse a system
which those interested almost universally employ.

In treating this subject I have been obliged to record my honest conviction of the superiority of driving
as an art, as well as of its advantages to the general
stock of birds.   But in a work of this kind one must
endeavour to be just all round, and recognise the fact
that there are many persons, some of them excellent
shots and sportsmen, who would not on any account
abandon the ancient and beautiful sport of shooting

grouse over dogs, or to whom the organisation of drives would be neither convenient nor practicable.

As a youth I duly graduated with Don and Ponto, 'Wallass' and Lady on the higher moors of Forfar, Perth, and Aberdeen, and approached a point with as much keenness as ever Colonel Hawker felt when sculling to a bunch of fowl on the ooze of Keyhaven, or advancing on a covey in the sheltering stubbles of Longparish. Yet when I had been introduced to the increased excitement, the superior marksmanship, the ampler results, and the more picturesque aspect of the birds in Yorkshire driving, I became contemptuous of those who were content to plod day by day after their dogs for a much smaller number of comparatively easy shots. But one grows more catholic with age. I have had many pleasant days since then with other Dons and Pontos, and should regret as much as anyone to see the extinction of so valuable a race of dogs, or the complete abandonment of so picturesque a science.

I recall few days' shooting with greater pleasure than a bag of fifty-three brace to my own gun, which I made on September 23, 1872, on the late Sir Charles Forbes's moor in Strathdon, Aberdeenshire, after many hundreds of brace had been taken off the ground by both driving and walking ; and that, considering the date, was a satisfactory performance. There is nothing in it, perhaps, even worth recording ; yet the fact remains that it is graven on my memory as a red-letter day, and ranks in my reminiscences of varieties of shooting with some of the best days of driving in which I have ever taken part.

Shooting as practised in England is, on the whole, less selfish than most other forms of sport, yet it is also tinged with a proportion of the vice. I may, therefore, be forgiven for saying that I think grouse shooting over dogs is eminently a sport which is best enjoyed alone—that is, by one gun only. It is true that the party of two is the more correct form, granted that the pair work together absolutely without jealousy, and with exact knowledge of one another's powers. But these conditions are rare, and it is not too much to say that in no branch of shooting are greater sacrifices of result made to the essential qualities of courtesy and consideration for the capacity of your companion. If two guns can kill forty brace over dogs, you may be quite certain that the better of the two could have killed thirty brace, if not more, over the same ground on the same day. A good hand at the work can, if he chooses to set aside the unwritten laws of politeness and fair play, take so much advantage of an inferior hand as to practically absorb all the chances, and obtain what satisfaction he may from achieving much the larger share of the bag. But a few hints may help a man who is not an adept to avoid finding himself always in the position of second best, or trying too severely the temper or good manners of his more accomplished companion.

We will suppose that your dogs are well handled and steady, and that there is a fairly good scent, a breezy, pleasant day, and enough birds on the ground to reward you for hard work and good shooting, while —for it is the object of this work to assist, if possible, those who have something to learn—you are alongside a man who is much your superior, possibly a past master of the art. The first thing to note carefully and incessantly is the wind. This you must bear in mind all the time ; otherwise, when you see a point, you will be quite at sea as to where the birds are likely to be lying. There is no doubt that a wind blowing across the ground you are beating is altogether the best ; and supposing that you have as your allotted beat the long 'face' of a hill, with cultivated ground or pasture along the lower side, and the march on or just over the ridge on the upper, with the wind blowing downwards, it will be best to begin at the bottom, and work across and across till you have beaten the whole face, and pushed all the birds

possible forward. You will thus drive them mostly on
to some stretch of lower ground beyond, which will
give you probably your best sport towards evening.
As you work the ground in this way the birds will
obviously be always lying above, that is, up wind of
the dog, and the moment you see him point you
should walk in a slant towards the ground above him,
rather than straight to him as the novice would. If
you do the latter, and your friend the professor is on
your right, he will cross higher up, and probably,
while appearing to let you go straight for the point
and the best chance, walk right into the covey and
get a double shot, while you, though still level with
him, are yet a long way below the birds. Again, you
must watch the behaviour of the dog narrowly. Should
he stop very suddenly in full career, turning his head
slightly back, then run quickly a few yards, do the
same thing again, but appear unsteady and inclined
to hunt further, he is probably up wind of the birds ;
in which case walk pretty straight to where he first
pointed. If, again, he simply points very steadily, go
slowly up to him, a little up wind as before ; if he
draws rather rapidly and keenly ahead, get after him
—slanting your course up wind of him—as quickly as
you can. These will be wild birds, probably old
ones, whom it is most desirable to destroy, and they

will be running or creeping uneasily before him, most likely working up wind also. In this case you may get a shot by fast walking or running where you would not by going slowly. Come in to the point where you can across the wind and above the birds, so as to push them forward as you wish. If you get in or past them from below, they will be likely to go up to the ridge and off your ground, or swing back.

Remember that a bird must always rise with his breast up wind, especially if it is blowing hard, and that there is no more killing moment than when he is just turning to go down the wind after the first rise. To be ready to take him like this, or in fact to kill any old or wild bird, you must have your gun ready to throw to the shoulder in a second, and must study your walking, so as not to be stumbling when he gets up. Husband your wind and your strength, especially in the early part of the day, as much as you can ; and fear not to take a good long rest at luncheon time, for the sake of your men, dogs, grouse, and yourself. Birds rest in the heat of the day, and the scent is weak ; morning and evening, but evening especially, is the time to make a bag.

On the same piece of ground, should the lower side be bounded by the burn only, with good lying on the other side, it will be better to work the face longways, taking a long beat along the lower side first, coming back almost on the empty ground and then repeating the manœuvre, just as you would often do in a turnip field when you wish to push partridges forward.   Again, if the wind be blowing exactly the reverse way—that is, up hill—I should advise taking the top beat first, or at least working the top side most as you cross and wheel, so as to protect the march. What I have suggested here applies when you have a long hill-face to beat, perhaps the simplest as well as the most frequent formation of grouse ground in Scotland. But when you have to beat an area of flat or undulating moorland *above* the hill-face, it is better to get straight to the higher part of the ground first.   Grouse lie on higher ground during fine weather, and you must break them up on this, so as to deal with them later on when scattered on the lower ground.   But in what I may term 'mixed weather' they will be more on higher ground during the morning and middle-day than in the evening.   In very wild, stormy, and wet weather, you had best, for the sake of your moor, not be out at all ; but if you are, it will depend entirely upon your observation of how the sheltered spots lie whether you get a bag or not.   When the wind is very strong there is absolutely no chance of your finding broods lying on the windy side of a hillock or ridge.

An odd old cock you will disturb sometimes from
the most exposed places, and this I have never been
able to explain, except on the theory that he has heard
you coming from afar off, and run on to the exposed
ground to look around for you.   But then, again, these
odd birds in exposed places sometimes lie very close,
and rise with such a cackle as almost disturbs your
nerves, so that we must suppose they have been able to
find some special little bit of warm shelter which suits
them, although on the windward side.   But the bulk
of the birds, and *all* the broods, will be found lying
with some protecting ridge or hillock sheltering them
from the wind.   In perfectly calm, still weather you
may almost do as you like, beating the ground regularly and extra closely, and so crossing it as to push
the grouse on to the part you reserve for the late
afternoon, with the proviso that you take the higher
ground first.   But whenever there is a breeze, and
still more when it is blowing really hard, the science
of making a good bag of grouse, given that you can
walk and shoot well, is entirely a question of the constant study and observation of the wind.   Remember
that your dogs rely on it entirely—you must therefore
bear it in mind, so as to understand their movements ;
your birds are guided by it in their choice of lying, in
their method of rising, and in their eventual flight ;

while your keeper, especially if Scotch, bases his
entire scheme and conduct of the day's shooting
mainly upon the same factor. A Scotchman reckons
by the compass — he never thinks of alluding to the
right or left of anything, but guides himself, and attempts to guide you, by North and South, East and
West. You must be guided by the same instinct to
this extent that, whether E. or W., N. or S., you must
bear in mind constantly as you follow your dog the
direction of the wind, and the effect it is having upon
the manner of his hunting, as well as upon the movements of the grouse.

When you are following your dog directly up wind,
should the ground rise directly in front of him get past
him as noiselessly as possible, and as you peep over the
ridge have your gun absolutely ready, and look out for
a rise directly you show your nose over it. You will,
in wild weather at least, get a difficult twisting shot,
which you will be pleased to kill. If under the same
circumstances you make any noise, or there is any
calling or whistling to the dog, you will see nothing
when you look over, but possibly a distant bird or
covey, noiselessly skimming out of sight ; or, if you
are not quite ready and smart, as you look over you
will be beaten by the unexpected and tortuous flight
of an old cock as he dashes away from you.

The variations of pace or direction in which you approach the point must necessarily be founded more on experience and the true instinct of the hunter than on anything that can be taught ; but the novice may at least be warned that he cannot rely upon the keeper and the dog, even when aided by good shooting, exclusively to make the best bag possible. Rapidity and silence in getting to the point are very essential. Supposing the dog to be young and not very steady, he will draw on the birds, and in a few moments probably get too close to them and put them up if they are sitting very light. You will say he can be checked by whistle or by the familiar 'To-ho!' and you can get up to them at your leisure. But they will probably be flushed by this noise before you get there; whereas, if you can get up to the dog very quickly and without any noise of any kind, you may get your double shot, and the dog, even if he runs in on them at the last, can be chastised afterwards. No dog is worth anything unless he will stand without even the uplifted hand; and to my thinking many a one is spoilt by being so used to this sign and the ejaculation of 'Ho !' that he does not believe in the necessity of standing steady unless he hears it. This accounts for the loss of a great many chances, and for the too frequent cry of 'Hold up! gone away !' which assails your disappointed ears when you come upon a bit of sheltered lying where the dog has been ranging for a moment or two out of sight. Unless, therefore, your dog is absolutely to be relied on to stand steady, you must, however much it may try your legs and wind, continually keep him in sight. This is frequently left to the keeper by the deliberate or indolent shooter. The dog disappears over a ridge, the keeper, becoming uneasy, runs swiftly and looks over, sees the dog drawing on birds, and immediately up goes the hand, and ' Ho !' he shouts. But the movements of the dog, the man's appearance on the skyline, and the shout are too much, and they are off. If you can get to the ridge and be down alongside the dog quickly enough the instant you see he has birds, you will very likely get your brace, where the slow man would have got nothing and never even seen the covey. On the other hand, especially in broken ground and deep heather, you cannot be too deliberate in quitting the ground where you have found close-sitting birds, or you may leave more than one easy certainty at a fine young bird from want of hunting carefully enough all round.

Some men seem to have almost as keen an instinct as to whether there are birds near them as the dog, and this can hardly be acquired, though close watch-

ing of the habits of pointers or setters and their
manner of hunting the ground will teach you much.
Often when you have found birds up wind of the dog,
especially if it is blowing pretty hard, it is worth while
to make a cast back to see whether he has not struck
the scent between two lots of birds, and whether there
are not some more of them down wind of him. Especially must all these points be attended to when you
are hunting the ground which you have filled by
driving broken coveys and scattered birds on to it.
Towards evening every bit of such ground must be
carefully searched, and you will soon acquire an eye
for the likely patches for grouse to lie in. Activity
and judgment are also much required when, as often
happens on high ground, you have to work an area
of deep moss-hags with steep sides of yielding peat,
and intersected by little ravines, which, powdered with
stones and, maybe, ancient roots, look like portions
of the bed of some primæval flood. Grouse on this
sort of ground rarely lie well, being mostly old birds,
or, if not, being on the move themselves from one
hillock to the other, and here you will do twice as
much execution if you utilise the ground in your
pursuit. Keep as much as you can on the tops of
the hillocks, leaping from one to the other; or, on the
contrary, if you see a doubtful or uneasy point, and

I

the ground favours you, running along between the hags, keeping carefully off the stones, and so getting noiselessly and rapidly up to the dog.

In all these instances it will be observed how very difficult it becomes for two guns to work harmoniously together so as to realise the best possible result ; but at least it should be agreed between them that, wherever speed is necessary, the man nearest to the point should get to it without waiting for the other—otherwise many chances must be lost. The two shooters should, therefore, be as evenly matched as possible. I think, where two parties go out on separate beats, it is better to send the two better or more active and the two slower together; each pair will enjoy their day more than on the mistaken principle of sending a good gun to 'nurse' a bad one. This, unless they are both angels from heaven, is a trial of temper and a mortification to both.

In very calm warm weather at the beginning of the season, where the cover is thick and the birds plentiful and tame, any two or even three men can take turn and turn about, and manage the amenities of the pursuit as easily as if they were beating a cabbage garden for very young partridges ; but this, though much affected by some gentlemen from town, and by dog producers—I will not call them breakers

—who seem to think more of their beasts' coats or
pedigrees than of their noses, is not the poetry of
shooting over dogs. It is when the breeze is cool
and keen, the heather wet from last night's rain, or
glistening from a slight touch of early frost; when the
distant range stands like Soracte, toweringly white
with snow; when the burns run brown and full, the
oats are ripened, and the hill-face is growing redder
and more golden; when the river trout are stiff to rise,
and the blackcock has almost his full tail—then is the
time when to follow a brace of good dogs, both you
and they in first-rate trim, and to make a bag of
grouse, is worth the doing.

For this reason, revolutionary as it may seem, I
would, supposing that you wish both to drive and
walk your ground, drive it first and walk it afterwards.
By so doing you will spare many young birds which
should be left for breeding, you will get more shooting and less waiting and exposure for your drives, and
sport better worth having and under pleasanter conditions, granted you pick your days, for your shooting
over dogs.

The plugging at very young birds in the early days
when the weather is hot, and many of them could be
(or are) taken by the keeper with his hand, when dogs
and men get knocked up before the day is half over,

and hardly any shot you get is any satisfaction to kill, while it is a disgrace to miss, is not to my thinking worthy of a keen sportsman or accomplished gunner, unless he be well past the prime of life and merely takes it by short spells as an agreeable pastime. On the other hand this is a pleasanter time for your driving parties, and the waiting in the butts, always a trying operation, is at least not made worse by showers of sleet and snow or biting winds.

After your driving days are over, in bright and cooler weather, when it is easier to walk and your condition is better, you will enjoy your day's point shooting more than you have ever done on the Twelfth, for every point will test your dogs, every shot will try your skill, and every bird will be worth killing. I cannot believe, judging from experience, that driving will make the birds so wild as to preclude all shooting over dogs. I have seen many a good day over dogs after the ground had been driven several times, and the birds lying as well, on a favourable day, as any one need wish; and I am convinced that driving them does not make them any wilder, nor so wild, as constant walking after them with dogs.

I am against walking the moor in line. This seems to be neither one thing nor the other; it disturbs a large extent of ground and terrifies the birds, while the result is usually far from satisfactory as to the bag brought home. It is impossible to keep a long line of men, extending, say, 500 or 600 yards, in proper touch with one another on rough ground. To preserve the formation while one man has two or three birds to pick up, and the others, far away from him, are too anxious to walk on, is usually found to be impracticable, and the whole thing ends in a maraud more worthy of a gang of poachers than anything else.

I shall not here attempt to enter into the question of the breeding, selection, or breaking of dogs. It is abundantly clear that to go out to make a bag of grouse, and to go out to train your dogs, are two distinct things, and your dogs should not only be well broken, but well exercised and in good condition, before you attempt a serious attack upon your game. This work is devoted to the grouse and not to the dog, and therefore I trust that the only apology I need offer is for want of ability to deal with the former in the way that so grand a bird deserves.

I confess to a preference for pointers where birds are plentiful and lying is good, and for setters under the contrary conditions, from their wide-ranging powers, and because I am, as remarked before, a strong advocate of rapidity of movement.

Three guns is an unreasonable number to send
out in one party, unless you have an abnormal stock
of grouse, and are anxious to kill all you can. The
difficulties of dealing properly with the point, of getting
up at the right moment, of all three shooting at the same
bird, and other matters of varying skill and courtesy,
are much increased. And if the grouse are lying well
it is rather hard on the moor. Yet it is too often
done. The young men of to-day mostly shoot pretty
well, some few very well, and at any rate are pretty
destructive at close-lying young birds ; and three of
them, with every appliance for quick loading and firing,
will, as I have already pointed out with regard to
partridges, kill far too many young birds, while they
are more than likely to spare most of the old ones.
These should always be selected where possible as
your first victims, and I think that when you are
working a wild beat on high ground, where birds are
not too plentiful, you should not, when you come
across a brood, follow it up to the death and massacre
the whole family, but rather deliberately leave a
brace of young birds here and there, and turn your
attention as much as possible to the more difficult and
fascinating art of circumventing the old inhabitants of
the ground, my opinion of whom I have recorded in
the chapter on Scotch Driving. The following extract

WELL FOUND AND WELL BACKED.

from Daniell's 'Rural Sports' reads quaintly in the present day :

'To shew the abundance, rather than the exploit itself (which by a Sportsman, must be hoped never will be repeated), the Earl of Strathmore's Game-keeper was matched for a considerable sum to shoot *forty brace* of moor-game in the course of the 12th of August upon his Lordship's moors in Yorkshire ; he performed it with great ease, shooting by two o'clock forty-three brace ; at eight in the morning, owing to a thick fog, he had only killed *three* birds, however the day cleared up by eleven, and the work of slaughter went on rapidly.'

What would the Rev. Mr. Daniell have said could he have lived to see the bags—more than once of over 1,000 brace in a day—which have since been made on this very ground, 'his lordship's moors in Yorkshire,' the now famous Wemmergill and its neighbours ?

We hope forty brace of moor-game in a day may often be killed again ; but it is a good bag even now to one gun over dogs, and no doubt there will always be a sufficiency of men able and willing to do it without forfeiting the title of 'sportsman.'

CHAPTER III

SCOTCH DRIVING

THERE are many things which distinguish grouse
driving in Scotland from the same sport in England,
and some difficulties to be overcome in the former
country which are not ordinarily met with in the
latter. Nevertheless, it will be my endeavour to show
that the distinctions inseparable from Scotch driving
merely add an attractive variety to the sport, and
that the difficulties are by no means insuperable.

Ever since the memorable season of 1872, of which
more hereafter, and which, following as it did upon two
very good seasons in 1870 and 1871, finally opened the
eyes of the shooting world to the great possibilities of
grouse, my opinion has been that on a very considerable number of Scotch moors a scientific and practical
system of driving, such as has been in force in Yorkshire for years, could and would produce results to
equal the totals ordinarily achieved in that county,

and possibly to rival those of the most famous English moors.

I have often been opposed in this view, and even ridiculed, by men familiar for years with the conditions of what I may call an ordinary Scotch shooting, and even by some whose experience embraced a large measure of both English and Scotch sport. Yet what are the facts? On many Scotch moors, notably in Ayrshire, where driving has been taken up systematically and scientifically, and where shooting over dogs has been abandoned, such respectable bags as 250 and even 300 brace in a day have to be recorded ; while even as I write comes the news of a bag of over 500 brace in one day, made on the moors of the Mackintosh, at Moy, in Inverness-shire.

There are three principal reasons usually adduced to prove that driving in Scotland cannot be carried out with ordinary success, still less to the point arrived at in England :

1. The unfavourable nature of the ground.

2. The opposition or unwillingness of Scotch keepers.

3. The difficulty of obtaining drivers.

The last of these is in most instances the only one that constitutes a serious source of trouble, and this only applies to sparsely populated districts, where the few inhabitants are obliged to take advantage of every moment of fine weather for their hay or corn harvest.

I propose to consider these objections in detail, and try to point out how they may be best overcome.

There are no doubt localities where the precipitous ground, intersected with deep ravines, and powdered with great rocks as though cast from a giant's hand, precludes any attempt at driving, excepting in a limited and desultory fashion, merely to give a day or two of variety. It is also superfluous to observe that where the grouse moor is merely a slight fringe to the higher ground or deer forest, driving need not be considered. But putting such districts out of the question, the great majority of Scotch moors are what, if I may coin a word for the purpose, I should call 'drivable.'

More than this, there are many which are more suitable for driving, and would yield larger bags, than a second-rate Yorkshire moor. We are, of course, not here considering the comparative attractions or merits of driving as compared with shooting over dogs, but assuming that the owner or lessee of a moor in Scotland would like to drive his grouse, and thereby improve his stock, but considers himself prevented by one or more of the difficulties I have named.

It is a very common error to suppose that all

Yorkshire, Durham, or Derbyshire moors are quite flat, consisting entirely of heather at a certain elevation no doubt above the cultivated districts, but which, once reached, stretches far and wide in a series of very gentle undulations or perfectly flat tableland. A journey along the Settle and Carlisle branch of the Midland Railway, or a tour over the moors on the borders of Yorkshire, Durham, and Westmoreland, will soon dispel this. The gills, sikes, and becks of these counties are comparable to the glens and burns of bonnie Scotland, and the sources of the Ribble and the Wharfe, the Swale and the Ure, the Tees or the Wear, owe their wildest recesses to volcanic convulsions hardly less violent than those which witnessed the birth of the Dee and the Spey, the Tay and the Tummel. Yet these southern rivers spring from and find their course through the heart of the most famous of the English moors, where more grouse have been killed in one day than many a Scotch keeper looks for in a whole season.

Again, the low moors of Ayr, Dumfries, or Lanark, as well as of parts of Perth, Aberdeen, or Inverness, are richer in wide expanse of rolling flat and typical driving ground than many of the dales and fells of Cumberland, Westmoreland, or the North Riding.

'Ah, but,' says one, ' my moor isn't like that ; you

couldn't drive my ground, it is too steep.' This may
be so, although he is probably mistaken ; but it is
impossible to know the particulars and comparative
conditions of every moor in Scotland and England.
Nobody's knowledge would be sufficient for this ; one
can only consider the general characteristics of a
district.   I only know that I have heard this sort of
speech from men who rent shootings in a district
where the conformation of the ground is far more
favourable to driving than many a Yorkshire dale,
and that merely looking from the train window on
the Caledonian, the Glasgow and South-Western,
ay, and on the Highland line, you will see miles
upon miles of gentle slope and broad hill-face clothed
in luxuriant heather which to a Yorkshire keeper's
eye would look ideal ground for driving.

The very inequalities of the moor, when properly
turned to account in conjunction with the habitual
flight of the birds, give opportunities which would not
be detected by those unaccustomed to study ground
as well as grouse with this object in view.   Where
the moor is very rocky, and the small 'knowes' or
knolls of heather are alternated with miniature precipices and ravines, furrowed and scored with the rush
of melting snow, or swept bare by the plenteous
volume of the summer spate, you will find the grouse

acquire habits peculiar to the class of ground, habits which, if you observe them, you can turn greatly to the advantage of your driving. They select rather bare and rocky spots for their alighting and surveying places, and when disturbed from basking or feeding on lower and more sheltered ground they fly to these, and almost always by the same route, according to the wind. I have had a very fine drive with hardly a bit of heather near me, surrounded by frowning precipices and huge boulders, and sheltered by a butt formed ot the great stones scattered in profusion all over the upper slopes of the hill.

Again, when grouse are pushed, as they often can be, across a deep ravine or narrow glen, soaring high over the low birch scrub and bracken, haunts of the black-game and the roe, you will see if you watch them carefully—but *very* carefully—that they only alight in certain spots on the opposite hill, or that, having a rough and rocky ridge to pass over, they invariably select certain passes or gullies to rush through to the same resting place.

Here is your chance. Your batteries must be carefully placed just *behind*, not *on* the ridge, each one preferably in a slight hollow or pass rather than on a knoll, and you will be surprised at the result. Unlike the typical grouse ground as this spot may

appear, and though you find no birds sitting on or
near the butts as you approach them, yet as the far-off
holloa of the drivers sounds more frequent, round the
rocks they begin to come, swinging through the passes
at a terrific pace with the wind, or beating slowly and
heavily against it, seeming to grow mysteriously out of
the rock in front, and vanishing like lightning over
the grey knoll behind, yet always making for the same
place, until you find by experience that, in proportion
to the birds upon the moor, your rock or ravine drive
is always one of the best and most certain.

The march between two moors is, in Scotland,
usually on the ridge or watershed, although you will
often find it defined by a river or a road.   Where it is
on the ridge, the shooting will probably consist of both
sides of some great glen, with the flat or rocky ground
above the 'face,' stretching as far as the highest
point of the watershed.   Now, grouse are very loth to
fly across a big valley, especially if it is cultivated, and
should the distance from face to face cost them a
flight of a mile or more they will hardly ever attempt
it.   I have seen a biggish pack of grouse start across
a broad valley, where they would have had to go two or
three miles before they could again alight upon heather,
fly about half a mile, funk it, and turn back again to
the hill they were disturbed on.   Their inclination is

always to fly *along* the hill, and round the bottom or side of a knoll, whether great or small, rather than over or across it. It is very wonderful to see how they save themselves in their flight, especially when they are going against a heavy wind. Could you be alongside of them, and travelling with them, you would note the marvellous way in which they give themselves the benefit of the ground to escape rising into the wind, passing round all the excrescences and through all the depressions in the hillside, clinging close to the heather, but always manœuvring, sidling, or creeping to reach the alighting place which they have in view.

This characteristic will aid you greatly in the choice of the place for your line of butts, which, as everybody now knows, is the important factor in driving. The birds are not likely to leave the hillside on which you find them ; consequently you have only to study the routes they will take in flying along it.

If the ground is so intersected by rocks, precipices, or deep gorges that your drivers cannot travel it at all—at least, without consuming the whole day in one or two drives—you may give it up ; but if your men can manage to get about the ground so as to give you, say, at least four or five drives in the day, there is nothing in the flight of the birds on steep ground that you may not turn to your advantage.

One often meets with a drive in Scotland where the grouse and black-game come over the guns at such a height that no shot will reach them ; and you are told that this hill is impossible to drive, as the birds always do this ; nobody can kill them, and there is no result. This is a wrong conclusion. It merely means that the guns are not in the right place. These birds must touch the ground somewhere, and when you have found their point of contact with the earth, or alighting place, then you have found the spot where you can kill them.

It is only *with* the wind or on a perfectly still day that they will trust themselves thus in mid-air, and then only under compulsion ; they will never attempt high flights against the wind. Great as is the power of their flight, and strong as their wings and tails are to steer by, they have as great a horror of being caught high up and rendered helpless by the wind as we should have of finding ourselves striking out in the rapid stream of a big river.

Now make an experimental drive—and you must make many such if you wish for successful permanent drives ; place a trustworthy man or two far away down wind on the hillside beyond where they come so high over you, and you will probably be agreeably surprised to find how easy is the solution of the problem. Your watchers will tell you that every bird came as though out of the sky straight for a particular rock, or peak of high ground, and swinging round the point into the lee, alighted in the shelter.

There you have the spot for your butts. Neither grouse nor, so far as I have ever seen, any other bird can pause and alight in his flight down wind without turning round and up into the wind to do it. They will seldom attempt this, and almost invariably drop into a sheltered spot where they can settle without fear of being dashed against the ground by the force of the wind.

So much for your down-wind drives, which are, in spite of anything you may be told to the contrary, much the most difficult to manage on steep or high and precipitous ground.

You will find it easy enough to push them back up wind, provided you attend to one or two essential points. The butts in this case must, as I remarked above, never be placed along a ridge or sky-line, but just behind it, so as to give the guns about fifty to eighty yards in front of them to see the birds coming. I have never seen a successful drive where it was attempted to push birds *up wind* to butts on a ridge, though it can be done with the wind. Again, though it is a very pretty sight to observe the birds, at first

K

tiny specks afar off, and as they grow bigger to the eye to watch every detail of their long flight, speculating as to whether they will come to you or your neighbour, yet this is not the most killing condition. You will always observe that more birds are realised when everyone remarks that ' I couldn't see them till they were right on me,' than when they could watch them coming the whole way. Just room enough in front to be ready, select your bird, and get the gun up is all you want, and for this eighty yards from the butt to the ridge is amply sufficient.

Then each butt must if possible be placed, though always adhering to the straight line, so as to command what I must describe as a pass—that is, a hollow or comparatively flat space. I have seen on a sharply undulating ridge each one placed on the top of the knoll, with the passes or valleys between. The result of this is that the birds swerve a great deal, and sometimes turn back, while the shots at birds *below* the gun as they pass through the hollows are about the most difficult you can have. When placed in the hollows it will often be impossible to see your next-door neighbour, but in this case you have only to be careful that when your line of butts is made, a big stone, stake, or cairn is put up on the knoll in the exact line between the two butts.

It is absolutely essential that the Scotch keeper to whom driving is an unwelcome novelty should be made familiar with the aspect of the birds' flight from the butts. You must make him delegate the management of the drive to his next in command, and be with you in the butts at least once or twice at each particular drive, that he may see what happens. He will then be able to observe why it is that one or two butts have all the shooting, or why birds which come apparently well to the guns are at certain drives never properly realised ; he will see the difference in difficulty between birds creeping through a slack or pass straight towards you, and the same birds when you only command the slack from above, and have to point down at them at a sharp angle as they curve round beneath you. Again, he will understand why you, after some experience of this drive, possibly conclude that by shifting the whole line of butts only a few yards you may convert a difficult killing place into an easy one. He will grasp the point, and be keen enough unless endowed with too great a share of Gaelic obstinacy, to reconstruct the line and watch the successful result. You must never be afraid to make new lines of butts or to shift old ones, nor permit your keeper to make any fuss over the question. Scotch keepers are sometimes very troublesome on this point ; they will not make butts themselves, but insist upon extra men being hired to do it. This should never be allowed. They have more than ample time during the months when there is no shooting to do this, and the more they get to know about the construction and position of the butts the better, while the work involved is nothing but good for them.

Highlanders are, as all the world knows, a very fine race of men, courageous and loyal, courteous and amiable, they make the best sportsmen and the best soldiers in the world ; but they are neither so practical nor so energetic under ordinary conditions as the northern Englishman, and laziness is their great failing. There is a great deal of work involved in erecting and maintaining several lines of butts, and it is necessary that the keepers should be kept up to doing this properly. They will soon learn that it is to their interest to do so, and that the visitor who is used to high-class driving, and possibly knows a great deal more of the management of a moor than they do, will be more liberally and generously inclined towards them if they thoroughly perform their manifest duty of keeping everything connected with the shooting in first-rate order.

It is impossible to kill grouse well from a badly

constructed or ruined butt ; and the man who has to wait for three-quarters of an hour in cold and windy weather with his feet in three or four inches of sodden mud, peat, or water, unprotected from the blast or from the keen eyes of the approaching grouse save by dilapi-dated walls of sod, sunken to the level of his waist, trodden down by sheep or cattle, and never touched since they were carelessly erected a year or two before, is not likely to feel favourably disposed towards the keeper who has charge of these things. His only alternative is to scrape out the mud with his feet, thereby blocking the entrance to and the drainage from the butt, and to build up the front wall by taking sods from the back one, the result being to make the place still more comfortless and untenantable for the next comer on a succeeding day.

Square butts are always to be recommended, es-pecially on high ground, and where sheep or cattle are pastured on the moor, as being much more permanent, while they afford welcome shelter in bad weather. The entrance should be at the side, and as narrow as pos-sible, so as to keep out the aforesaid animals. The walls should be built high, as remarked on in the fol-lowing chapter, and the measurements there given adhered to.

Old birds on the high ground are very wary, as

well as very accomplished in their flight, and if they catch sight of you will swing away and often turn altogether from the line. These are exactly those which you should be most desirous to kill, and a well-made and commodious butt, in which you can keep well out of sight, is really most essential in the more remote drives, where birds are few and keen, than anywhere. Yet you often see in Scotland the error committed of taking less trouble over these than over the lines near the lodge and on lower ground, where the driving is easier. The second difficulty I named above— viz. the opposition or unwillingness of many Scotch keepers—has to be reckoned with in this department. They must be taught that these things are not fancies, nor mere aids to making the sport easy or luxurious, but absolute essentials of a successful drive, while the proper manner of carrying them out is the result of the experience of fifty or sixty years on the English moors.

It is the same with the manner of conducting the drive. Many of my readers must have noticed how impossible it appears to persuade a line of Scotch drivers to preserve the proper horseshoe or half-moon shape, or that their flanks are really the most important parts of their force. Instead of getting well round the ground, and no driver showing himself or beginning to move until it is practically inclosed in a great half-circle, they drop carelessly, after going just a quarter of a mile short of where they should have gone to, into some sort of line, and then all come straight on, the centre often farther ahead than the flanks (!) and the birds, of course, pouring out on each side. It is a matter of luck that any birds come to the guns at all, a very poor bag is made, and then it is voted that driving doesn't really answer, and that you mustn't expect what they get in Yorkshire, &c.

This can only be remedied, to my thinking, by the command of the drive being taken by some person who understands it, whether the host, or anyone else whom he may import to instruct the keepers and beaters. His authority must be absolute, and they must be brought to understand that successful driving is entirely a matter of discipline and organisation. The most excellent instruction as to drivers, formation, flags, &c., has been set out in the Badminton Library, and in Payne-Gallwey's 'Letters to Young Shooters;' but when do you ever find it acted upon?

On the best known Yorkshire moors, where the system has been brought to perfection, all this instruction is superfluous; but why is it that in Scotland, where it is so much needed, you never find it followed out? The average owner or tenant buys these books,

reads them, discusses and criticises them, and then
puts them away on the shelf without ever making the
experiment of thoroughly putting into practice what
has been so carefully thought out and set down by
men of such experience as the authors of those
volumes.

I can add hardly anything to what they have
written, but I can at least point out that if they were
less criticised or neglected, and more acted upon,
grouse driving on the average Scotch moor would be
far more profitable to the owner and pleasanter to
his friends.

The matter is new to the Scotchman, and he is
inclined for various reasons, to be alluded to presently,
to view it with little favour.   But if he has to do it at
all, he may just as well learn what remarkable results
he may achieve by carrying it out systematically and
properly.   The new system must have a fair trial to
be properly adopted or condemned.   It is the *head-
keeper who must read the Badminton Library* and
master its details ; but how many keepers have ever
had a serious book on shooting given to them by their
masters, or enjoyed the chance of discussing such a
work with anyone who understands it ?

Take a simple instance like the colour of the flags.
It has over and over again been urged that the

colour of the flags carried by the head man should
be different in colour from those the drivers carry, the
flank men, again, having a distinctive flag of some kind ;
yet you usually see flags served out indiscriminately,
and it is consequently impossible at a distance for
either the shooters or the drivers to tell where the
centre of the line or the flanks may be. This the
drivers, at least, embracing as they sometimes do a

FIG. 1. FIG. 2.

mile and a half of line, ought to be able to do, and
each one regulate his own pace and direction thereby.

I would recommend white flags for the rank and
file, and a red one for the head man or centre of the
line, with red and white ones for the flankers and
pointsmen. The white is the most visible on the
moor, but the red and white ones, especially if made
as in fig. 2, are very conspicuous, and therefore good

for the flank men, while the solitary red one will be
easily found in the centre of the line.

Now, all these details are important, nay essential
to success in driving. But if they are neglected, or
obstinately combated by persons who have no knowledge or not sufficient keenness to wish to realise the
largest head of game that the ground is able to produce,
then their grouse driving will always remain an unsatisfactory and haphazard performance, while every excuse
except the real one will be advanced to account for
the poor results achieved.

To drive grouse unless they are driven properly—
I may say scientifically—is a waste of time, money,
energy, and temper ; and, as I have urged before, the
detailed advice and instruction of initiated and experienced authorities is far more necessary and useful to
those who are taking it up under adverse or new conditions than to those who have studied it under more usual
or favourable circumstances. Your horseshoe formation, your good flanking and carefully placed butts, are
far more necessary on a wild Scotch beat than on a flat
and easily driven Yorkshire moor. Yet it is frequently
made to appear as if all these things were considered
immaterial by those who ought to study them most
carefully, and would profit most by them.

Now suppose the wind to be blowing directly

across the valley, and—for I wish to take the most difficult instance—rather against than with the course of the drive. Here your result depends entirely upon the disposal of the men and the conduct of the drive. You are driving along the face of a hill, and the cross-wind is blowing fairly strong from the ridge or crest of the hill downwards. The natural result of this will be, unless you manage properly, that birds flushed on the higher part of the face will be inclined to turn round and downwards, flying back high over the heads of the beaters. This is the danger to be guarded against. Once the birds have made up their terrified minds to do this they *cannot* be turned, neither could they turn themselves, with the strong breeze behind them, if they would.

It therefore follows that this instinct of theirs must be guarded against from or before the start. The head man, with the red flag, starting from the centre point and heading straight for the centre of the line of guns, will, instead of having seven men on each side of him (I am allowing fifteen drivers and pointsmen, all told), have five on the windward and nine on the leeward side.

I have made a diagram, which I hope will convey what I mean. At the bottom of the hill is the burn running along a deep gully. The butts extend at the

point chosen from the burn to the ridge, the highest
No. 8, being just under or on the ridge, as experience
shows to be best.   The drive widens out into a corrie
or flat at the beginning, in which lie a large proportion
of the birds, taking advantage of its sheltered position. In this drive there will be no pointsman or flanker
near the guns on the windward side, while on the leeward side five or six of the men will be pushed along
the burn-side before the drive begins, the efforts of
the pointsman, standing on the highest knoll he can
find, being supplemented by the man with the ponies,
who can always be utilised as a flag nearer the guns.
It is of supreme importance that this formation should
be completed before the driving begins, and it must
be borne in mind that the upper drivers, on the windward side, will, in addition to the wind, have the added
power of showing against the sky to the birds below
them.   Their movements must, therefore, be cautious,
and they must not get too far ahead or make themselves too conspicuous, as they might if it were a still
day or they had the wind in their favour.

When the base or centre, A, of the drive begins to
move, all the men on the leeward or burn-side must
come into sight at once, and the aforesaid men on the
windward flank must creep *under*, not on, the ridge to
get round the sheltered corrie without going very far

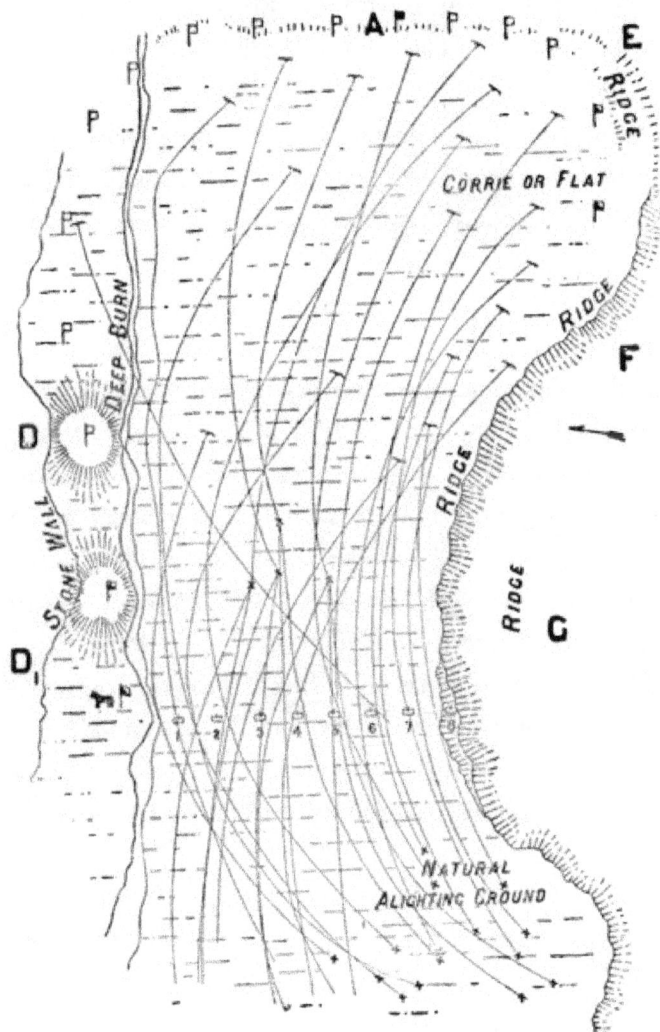

FIG. 3.

ahead of the centre. All the birds in this corrie if
flushed by men behind them will hang right along
under the ridge in the shelter, describing a curve
which the force of the wind will impose upon them,
and coming well over the guns in order to reach the
alighting ground they make for beyond the line of
butts.

Now, if this drive be mismanaged in the archaic
manner I alluded to before—that is, with all the drivers
in a straight line—nearly every bird in it will be lost,
except a few lying at the bottom of the corrie, who may,
if flushed luckily, hang on under the ridge and come to
the upper guns. But most of them will never come
to the guns at all ; those in the upper part of the
corrie will, many of them, slip out at the head, and go
up wind into the next valley or shelter. Those lower
down will, most of them, feeling the force of the wind
directly they rise, bear away over the burn and either
remain on the other side beyond the stone wall, or
curve in again if this ground is not moorland towards
the alighting ground beyond the line of guns, without
giving a shot. Many others, hearing the guns in
front, and seeing nothing to stop them on the burn-
side, will rise in the wind and go clean back towards
the point n. The drive will consequently be an utter
failure.

Again, if driven in the ordinary horseshoe shape, with both flanks equally forward, a lot of birds will be lost, still owing to the curve they will describe because of the wind, at and between the points D and D. Besides this the flankers on the ridge side, especially if showing strong against the sky, will turn back any birds which get up below and behind them, and these will again make away over the drivers' heads to the point B. The only birds which will come well to the guns will be those that rise in the middle, having caught sight of the burn-side flank and not seen the ridge flank. But the drive will not be a success, half the birds not having come forward to the guns, and what is worse, the next drive, in which these birds are counted on to make a still better one, will be spoilt also.

In giving this illustration I have endeavoured to take an instance of a typical drive in a Scotch glen, and founded it not upon any one place in particular, but upon the common or usual characteristics of such ground.

To drive the same piece with a cross-wind from the opposite direction—that is, blowing up the hill—is an easier matter, and I do not think requires a fresh diagram. The flankers along the burn-side need not be so numerous or conspicuous, though this wing must still be pushed on a little. The general tendency of the birds in this wind will be either to creep across the wind and up the hill, or to turn back as before over the beaters, making their exit in this instance somewhere over the point A, instead of towards B. The flankers on the ridge side will this time be the important people, and will have more to do. They must push more forward than the other flank, and coming along over or above the ridge turn those birds which are inclined to go over gently on to the guns. This will not be difficult to do, provided they are stationed there in time, but as the birds are flying up-hill, and the wind slightly more against them than with them, it will be time enough to turn them after they have topped the ridge. This is the reason why they should, as I said, be themselves over or behind the ridge ; the birds will then swing down from them in a fresh curve and come over the upper guns, hanging a good deal in the breeze and giving easy shots. If the men came in full view along the ridge, they would turn a good many of these birds back over the centre A.

In both these drives the butts numbered 4 to 7 will probably have the most shooting, though as the lay of the ground varies in detail, as well as the points from which the birds have been flushed, so will the curve described in the former drive vary also, and the lower guns may possibly be the most favoured.

Now, in this drive I have depicted a sharp ridge on the upper, and a stout wall or boundary to the moor on the lower side.

But without supposing any change in the shape or configuration of the ground, we may note a few alterations in the formation of the beaters which would become necessary if some of its characteristics were different. For instance, if instead of the sharp or rocky ridge you have a rounded shoulder, merely enlarging the area of good lying ground over the top and extending to a more or less flat district with good spaces of shelter probably ending at a march of watershed higher up ; in this case, unless too much raked by the wind, a good many birds will be lying on the upper flat, and some more on being flushed in ther corrie will be inclined to make up to it against the wind.

What I have termed the ridge flank must therefore be extended before the drive begins beyond the point E, and may want an additional man, who had better be spared from the other flank between A and B. This flank must now take great care to get right round this upper ground, especially as most of the birds lying on it will probably be old ones, which

L

it should be your invariable object to kill if possible,
and instead of coming along under the ridge as in
the first instance suggested, take a wide circuit round
from E to F and approach the guns in a direction
about from F to G.   By this means the drivers will rake
in all the birds on the upper ground, and as they will be
far enough over the shoulder not to show on the sky
line, they will not turn back birds flushed below on
the face.   They must go warily, and the burn-side
flank and centre must go slowly, to give them time
to get cleverly round.

Again, if on the lower side there is no stone wall
or boundary to the moorland, but an expanse of
equally good ground across the burn, it will be necessary to extend the lower flank and sweep some
of this ground in, always, however, keeping the flank
extremely forward, practically joining on to the
pointsman, on account of the wind.   In this case the
lower butts should get better shooting, and it may be
well to have an extra butt across the burn in a line
with where I have shown the ponies.

In this diagram I have made curved lines showing
the probable direction and curve of flight birds would
take from where they are flushed to the alighting
ground, those flushed very early in the drive in some
instances settling at the points X.   On rising again

these birds would be taken with the wind down to the lower guns, in the beginning of a new curve of flight to fresh alighting ground farther off.

Now, the higher level of ground which I imagined above, and which is the most frequent accessory condition to a Scotch moor, embracing as it sometimes does a large part of the acreage of the shooting, on which there is little or no heather, but large expanses of grass varied with deep and barren peat bogs, and interspersed with rocks, caves, and gullies, yet not high enough to fairly reach the haunts of the ptarmigan, the eagle, and the fox—the level, in short, that is known as 'the tops,' rather than the ' high tops '—is an important factor in Scotch driving, and from the point of view of improving your moor must be carefully considered.

On these heights almost invariably throughout Scotland, but more especially where no driving has ever been systematically tried, abides a race of old grouse, of wary and predatory habits, amatory and pugnacious dispositions, evasive and exclusive conduct. Now, these old stagers it is of the utmost importance to destroy ; but to do so is no easy matter. It is my firm belief that the presence of these useless, and it is no exaggeration to say destructive, birds has a great deal to do with the scarcity of broods, and the low

average of stock to be found on elevated Scotch
shootings. It is well known that in deer forests,
where the great object is to get rid of grouse, the best
means to arrive at this end is to leave them alone
altogether. The result is that in a great measure they
die out ; at any rate, their numbers dwindle to the
lowest possible point. There are two reasons for
this : one that the race becomes vitiated and reduced
by in-breeding, the other that the older birds interfere
with the matrimonial arrangements of the younger, to
the prejudice of the offspring.

The latter evil prevails more than the former
among the birds I have mentioned as inhabiting the
higher portions of Scotch shootings. In the pairing
season the old warriors come down from the heights,
fight with and vanquish the younger ones, and absorb
the young hens ; the latter lay nests full of eggs, but
they are sterile ; while the more youthful and capable
cock bird, who would become the parent of a healthy
brood, is either driven off the ground altogether or
obliged to remain in a state of combative celibacy.
The old hens also, who are beyond the age of laying,
attack any young hen who may nest near them, driving
her off her nest, thus causing the eggs to get cold and
the incubation to be abortive.

The old barren hens are bad enough, but the old

OLD GROUSE ON THE TOPS.

cocks are the worst, and both *must* by some means or other be destroyed. You would never dream of keeping birds of this age in a poultry yard for profit, where the inevitable test of *l. s. d.* forces you to be practical. Why should you allow this loss of stock on your grouse moor? We must therefore condemn them ; but how is the sentence of death to be carried out ? It is not easy. The nature of the ground they frequent in the shooting season, and their alert and wily habits, sentinelled as they are during their baskings and feedings, tortuous and swift as is their flight, are ample protection against the ordinary methods of the average shooter, keeper, and brace of dogs. I would rather poison them than have them on my own ground, and on expressing this revolutionary idea to a friend of mine, one of the best known living authorities on such subjects, I was delighted to hear him cordially assent.

But as I have not studied the Borgian method, and am not therefore in a position to actually recommend it, I will confine myself to other and more practicable means. These birds could be immensely reduced in numbers, if not decimated, by indefatigable stalking ; but this would consume an immense amount of time, involve constant disturbance of the other birds on the ground, and entirely engross the keepers' energies.   The only method left is, therefore, to drive them.

I have already observed that the average shooter, endeavouring to secure them in the ordinary way with pointers, would find them more than his match ; indeed, he would kill very few of them.   I will go farther—he would probably never see most of them, unless he were a very first-rate, keen-eyed, and active sportsman, and devoted much time, instead of delegating this to his keeper, to sneaking quietly up the gullies, and taking advantage of inequalities in the ground to creep upon them unawares.   This method is often practised in the latter part of the season in Yorkshire, under the name of 'gruffing,' from the local term 'gruff,' signifying the little deep gullies in the moor along which the grouse stalker manœuvres, and is very good fun.   But as I have remarked, this takes so much time that it could only be effectively practised by those who reside all through the season close to their own moors.   For the average grouse shooter who resides in the low country, and only visits the moorland from August to October, it is not practicable to any effective extent.

There is but one way for the sportsman—to drive these birds.   The average Scotch keeper does not believe that the stock of birds on his moor in a good

breeding season could be increased. I must beg to
differ from him. He does not, as a rule, even know
how many he has on the ground ; and the aforesaid
packs of very old birds on the higher ground are to
him a mysterious, unknown, and inaccessible quantity.
He may walk all over the tops, with dogs or without,
but unless he creeps and crouches like a stalker, and
studies the instinct of the birds which causes them
always to lie in the leeward or sheltered sides of the
hills or knowes, peeping, with half his face and the
whole of his body hidden, over the brows, and advancing with noiseless tread, he will not even catch
sight of these wary old fowl. Nothing will fairly show
you what stock of grouse you have upon a moor except
driving it ; and unless you drive the whole of it,
especially late in the season, you can never be sure
what is the quantity of birds left behind or outside
your drives which you may not have seen. If you
are petermined, whatever your conditions, to kill the
majority of your birds over dogs, you still ought to
drive the tops, and do what you can to reduce the
regiments of antique fowls which inhabit them You
are not asked to eat them ; they will do to send to
your friends (?), or to swell the market which supplies
the suburban taste for game through the medium of
third-rate restaurants ; but kill them if you can.

On a Yorkshire moor you are driving *on the tops*
all the time.   If there is a high point on the moor,
rocky and precipitous, it is in extent probably a mere
fraction compared with the acreage of good moorland
around it.   On a Scotch moor you have usually a
large acreage above the line of your highest driving
ground, but you rarely, if ever, see the tops driven.
The two accompanying sketches may help to suggest
the difference of conditions to the eye.   In fig. 4,
'Yorkshire,' you have a supposed rough outline of
an extent of moorland, the horizontal line showing
(in both drawings) the highest level reached by your
drivers.   In fig. 5, 'Scotland,' you will observe that
as you only drive along the hill-faces where the heather
is good, this line lies below a large tract which I have
marked as 'tops,' dominated at the back by the
ptarmigan hills or deer ground.   It is the birds on
the 'tops' that must either be absorbed into your
usual drives by extended manœuvres, or made the
subject of special drives on intermediate days, with
extra lines of butts for the purpose.

To my thinking, much more could be done than
is usually attempted by the former method.   I would
suggest that the drivers should be on the ground a
long time before the guns are in position, and should
sweep across the tops, driving all upon them on to the

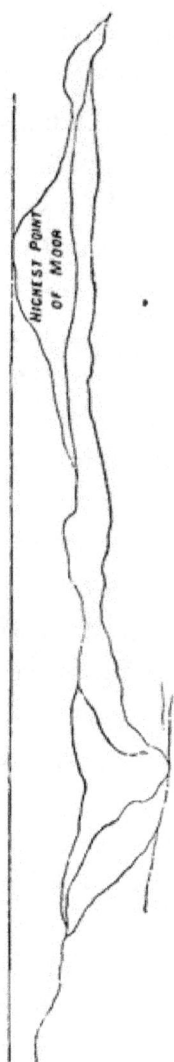

FIG. 4. Yorkshire.

HIGHEST POINT
OF MOOR

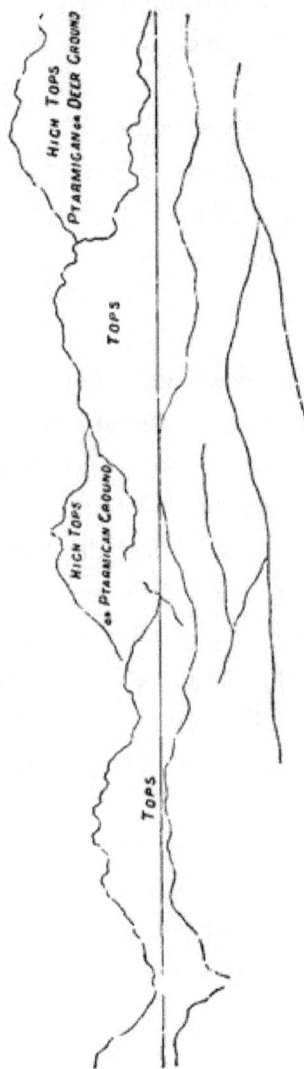

FIG. 5. Scotland.

HIGH TOPS
PTARMIGAN or DEER GROUND

TOPS

HIGH TOPS
or PTARMIGAN GROUND

TOPS

lower ground, before they form line for the individual
drives. Two men at least—more if available—should
then be told off who would keep on the high ground
all day, always walking across it, keeping the birds
from finding refuge there, and constantly pushing
them on to the lower faces. This would be a very
effective method, and I have never taken part in driving on a Scotch moor, whether in Aberdeenshire in
the palmy days of 1872, or on a west-coast shooting
in more recent and inferior seasons, without feeling
that the ground, without some such manœuvre as this,
was not being properly covered, and that the birds
had a shade the best of the contest.

Late in the season the birds all over the ground
will pack, and unless you can get at these packs and
break them up your sport is poor ; they will after
they have been driven a few times betake themselves
bodily to the tops, leaving you with nothing but a
few stragglers—all young birds—to make your bag
from.

Not having a moor of my own, and feeling, therefore, that in spite of varied experience on other
people's ground I am still liable to the criticism of those
who own moors, and who might think that my remarks
are not practical or applicable to their particular cases,
I have been at the pains to obtain an exhaustive

account of what has taken place on the moor which, up to now, has beaten all the records in Scotland. I allude to the estate of the Mackintosh at Moy Hall, Inverness. This gentleman has been kind enough to send me a very exact record of the progress of his moor from the days when no driving was done until the present time, when he finds himself able to rival the records of most of the English moors with very few exceptions. My readers will, no doubt, find it difficult to believe that I have not founded what I have written above upon the account which the Mackintosh has been good enough to send me. I can only, therefore, give them my word that I have not the pleasure of knowing that gentleman, that I have never set foot upon the Moy Hall moors, and that all the foregoing pages, in which I have endeavoured to show how the results of Scotch moorland could be improved by driving, were written *before* receiving this admirable paper. I may, perhaps, be allowed to say how gratified I feel to find that the Mackintosh's narrative of experience so closely corroborates what I have urged myself. The matter which he has sent me, and for which I cannot sufficiently express my gratitude, is so excellent and practical that I think I cannot do better than print it *in extenso*:

Moy Hall, Inverness : November 30, 1893.

This moor contains about 11,000 acres, and lies in Strathdearn, in the valley of the river Findhorn, at an altitude of 1,100 feet above sea-level. It is nearly square in shape, and the surface is undulating and pretty smooth. It is very well watered by springs and burns, and lies to the sun. As it has been in the proprietor's own hands since 1878, the heather is well burned all over the ground—a matter of vital importance in keeping up a large stock and insuring healthy birds. Too many moors are well burned in parts only, generally near burns, and the other beats neglected. Good burning can only be done on the high ground in exceptional years, and only then for a very short time, so that it is all-important to put on a large force of men to do this when the chance can be got. Little patches, but very frequent, should be the rule. This spreads the birds more, and prevents old birds from driving the younger birds off the strips when they are feeding. Then again, every care should be taken to make as much as possible of the water on the moor. Every trickle of water should be puddled up, and a succession of small drinking places made. Nothing can be worse in a dry rearing season than to have all the birds crammed together in one or two places. In fact, as in modern warfare, the spade has as much to do with obtaining good results as the gun has. What with looking after the springs, altering and repairing the butts, the spade is not out of the keepers' and watchers' hands from April till August. Another matter of vital importance is the killing down of old cocks. These worst of vermin can always be killed in November in certain favourite places. Every old cock killed then is worth a good many eggs in the following spring. The head keeper alone should be entrusted with this work, however. On too many Highland moors not nearly enough trapping is done for the smaller vermin, such as stoats and weasels. The traps should be left standing so long as they can spring.

In the opinion of the writer the cause of there having been so many disappointing seasons on a great many moors of late years is because what should be the breeding birds are killed early in August, and gradually a worse and worse class of bird is left. Grouse in many places have not laid the large number of eggs they used to go, even though the seasons for nesting have been very good. The large shootings which existed, say, in the Seventies have been broken up into smaller ones, roads and paths made to the distant beats, and as nowadays everyone shoots 'pretty well,' too often the old birds escape and the young birds are bagged. Especially is this the case with moors which are let from season to season, and nowadays the new class of shooting tenant does not much care about a lease. To give these moors a chance they should either be let on lease for a limit of birds, or else rested for a season, and then judiciously shot over. Where the moor is in the owner's hands or let on a long lease the case is different. If a man is very fond of dogs, pointers and setters, by all means let him use them; but if he wants to give the greatest amount of pleasure to the largest number of his friends, then let him harden his heart and make his moor into a 'driving moor,' not shooting over dogs at all, except perhaps in some odd corner or two. He can really get far more pleasure, and profit as well, if he sees his dogs broken himself before the shooting season, and then sells them to the public or to such of his friends as wish to shoot over dogs. There can be no manner of doubt that, once dogs are given up and regular and systematic driving taken to, the stock of birds is doubled or trebled, and, better still, the average healthiness of the birds is raised. This can easily be seen if there is a 'driving moor' next to a moor which is 'dogged.' On the Moy Hall moor there has been practically no disease since 1873.

Driving was first resorted to in 1869, and only then when the birds were too wild to sit to dogs. On September 8, 1869, the entry is ' We drove the birds ; ' the result for two guns was twelve grouse—not much, but a beginning. The next mention is on August 30, 1870, when, with four guns, forty-two grouse were got by driving; and there are two other days in that year when the same number of guns shot twenty-seven and thirty-four birds. No attempt was then made to go over the main part of the moor. Driving was only resorted to on the flats and round the cornfields. Of course no butts were at that time erected. In 1871 four guns got by driving 60, 57, and 121 grouse. On September 15, when the 121 grouse were got, the entry is, ' Everything went well ; we got fifteen brace at one drive, and eighteen brace at another.'

In 1872 there is the first entry of the individual scores of the guns. Twenty-nine birds was the highest score. In the years of 1871 and 1872 the total number of grouse killed during the season was 2,836 and 3,002 (birds).

From 1876 to 1879, owing to the moor being let, no driving was done. In 1879 this form of sport was regularly taken up ; and on September 1, 103 grouse were killed in six drives. The highest score at one drive was thirteen birds for forty-three shots.

During this season there were fourteen days of driving ; the best day of the season on Moy Hall was 162 grouse. On the adjoining moor of Meal-burne, belonging to the Mackintosh, on September 10, 270 grouse were killed in one day's driving by ten guns. This moor is peculiarly suited for this kind of sport, and up to date of 1893 the largest one-day's bag in Scotland, 454 brace, was got by nine guns. During 1879 the bag at Moy Hall was 5,172 grouse, showing how much the driving had done to secure birds which would otherwise never have come to the gun. On September 13, 1883, the first record of over one hundred brace for one day was got, 255 birds being bagged by eight guns. During three successive days 540 grouse were got, or an average of ninety brace per diem. In 1884 an average of ninety-four brace was got for the first four days' driving, the best day being 256 grouse, and thirty birds being the highest score at one drive.

In 1885, in the first four days' driving 527½ brace were killed.

In 1886 the first four days' driving resulted in 580 brace.

In 1887, owing to the death of the late Lord Lovat when actually engaged in a day's sport, there was no shooting until September 19, when 1,608 grouse were killed in three days, or an average for three successive days of 263 brace. One gun killed no less than eighty-two birds in one 'single drive' on September 20, and had he been shooting with three guns would have got many more. His total bag for the same day was 143 grouse. The best drive of the day was 271 grouse.

In 1888, during four days' successive driving, an average of 323 brace per diem was killed. During this season, which was a very good one, 5,822 grouse were killed on the moor.

In 1889, an indifferent breeding season, four days' driving gave 777 brace. In this year grouse were shot over dogs for the last time. Up till that time the moor had been regularly shot over dogs until the end of August.

In 1890 the first three or four days' driving resulted in 744 brace.

In 1891 864 brace were got in four days, but there was much more shooting, as 1,806 brace were got in the season.

In 1892, on September 1, nine guns got 575 grouse, and on the 2nd 803 grouse, the other two days of that week being so wild and stormy that there was no shooting.

In 1893 2,642 grouse were killed by nine guns in

M

the first four days' driving, an average of 330 brace per diem. The best individual score for one day was 184 grouse. There were six drives each day, and had the weather only been a little better, the results would have been much higher. 4,480 grouse were secured this season, all, of course, by driving.

The writer considers that since 1888 there has been nothing like a brilliant season. This past season the birds have been healthier and better scattered than they have ever been.

The great secret of success in driving is to select those places in the flight of the birds where they can best be killed. In Scotland this is far more difficult than in England, and no double drives, to give good results, are possible where the ground slopes, however gently. It is only on a dead level where a double drive is much good. The writer is all in favour of 'massing' the guns, and making the birds fly as concentrated as possible   In some of the drives the butts are only fifteen yards apart, and in none more than forty-five yards. All the butts should be (1) in a dead straight line, (2) should be close together and well concealed, being invariably placed within gun-shot of a ridge in front when on a hillside, and, if on a flat, then the outside turf should be carefully placed at the front of the butt.

The writer is all against upright, built-up butts. These must be dark-looking, and the birds 'shy' at them, without the least doubt.

The butts should be half sunk, well drained, and *perfectly invisible* from the front.

For driving, about thirty beaters and six side boys are used. Only single drives are taken, as the distances taken in are very large—in some drives about three miles round the arc of the beaters. Not a word is allowed to be said, except by the head keeper, who is always in the centre of the beaters. The six side boys are placed in 'pegged-out' positions, and only use their flags on the down-wind side.

Some of the drives are very peculiar. In the 'Top of the Delta,' which is about the best on the moor, the grouse are driven to the end of a sloping hill, and *parallel*, and not at right angles to the butts. By this way as many birds are shot coming from behind the right rear of the butts as from the direct front. The butts at this drive are very close to each other, and the bags made at it are large—350 birds, for instance.

In another drive, 'The Rocks,' the birds are driven at first entirely away to the left of the line of butts, and at least half a mile to their left. When once congregated on a certain flat, they are then

M 2

'dribbled' round a gentle slope at one side of this flat, the beaters hardly moving, but every one or two men moving from time to time as the firing moderates.

In fact, the more 'dodgy' a drive can be made, the more sport there is in seeing it done. Many of the writer's friends, who shot regularly on English and Lowland moors, describe the birds in the Highlands as being much harder to shoot. This, of course, is owing to the ground. In some drives birds come perfectly straight, either low, highish, or very high; in others, on the same day and with the same wind, they will fly like snipe, with a wrench and twist which sadly upsets 'averages.'

As regards scoring, the writer considers that the best fairest, and quickest way is to draw for butts, shift two each drive, and ask each gun after each drive is over, 'How many birds did you see *fall* to your gun?' In these days of nitro powders everyone can see if he kills or not. If he does not know whether he has killed or not, he had better give up grouse driving. The total of that drive is then given to the gathering keeper, who then has some idea of what was *claimed* and what was picked up. As the drives are all single drives, birds are easily gathered by the guns, and after they have left to go on to the next line, the ground is well hunted, and far back, by a keeper. Not a shot is allowed to be fired except during a drive. Walking in line and shooting home, as is often done, does really more harm in frightening birds than any amount of driving.

The shooting at Moy Hall, in a fairly good year, is as follows :

First week, about third week in August ; second week (after one week's rest only— more is useless), about first week of September—these of four days each ; another two days about September 21, and another two days about last of October. These last are, of course, 'sandwiched in ' with other kinds of shooting. The man who will kill most at his moor by driving will be he who (1) gets good guns to shoot his birds ; (2) who disturbs his moor least by small days or stray guns being enlarged upon it ; (3) who is constantly on the look-out for fresh hints —given by the birds themselves.

(Signed) A. MACKINTOSH OF MACKINTOSH.

With most of the above I cordially agree ; in fact, the experience of so close a student and excellent a sportsman could not, for his particular ground, be improved upon. I cannot quite endorse what he says about built-up butts, having seen them work so

well for a considerable succession of days. But even
on this point one should, in considering individual
moors, be open to conviction, and my solution of it
would be that where on wild or rough ground such
long drives are taken as are here mentioned, birds
would be brought off their own ground entirely, and
coming suddenly upon butts which they have never
seen, would be likely to shy at them. At any rate first-
rate sport has often been seen from both kinds, and so
long as the sunken butts can be well drained I think
there is a good deal to be said for them.

Placing the guns so close as is advocated here
seems to me to have disadvantages which on some
moors would outweigh its advantages. Under any
circumstances to concentrate the birds within so small
a space is quite beyond the efforts of most Scotch
keepers and drivers, although I admit that when once
a perfect system has been established, such as obtains
in Yorkshire, it would in some places be of great use
to the bag. But in most Scotch drives the flight of
the birds spreads over a wide space, requiring six or
seven guns to cover it, and in such cases the flanks
are sometimes as good as the centre. Again, having
neighbours only fifteen yards off on each side of you
would bother many people, besides destroying the
feeling that you are free to shoot at any bird that

comes within range, which constitutes one of the most attractive features of grouse driving.

The opposition of the keepers is, as mentioned above, a serious drawback to the success of driving in some parts of Scotland. With regard to this it seems to me necessary, while making allowance for the traditions under which they have been brought up, and their dislike of change, not to lose sight of certain interested motives which generally underlie their hostility to the new system. Scotchmen, though as a majority they vote on the Radical side, are by instinct the most conservative of highly civilised races. Their laws and customs, language and dress, show the tenacity with which they cling to the traditions of an ancestry of which any nation might be proud, and a gathering of the clans would to this day evoke a response which probably no cry could raise in any other country.

In the training and management of dogs the Highlander has always shown himself to be particularly apt. He seems in some degree to share the keen instincts and finer qualities of the dog, and the devotion of the animal appears to bring out the gentler and more sympathetic side of the nature of the man. The pointer and setter, no less than the collie, the deerhound, or the 'dandy,' respond more faithfully

on the average to the handling of a Scotchman than
of his English counterpart. The best dog-breakers I
have ever seen have been Scotchmen, and one cannot
but admire their reluctance to abandon an art in
which they excel for what is to them a more irksome
and laborious manner of providing sport for their
employers.

But while we may and ought to sympathise with
their genuine devotion to the dog, as well as the
honest and painstaking assiduity which they bestow
on the development of his qualities, we need not be
blind to the fact that there is in the large majority of
cases the interested motive which I mentioned above.
They many of them think more of the *bawbees* than
of sport, and fear they may lose under the new *régime*
a source of profit which they enjoyed under the old. It
pays very well to breed pointers and setters at some one
else's expense and sell them for your own profit. The
kennel of a Scotch shooting tenant is usually a heavy
item of outlay to him, but in most cases a profitable
business to his keeper. It is the fear lest they should
lose this which influences most of them, and causes
them to take refuge in the unworthy course of advis-
ing their masters that driving is impossible on the
moor, that they cannot get men, or that they will
drive all the birds off the ground or kill too many

of them. Now, since this source of income to keepers, though not over honest in its source, has been, so to speak, legalised by the custom of two or three generations, it seems to me both wise and right to compensate them to some extent if for your own pleasure or profit you do away with it. The obvious and best solution, unless you are prepared to raise their rate of wages, is to encourage them to breed and train retrievers, with a few spaniels or setters. Good retrievers are very scarce and fetch high values ; most grouse driving is deficient in interest as well as in result, to those who are fond of hunting dogs, for lack of them. The same keeper who has for years maintained a high-class kennel of pointers will soon take an equal pride in his retrievers ; and a couple or two of setters should still be kept for wild days on outside beats, or to assist in finding birds after the big drives.

The dog-man, whom I have urgently recommended as a necessary ally in partridge shooting, is equally if not more necessary to well-conducted grouse driving. To him should be confided the task of finding all the dead or ' pricked ' birds which fall wide of the line of butts or far behind, and it should be his business to remove all excuse for the apparently innocent, but usually crafty, marauding to which some of our friends resort to supplement their bag.

The third difficulty, that of getting enough men to drive, is in some places insuperable. But here we must remember that, as in the case of the kennel question, liberality will do a great deal. A frequent evil to be found in Scotland is that the shooting tenant, having given a rent out of all proportion to the value of his moor, becomes stingy in other matters to recoup himself for his bad bargain, and so between the two conditions he gets less and less sport as time goes on.

As I have urged in another volume,[1] liberality to all concerned is an essential condition of a pursuit of pleasure such as shooting, and I have always noticed that those who exercise this quality judiciously but freely, and combine with it a firm and kindly discipline, get the best sport. This is eminently the case in Scotland, where the people, specially responsive in nature, will be grateful to you for the one and admire you for the other.

Good wages, a hearty lunch, and a brake or other conveyance for drivers who have to come far from their homes, I have seen work wonders ; while with the contrary conditions I have witnessed a general mutiny, and more often a sulky recalcitrant spirit, which, carried into practical effect all day, has entirely

[1] *The Partridge.*

spoilt the sport. Where labour is scarce and drivers difficult to get, it becomes the more necessary to train the few you have to intelligent driving. It is wonderful what can be done with a small number by taking shorter drives, and teaching the men to cross about— that is, while keeping their relative positions in the line, to zigzag so as not to miss the likely bits of holding cover.

To sum up, I commend the study of driving to those who rent or own Scotch shootings, feeling sure that if by any of the means I have tried to indicate they can infuse a keenness for it into the people they have to deal with, commanded and directed by superior practical knowledge, they will be much gratified if not astonished by the result.

CHAPTER IV

ENGLISH DRIVING

SOME twenty years ago Messrs. Blackwood did me the honour to publish in their well-known magazine an article I had written on grouse driving ; a subject of which I had considerable experience during the remarkable seasons of 1870–1871, and above all 1872.

In it I tried to portray grouse driving as it was, and is still, on English moors, and to defend and recommend it as a system alike the most attractive to the sportsman and profitable to the stock of grouse. Many letters followed my little effort, and one gentleman, who disguised his identity—of which I am still ignorant—under the signature of 'W. C.,' fell foul of the advocates of driving, and of myself in particular, in the columns of the ' Field,' with all the artillery of envy, malice and uncharitableness, supplemented by an ignorance of the subject that was remarkable even among journalistic contributions to sporting literature.

Sentiment against this 'inhuman butchery' so overcame Mr. 'W. C.' that his feelings found vent in poetry, and the lines in which he may be supposed to have summed up his peculiar views on the matter are really worth reproducing, if only as evidence of his literary power and sporting instincts :

> Let gay ones and great
> Make the most of their fate
>   As from mantlet to mantlet they run ;
> I envy them not—
> No, not a jot,
>   If you give me my dog and my gun.

I should have been concerned to see, even at that date, anyone who elected to run from 'mantlet to mantlet' during a grouse drive, and the light of subsequent experience only tends to confirm the view which I held then, that a dog and a gun are almost as useful to a sportsman engaged in that pursuit as in any other, and none the less if, as appears to have happened to the fortunate 'W. C.,' they have been given to him. Mr. 'W. C.' finally crushed me with the remark that I was evidently more familiar with the pen than the gun, a compliment I enjoyed the more as I had never written anything for publication before, and had used a gun ever since I was strong enough to carry it.

It is no longer necessary to defend grouse driving against this kind of onslaught, even when emanating

from so powerful a source as ' W. C.,' but this gentleman
was only one of many who always attacked anything
like well-organised shooting or large bags, partly because they had no knowledge of such things, and
partly because at that time they furnished almost the
only 'copy' which editors of journals could procure
on shooting matters.

Nowadays all the best performances and records
are pretty well known, most of them having been
published in books or newspapers, and I think the
Badminton Library has finally silenced the class of
criticism so ably represented by my friend ' W. C.'

The journey to the English moors, picturesque as
it is, has details of a different character from those
described in a previous chapter ; and what is a very
important fact, the travellers are much more numer-
ously recruited from local sources.

The Manchester man and the Sheffielder, the
dalesman and the tyke, are devoted to their grouse
driving, and as proud as possible of the great bags that
have made their moors so famous ; while their love
of the sport is largely shared by the lower classes in
the North of England. Herein lies the great difference
between English and Scotch driving, as well as the
secret of much of the superiority of the former over
the latter.

It takes a great deal to astonish a Yorkshireman ; this is one of his most distinctive attributes ; and if any competent Yorkshire authority such as Lord Walsingham or Mr. Rimington-Wilson told a man of York that an effort to kill 2,000 brace in one day was contemplated, he would be delighted, not surprised at the idea, and only ask for the privilege of helping to do it. There is therefore no difficulty about obtaining drivers, and those of the most willing sort. Many of them will be glad to help without any payment, and the older hands among them will have besides a complete knowledge of the mysteries of flanking, wind, &c., a shrewd judgment of the comparative merits of the shooters engaged, and often a wager on the probable scores of their favourite champions. Last but not least, if the head keeper is a good man, they have implicit confidence in, and great respect for, him and his prowess ; and as a consequence he can keep them all under discipline, and turn them all to account in the management of his birds.

It will readily be seen what an important factor this spirit among the inhabitants becomes towards the success of those great days on the more renowned moors, which seem to provide an ever-recurring sense of wonderment even to those who have often taken

part in them, and to be absolutely incomprehensible
to those who have not.

Many a time, in other parts of England or in
Scotland, have I felt that it would be wiser to be silent
concerning these phenomenal deeds, and that my
character for veracity or honesty would never survive
the relation of even half what I had often seen. I
have never forgotten a lesson I received when, as
a youth at a private tutor's in Oxfordshire, I used
to be asked to take a laborious part in the slaying
of from ten to twenty brace of partridges in the company of seven or eight old farmers. I had returned
to my tutor's after the summer holidays, during
which I had been fortunate enough to be allowed
to take a gun in a day or two's grouse driving on
the moors of Mr. Walter Stanhope at Dunford
Bridge. When the Oxfordshire farmers asked me
where I had been, I said 'grouse driving.' This conveyed very little to them, but one of them lazily asked
what sort of a bag we had made. I naïvely replied
the truth, from 150 to 170 brace each day. We had
just finished lunch, and our morning's bag of 7½ brace
of partridges and a hare was proudly laid out near us.
But this reply of mine cast a gloom over everything,
and one of these sandy-haired, beefy-faced veterans
laid his hand on my shoulder and said, ' Ah, young

man, when you be older, you'll know better than to tell such tales as that to a lot of men.'

Many years after, a servant of mine, a veteran of the navy and the Taku forts, and afterwards of the London Fire Brigade, had to fight for his life in a Scotch lodge because he had incautiously related, and on this occasion quite truthfully, the results of a week at High Force, where he had just been with me, and where we had averaged 600 brace a day for four days. Previously nettled by his disparagement of Scotch moors as compared with English, the local champion, who happened to be the coachman, was fairly roused by this astounding record. 'Ye're a d——d leear,' he cried, and fell upon the Southron. They were separated, but not until Flodden and Bannockburn had been fought over again, and the gun-room floor was covered with blood.

These things are more widely known now, but I misdoubt me that many a Scotch keeper who listens with open-mouthed gravity to the tales of Studley and High Force, Broomhead or Wemmergill, conceals under the politeness of the Highlander an incredulity which cannot be shaken, and which deters him for ever from any effort to emulate such fabulous achievements, or eclipse the respectable moderation of the records of his own glen.

N

Although the opposition to driving mentioned above is now out of date, there are still many people to whom the mere making of a large bag appears to constitute a source of irritation. I have never been quite able to understand this frame of mind. There is nothing to prevent such a man from making a small bag if he wishes it, either on his own or his friend's ground, and surely he might remember that those who take part in these (to him) colossal days are, for the most part, just as keen and accomplished sportsmen as himself. From the days of the great Hawker until the present time, all the evidence tends to show that when a man is once out with a gun he will invariably kill as much as he can. The man who will come home early in the day for fear that he should kill too much game is a person whom, at any rate, I have never met, and in whose existence, I must confess, I find it difficult to believe. But there is one point of view on which I should probably agree even with the unrelenting opponents of large bags. I do not think it desirable for boys or youths to take part in them until they have been properly trained to the contest between themselves and the animal they are pursuing, which constitutes the true definition of sport. A boy who is learning to shoot may be taken out grouse driving once in a way, but it is far better

that he should serve his apprenticeship in the pursuit
of grouse by walking, stalking, or shooting them over
dogs in the usual manner.   When they are very wild
he will, no doubt, if left to himself, organise little im-
promptu drives with the few men who may be out
with him, and in the course of a windy day he will
get many shots which will teach him something of
the calculation necessary to kill a driven bird.   To
partake in the pleasure of a well-organised shoot which
produces a large total is not necessary to human happiness, however keen a shooter a man may be, but
it is one of the delightfully exciting incidents of one's
life ; and if the moor, manor, or covert produces
naturally a large stock of game without doing harm
to any individual, it is surely better to realise from it
to the proper extent.   This result will not be achieved,
as I mentioned before in the first volume of this series,
by anyone not educated to all kinds of shooting ; and
the raw youth who has never pursued birds on his
own account, nor handled a dog, nor trained himself
to shoot carefully and accurately, but, on the other
hand, has been allowed by too indulgent elders to
take part in big days until he is nearly *blasé* with
heavy firing, is neither a desirable object nor a
pleasant companion.   I am glad to think, however,
that these are the minority, and that the English lad

N 2

is still keen enough, as a rule, to go out on his own
account, and show his prowess in circumventing and
securing birds without the aid of an array of beaters
or drivers.

Let me conduct such a one with me on to the
moor, and, presuming that he already knows something of the habits of the grouse, of the handling of
his gun, and of the ways of his retriever, let me see,
with all diffidence, if any hints that I can give will be
of any service to him.

Now mount your pony, and let us be off together.
The other guns will follow soon, and we shall, at any
rate, be first on the ground and into our places early.
The drivers will start three miles from the first line
of butts by time. It is, therefore, important that we
should be on the spot punctually, or the birds will be
coming over before we are there. Look to your girths
before you get up, or your saddle may go round with
you, and leave you in the middle of the road as we
go down the hill. Through the little village we clat-
ter, hustling the ducks and chickens out of the road-
way, at that short and uncomfortable canter which
appears specially to distinguish the hill pony. Round
the bend at the end of the street, almost grazing our
knees against the stone wall, as our ponies hustle
round the sharp turn, over the grey bridge that spans

with its single arch the narrow, but violent, torrent of
the beck, brown and swollen from last night's rain ;
and once on the opposite side the ascent begins, the
road widening out here and there into a green lane
or common, where the geese hiss and cackle at us,
barely floundering away from under our horses' feet.
We begin to leave the region of the sycamore, the
mountain ash, and the larch, while the foxglove and
blackberry grow scarcer by the roadside. Now we
emerge into a great inclosure of, say, a hundred acres,
in which, though there are still patches of succulent
green pasture, dotted with mushrooms or here and
there spots of grey stone peeping through the sward,
the coarser grasses and rushy tussocks of the moor
begin to predominate. A whole herd of young cattle
come dancing round us, and the temper of the old
bull who watches us, sulky and motionless, as we
ride by, is a source of inward anxiety, until we reach
the gate in the high wall which is the boundary of the
real moor. Now we are fairly in the open and on
the heather, a flock of anxious peewits hovers close
round our heads, screaming and turning over in the
air ; the wheatear evades us in a succession of short,
jerky flights, curtseying at us in derision at each pause
upon a stone, and so, making our way through moss
hags, over stones, and carefully round boggy places,

but still always ascending, we reach the first of the line of butts. Now dismount and take your gun. You have drawn No. 4 butt, which is sure to be a good one ; and as we walk up to it from here, you may kill a grouse, which, as the drivers are still miles away, can do no harm.

'Yak ! kak ! kak !' from close underneath No. 2 butt. Well done, very good shot ! but look beyond there up the face at all those birds rising and going back into the drive. No matter, they will come on again. There is plenty of time, and you may gather from where those birds rose, about three hundred yards away, how difficult of approach the Yorkshire grouse is even in the early days of August. But here we are at our place, so let us get in and be ready for action. Now take the centre of the butt yourself, put half a dozen cartridges in your right-hand coat-pocket, that you may be able to put one quickly into the gun in case your loader should not be ready with your second when birds are coming thick. Let him place his bag of cartridges, well open, on the seat in the left-hand corner of the butt close to his hand, and I will crouch behind him rather to your right. Neither of us is likely to jump up, so that you can swing the gun round with freedom on both sides to shoot behind. Look with care to the height of the front of the butt —it should be just high enough to shoot over in comfort when you are standing upright —make it up with the spare sods lying about, and especially on the left-hand side, as from that side you will show to the birds against the sky, and you *must* keep low as they come up hill. Now lean both of your guns against the front of the butt, being careful in so doing that no little pieces of peat fall down the muzzle See that the barrels of both are clear, and that both are loaded, and now let us take a good survey of the exact position of our next-door neighbours, and of the ground in front of us. Ours is the first butt under the ridge to our right, No. 5 being on the point of the ridge, and No. 6 beyond it out of sight. The three butts on our left stretching down the hill, No. 1 being the bottom one, all look at first sight to be better places than ours, but I think we shall find on examination of the favourable slack in front of us under the ridge that we shall get as much shooting as anybody. The sun is now quite hot. The grasses and heather buds on the ridge are waving and shivering gently in the breeze against the bright sky. In the valley I can just hear the splash of the beck over the stones, and clearly as we can see every detail on the opposite slope, and the flat above it, and even that rocky ridge, crowned by the delicate blue of a far-off

range, no sign of a driver's flag, with the exception of
the two pointsmen not far off on our left, is visible.

A hoarse exclamation, ' Lie down, will you ? ' from
a loader to his dog, comes to us faintly on the breeze
from the top butt ; a snatch of a skylark's song from
the pastures, an occasional bark from a sheep dog in
the valley, the single plaintive pipe of a young golden
plover, seeming to come now from the flat in front, now
from behind, and now from somewhere in the sky, are
all the sounds that reach our ears.   All is deliciously
still, and the atmosphere, fragrant with heather buds
and stimulating to the nerves, the brightness and
purity of the light, with the enchanting prospect of
heath and fell, of mountain and cloud, of the peaceful
valley watered by a shining river, its humble interests
all clustered round the grey church tower and bridge
of the little market town two miles away and five
hundred feet below you, would be worth the journey
up here, even if grouse and shooting did not exist to
make it, to your eyes, complete.   Faintly a very distant
rattle, the well-known music of the railway, catches
your ear, and there, creeping gently down towards
the town, is the little toy train, tracing its accurate
line in picturesque contrast to the windings of the
river, and giving with its long soft trail of snow-white
steam a new note of interest to the slumbering land-

scape. Toy-like as it appears from here, that is a northern express going at fifty miles an hour, and it has even now passed out of sight.

There ! On the rocky ridge afar off is a flash of something white ; it is—no, yes—a driver's flag ; there is another, showing black against the sunlit moor to the right—yes, there they are, all or nearly all in sight, and in the shape of a perfect horseshoe. 'The birds will not be here for some time yet,' you say. No, but I should take my gun and be on the watch for an odd lot often comes over very early off the flank of the drive.—Look out, here are birds !' Black and mysterious looking, a little pack of some five-and-twenty suddenly show on the ridge about a hundred yards in front. Rapidly and silently they come along the ridge straight for your neighbour, No. 5. Whistle to him, it is only fair play—but it is too late, for *him*. Some hasty movement of his or his neighbour's beyond, and in an instant they have swerved and are coming right down on us. 'Take the first one.' One —two—well done ; that second one isn't down yet, but badly hit ; ah ! there he comes, stone dead I should say, just this side of that little knoll with the shining bit of white grass below it. I shall get him for you all right after the drive, when we hunt the ground behind. By this time you are very much on the look-out, and so I now see are our neighbours, but there probably won't be any more for some little time. That little pack were all old birds, sitting on some bare place upon the ridge, and had got up thinking to sneak away long before the drivers came really near. And let me point out to you that, had your neighbour been 'watching out' as we were, the lot would never have swerved, but would have gone straight by him, an easy chance ; whereas as things are, he is either unconscious or furious, no matter which, and you are a brace of birds to the good, which he will only put down as an item of your extraordinary good luck.

Now keep a sharp watch, and especially to your left. The birds that come over the ridge on the right must show well against the sky, and those in front will tell black against the sunlight of the opposite face; but those that come up the hill from the left, having crossed the gully without our seeing them, will be creeping very low over the heather, so that with the sun shining on their bodies they will be very difficult to see against the ground, and get right up to us unawares, unless we are careful. Here they come, just from the point I warned you of, seven or eight of them, close to the top of the heather and very slow, for they have a little wind against them, have come a

long way, and are flying up hill. The slant of their
course will bring them obliquely across you, heading
straight for No. 5—and here is a good chance to get
four with your two guns. Take the outside one on
your right, they are sure to swing away a little when
you fire, but those on your left will still cross near
enough to deal with easily. Good ! he is stone dead,
the second also, an easy cross shot straight in front,
the third a miss, though an easy chance, and the
fourth cleverly dropped by a longish shot just as they
were swinging back all together. No. 5 kills one, close
to your last, for they are now almost in front of him,
and they are gone ; back over the ridge.

That third shot was a pity, and arose from too
much haste and flurry in changing your gun ; quite
unnecessary, for there was really plenty of time, as
there was another bird much nearer to you than the
one you fired at with your fourth barrel. Bear this
in mind another time. Here come two straight to
you from under the ridge ; take care, for these are
coming thrice as fast as the last, the side wind helping
them a little, and rather higher. Slightly to your right
they come over at express pace ; ah ! your first barrel
was neither high enough nor forward enough, as you
see by those little floating white feathers from under
his tail, but swinging quickly you killed him well

with your second behind the line, and he has fallen
stone dead in that patch of rushes by the little
trickle of water. 'You ought to have had them
both.' Yes, you ought, but the first barrel at a fast
grouse at about twenty feet from the ground always
demands just sufficient forethought to remember to
lift the left arm well up and to shoot well over him.

Now they are coming more frequently, and mostly
very straight to us from the ridge to our right, and
from the front. Look out again from the left—you
see those had got to within ten yards of you, coming
from below before you saw them, and that is why,
instead of getting at least three, if not four of them,
all easy shots, you in your hurry missed your first,
killed your second behind, and fired two most ridiculous
shots at him with your second gun after they were too
far off. Your eyes should run over all the ground in
front of you, from the extreme right to left and back
again, *incessantly*. Especially you should watch two
points—that where the ridge sinks into the skyline
eighty yards ahead, and that on the left where they
come creeping to you from below. You ought by
now to be getting to know the instant a bird is
in sight whether he is really coming to you or not.
Observe how those that you first see in front of
you nearly all swing with the wind down to No. 3 on

your left ; and on the other hand how the same curve in their flight causes all those which first show at the point of the ridge I just mentioned to come right on to you, though first seen straight in front of No. 5.

Look out for those two in front, they are going to settle, and you should always shoot at a settling bird, even up to a longish range. You missed the moment, and probably the bird also. Just when he tucks his tail in, and is sinking down into the heather, with his wings open and neck and breast exposed, he is very vulnerable, and may be killed at a long way off. There, he has run on to that stone— now take him sitting, it is better to put him up in any case, for he will only attract others to settle near him. Ah, you shot over him, and he is off. There is only one way to make sure of a sitting bird, a trick I found out for myself at pigeon shooting : aim carefully three or four feet under him, raise the muzzle gently till it just covers his toes, at that moment pull, and you will never miss another sitter.

Now there is a fine lot—they seem to be streaming at you from all points in front, there must be two or three hundred of them. Keep cool, take the one coming straight for the right-hand corner of our butt and who leads the pack, first. Well killed ! the second snapped rather too hastily in front, the third well

killed ; but why, oh ! why did you turn round ? the
fourth one you shot at and missed was ridiculously
far, and then one nearly knocked your cap off meanwhile. Again you change guns, and kill one out of
two hastily shot at behind the butts, and as you again
get your seventh and eighth barrels to work you find
that birds have been streaming straight to you all the
while, tailing off after the main body of the pack.
Result—five birds with your eight barrels, while, shooting as well as you do, you ought to have very easily
killed with all the shots and secured eight birds. As
long as there are birds still coming on you should never
turn round at all, but keep on plugging away always
at those which catch your eye as coming easiest, and
letting them get tolerably near you before firing. As
in watching a first-rate professional at billiards you
will be astonished at the number of easy strokes he
gets, and notice how seldom he takes a difficult one,
so a high-class performer with the gun will achieve as
much by his rapid selection of easy chances as by
accuracy of shooting. There will always be plenty of
difficult shots during a drive on which to employ his
more brilliant efforts, and which he will kill with all
the more certainty from 'getting his eye in' at the
easy ones. But this is a part of the art that is not
learned in a day, even by the most brilliant natural shot.

WHY TURN ROUND?

Now here come three, one a little ahead of the other two and straight to you, the others abreast and a trifle to your left. Take the leader first, shooting rather soon, at what looks like forty yards, and with particular accuracy; change guns quickly without firing the second barrel, and kill the other two with your second gun, one by sharp work just in front and the other an easy one behind. Good, you have got all three; and no doubt you see the advantage of this manœuvre. Had you stuck to your first gun after killing the first, you would have had to pause a little to get the next with your second barrel, and while you were changing guns the third bird would have got so far that you would almost certainly have lost him.

Now the holloaing of the drivers sounds quite near, and in fact, though you cannot yet see them, for they are still climbing out of the gully and under the fall of the ground in front of you, they are probably not more than 150 yards off, a distance at which you may easily blind a man. You must now only shoot at birds a moderate height up in the air, or low to your right against the ridge, or behind. What remain are coming singly and easier, but look out for a small burst off the ridge, for remember we saw a good many settle there from time to time. There they come, but they won't quite face it, and hang back, giving

long, high, crossing shots, and going clean back
over the drivers. High, and well forward, and you
have killed a beautiful double shot ; don't forget to
pick these up afterwards, for they have fallen a long
way from any of your other birds.

The drivers are showing all along the line, their
flags are rattling in the wind, and it is nearly over.
Do you remember where that bird settled about sixty
yards in front, just in that deep bit of heather ? They
will go past him, for I don't think he has ever risen ;
call to them, waving them to where he was. Yak-kak !
there he is, and as he comes straight on and rather
high you have killed him easily and safely over their
heads. He is about the last, and I think as the
drivers are now only forty yards off, we may go out
and pick up.

It is better now to make the loader hold your dog
until we have picked up all the dead ones near the butt
on the burnt ground. It is bad for him to see so many
dead on the ground and he will have had enough work
by the end of the day. Having done this the man can
go off after the bird we marked at the very beginning
of the drive, which is quite dead, and you and I will
look after the others with the dog, particularly those
two or three which fell, not killed dead, near the little
burnside. Twenty-seven you had down, besides one

of these not counted, which will probably rise again. Well, we must pick them all up. Now we have gathered twenty-one, and your loader has the far-off bird which makes twenty-two. Wait a moment till he rejoins us and is out of the way, and we will try for the three in the burn. Now be ready with your gun, and mind to work your dog up to them from this side, for right and left and behind us are men all over the place picking up, and unless we drive him away in the forward direction you will not be able to shoot safely. Ah, I see the dog winds him ; look out, there he is, and safely killed without trouble. One of the others proves to be winged, and to have run a long way down the burn till he is gathered right behind No. 3, but though the latter looks rather askance at us for being off our own ground, the bird was fairly footed by the dog all the way from where he fell. The third is lying stone dead in a little pool, so now we have twenty-five ; but stay, we had almost forgotten the two you killed right away in front, as they were turning back. Now we have got both of them, though the second took the dog a hundred yards down the gully, leaving a long track of feathers like the ' scent ' of a paper chase on the tops of the heather. But where have we left the twenty-eighth ? ' We must have been mistaken,' you say, ' for we have hunted the

O

ground all over.' 'I beg your pardon, I am quite
sure of my count ; so just look with me carefully close
round the butt, where a bird often gets left.   Here he
lies, down a deep rift in the peat, in a little stagnant
pool of brown water, which is why he had no scent,
almost hidden by overhanging heather, not five yards
from the butt ; so there is our correct number.   You
can see from this the value of accurate counting, for
without me you would certainly have gone away
satisfied you had picked all up, and left that last
bird to rot.'

As we have not been called on yet by our host, we
might just look at where the second of those two
settled in front, for the one which ran on to the stone
and got away was not the bird you fired at settling.
I thought not, and there to our joy is the other one,
not quite dead, crouching deep under the thick
heather, and found very prettily by the dog.   That
was lucky, I thought you had missed him, for he
seemed to drop all right into the heather.

So we have made it up to twenty-nine, a fair good
drive, and though your shooting was really very good,
you must remember that on several occasions you
missed the chance of easily getting more, merely by
undue hurry, or not making the most of the position.

Now we shift across, and rather uphill, about two

hundred yards only for the return drive. For some years we used to drive back over the same butts ; but grouse hardly ever return to any ground by the same line as they took to leave it, and here they always come back higher up, with the exception of a few lots which will return much lower down, and which it cannot be hoped to include in the drive.

The reason of this is the wind—the invariable factor in determining the line of the flight of grouse. This time they will be coming back off higher ground, the wind, though still across, being rather more behind them, an important fact to them, and with the sun also more behind them, an equally important one to you. You have now to keep, if possible, more carefully on the watch than before, and from the first moment after getting to your place, for some will return to their own ground almost immediately. Here you must carefully scan the face of the hill opposite you, bothered as you are by the sun, now on your left ; for they will be very difficult to see against the dark rising ground, and come very fast. You will get no shots against the sky except at such as come high.

They return on higher ground here for two reasons, one being that the majority of those in the last drive actually came off higher ground over the ridge to

your right than you supposed, which was swept in
sideways by the flank, and to which they wish to return ; and the other that the wind, the more imme-
diate reason, being here on their quarter, they can the
more easily slant across it, and are not obliged to
curve round under the ridge, as they would do if it
were at all against them.   Remember that here they
will *all* come very fast, and though nothing would
really turn them, they will swerve and twist a good
deal if you make hasty or jerky movements just as
they approach you.   This is another fruitful reason
of the wonderful 'luck' usually ascribed to a first-
rate man.   The duffer next to him exposes himself,
bobs or shifts about, and turns many a bird from
himself right towards the motionless form of his more
accomplished neighbour, such birds 'counting two
on a division' as politicians would say.   Here again,
if they are coming straight, as most of them will,
there can be no question of killing three or four,
except out of a big or streaming lot.   Make sure of
your double shot, one in front and one behind, letting
the first one come pretty close to you before firing,
and swinging round like lightning for the second.   To
this end make sure that your footing is secure, and
your loader so placed as not to interfere with your
movements, for when birds are coming very fast down

wind you have to turn round with extreme quickness, and must be free in your movements, with your feet on level ground. When you come to the pick-up, bear in mind that your dead birds will all be much farther back than you would suppose, and that you will have none, except cross shots, in front of your butt. Take your dog right away back at once to a point a little farther off than your farthest bird, and then hunt him up carefully towards the butt, so as to give him the full benefit of the wind.

In conclusion, never wait to kill a bird behind the line while it is possible to kill him in front; but be careful not to dwell upon or follow birds coming into the line, this being the most fruitful cause of accident.

Thus may one endeavour to instruct those who are beginning to practise this most engaging of all forms of shooting. There are a few further points I would urge, on some of which I must disagree with what has been written elsewhere, though I am against splitting straws with persons who have undoubtedly brought much study to bear upon the subject. I cannot agree with one well-known authority, who advises men never to shoot at birds which settle in front. I would always recommend shooting at them even up to seventy or eighty yards off. First, as remarked above, they can be killed up to a good distance;

secondly, because they will always attract others to settle near them. Whether the fresh arrivals detect the presence of those already there by sight or smell I cannot say, but it is certain that if birds have settled in front of you, and you do not disturb them, a great proportion of those following on after them will drop down to them. I have often seen them rise and come straight on over the guns after being shot at when in the act of alighting or sitting, showing that they did not detect where the sound proceeded from. Late in the drive, when the men are getting comparatively close, it is better to leave them alone, on the chance of their coming forward : early in the drive always shoot ; if they go back, they will probably alight again before reaching the drivers, and be forced forward a second time.

When you are shooting grouse with one gun only, and a big lot of birds are coming to you, fire your two barrels *early*, duck down below the butt, and as long as there are still grouse within shot, put in one cartridge only. You will do more execution this way than by waiting to load both barrels. I once killed five birds out of one lot of about fifty in this manner, and I ought to have killed six, for I missed the third shot, about the easiest of all. I need hardly say they were coming slowly against the wind, and swerved a

little across me after the first shot, or it could not have
been done. Keep your cartridges in your right-hand
pocket, and have your bag on the seat, wide open, on
your right, unless it is raining, when you must see
them bestowed in the dry, but the strap of the bag
left unbuckled ; and always feed your gun direct from
your right-hand pocket. I must say that since giving
them a fair trial I am distinctly in favour of brass-
covered cartridges, and more especially for grouse
driving, when one is so often overtaken by heavy
showers, during which the necessity for quick firing
makes it impossible to keep them all dry. For those
who use ejectors, they will be found, in the long run,
an economy, in spite of their trifling additional cost.
The ejectors of my present guns (Purdey's) have never
been out of order but once, and that was when I got
a sodden paper cartridge stuck fast, and used too
much force to extract it. We usually have to pay a
penalty for every improvement in this world, and the
use of hammerless guns with ejectors is no exception
to the rule. The mechanism of the piece is more
complicated, and requires more care in cleaning and
general treatment ; but with these precautions and
brass-covered cartridges there is no reason whatever
why guns of this improved type, turned out by a good
maker, should get out of order. They should not be

cleaned with anything but vaseline, which never cor-
rodes, and only a moderate quantity of that ; the
great secret being to keep all accessible parts of the
action as clean and *dry* as possible. A heavy-handed,
ignorant under-keeper, whether English or Scotch, is
rarely fit to be trusted with the handling or cleaning
of such valuable articles as the best breech-loaders of
to-day.

Whatever may be said to the contrary, the general
verdict of those who have the best opportunities of
judging is in favour of the best guns by the best
makers. You will often hear it said that these
makers' charges for their best quality of guns are
'outrageous,' and all sorts of ugly words applied to
those whose position in the trade enables them to set
the market price of these articles. I must put in a
plea for the good gunmaker. It would be invidious
to particularise, but there are several makers in London whose names are in everybody's mouth, and who
turn out guns, undoubtedly high-priced, but which,
to my thinking, are well worth the money. Everyone
who knows anything at all of the subject, knows that
the profit on the best quality of gun is not heavy,
much smaller, in fact, than on cheaper articles
of all sorts supplied by the trade generally, while
most of the most valuable part of the work is not

visible, and would not be detected by the inex-
perienced. A great deal of personal care, as well as
honest and dearly paid labour, is expended on a pair
of 'best guns' by one of these firms ; and I fail to
see why a man should grumble at giving, say, 140*l.*
or 150*l.*, or even more, for articles which, properly
cared for, will last him his lifetime, and for which the
demand is constantly and widely increasing. A well-
built gun, besides its practical use, is, to a certain
extent, a work of art, and it should be borne in
mind that as an article of British manufacture it still
holds its place against the competition of all other
countries ; and that whether you care to give the
price or not, there are plenty of Frenchmen Italians,
Austrians and Americans, without reckoning our own
colonists, who are ready enough to do so. The class
of gunmaker I am alluding to is one who makes
your piece to order, and specially to fit your
individual characteristics, who pays very high for
skilled labour, and bestows personal judgment and
care, the outcome of actual knowledge of working
at the bench, upon every detail of your order. There
is another class, who advertise weapons of extraordinary cheapness, but are merely agents for great
manufacturing firms, who have a large stock of guns
always on hand, and stand in the same relation to

those mentioned above as the reach-me-down clothes
shop to the high-class West End tailor.   These
I cannot recommend.   I must not conclude this
necessary digression on choice of guns without adding
that he who lives in the country entirely, and cannot
afford the price of the first-rate London firm, will do
better to employ a provincial maker of known re-
pute.   Of these there are several in England and
Scotland of whom very excellent judges have reason
to speak in terms of high praise, and whose work is
far better than that of the wholesale heavily puffed
firms, trading under assumed London names, who
falsely profess to give you the same article as the good
makers at one-third of the price.

A few words on this subject have not appeared to
me out of place in a chapter on grouse driving, since
it is precisely in this branch of sport that guns are
put to the most severe tests.   The atmospheric conditions, exposing the workmanship of your piece to
great extremes of heat, wet and cold, with the con-
comitant condition of very heavy firing, rapid working
of the mechanism, and maximum of expansion or con-
traction of the metal, try the workmanship of a gun
severely.   A weapon which 'jams' in the middle of a
good grouse drive would spoil the temper of an arch-
angel.   In the arrangement and conduct of your drives

I must repeat, with even greater emphasis, what I have said in the volume on the 'Partridge' concerning wind ; but you are far more in the hands of your head man and his drivers on this point than in any partridge drive. The latter have often to foot it some miles, even before you are out of your bed, to get to the remote point whence they will start the first drive. This involves organisation, since, living possibly some distance apart, they will not all start from the same place, and probably consist of two parties, each of which must be under a responsible lieutenant who thoroughly knows the ground. Consequently, should it be advisable to change the beat for the day on account of wind, or even the method of beating the ground, you must be able to rely absolutely upon the judgment and decision of your head man.

It is almost indispensable that he should be a moorland man, born and bred, though I admit that I have come across one or two notable exceptions to this. If he doesn't know the moors, literally up hill and down dale, every turn of the wind, every habit of the grouse, and every dodge of the driver, he is of no use to you in Yorkshire. He will command neither the confidence nor the obedience of his drivers, who, being all dalesmen who have travelled the moors and fells all their lives, know a good deal on their own account, and have it largely in their power to frustrate the most elaborate manœuvres. If you have to select a new chief, it is far better to promote the most trustworthy of the men who have been driving on the moor for years, rather than to put a man over their heads who has been mostly used to low-ground shooting, merely because he is considered 'fit for a head keeper's place.'

Very difficult manœuvres have sometimes to be executed, and unless your moor is very large in extent it is only by the most delicate and experienced hand-ling, in which every man must honestly co-operate, that the birds can be kept upon your ground. Five thousand acres is not nearly enough to hold large packs in a high wind, unless they are very well ma-naged. Suppose, for instance, that a large number of birds are packed at the head of a valley and on the ridge, close to the march, and there is a strong wind blowing *towards* the march. Unless your men get round very gingerly, keeping out of sight as carefully as a stalker getting up to deer, on the down-wind side, the game is up, and possibly your whole day's sport spoilt.

I have seen this very manœuvre beautifully carried out, and even the birds, having somehow taken the alarm, rise and make a big circuit round near the march

'NOT TO BE TURNED.'

A.Thorburn

before the two flanks of the drive had met; the whole of
the men on the windward side lay flat down the instant
the birds rose, and that without a word of command.
The pack settled down again, and the down-wind side
got well round and brought them on over our heads.
What would an obstinate Scotchman with recalcitrant
drivers say to that !

If, again, the head man is one in whom his drivers
have complete confidence, and who has trained his lieu-
tenants to carry out his orders whether he is present or
not, he can enjoy the inestimable advantage of placing
himself on the flank close to the guns, or of going
into one of the butts with his master or some other
shooter, and observing the exact result of his plan of
campaign, and what alterations, if any, should be
made in the line of butts. It is also an excellent
thing, should opportunity serve, to let him visit other
moors where good driving is carried on, and where he
may pick up a new wrinkle or two, or get rid of ideas
which may be too local.

I urge these points because it is impossible to in-
oculate a man with the instinct which alone makes a
first-rate grouse driver. The theory of the disposition of your drivers, the horse-shoe formation, the
placing of the flankers, and the method of progres-
sion, is now thoroughly familiar to all immediately

concerned in English driving. I have gone into it in greater detail in the chapter on Scotch Driving, in order, if possible, to be of use to those who wish to introduce it on Scotch moors, or to persuade such as oppose the system from ignorant, conservative, or interested motives, of its practical value to their ground.

In the construction and placing of the butts a few points should be noted. The larger and more commodious they are the better, seven feet square on the inside being about the most convenient size ; and there should be a seat of heather sods or flat stones in each corner. Some spare sods should always be cut and left close outside them, that there may be something for a tall man to build up his front wall with, should it be too low. The floor must be absolutely level and well drained. At Mr. Rimington Wilson's at Broomhead, on the Sheffield range, the butts have board floors, a great comfort to the shooters in many ways ; but on many moors the carting of timber up to the butts would be impracticable ; and on this particular moor on the principal days the driving is all done to two lines of butts close together, one on each side of a little gully, which has probably witnessed the slaying of more grouse than any spot of its size in the British Islands.

A point of extreme importance, for the safety of

the shooters, is that all the butts should be 'dressed' square with the line ; that is, that the front should be at right angles to the direction of the drive.   I have often, when in a butt set askew, found myself bothered in the hurry of quick firing to remember the exact line, and on reflection am convinced that many of the accidents that have occurred in grouse driving have

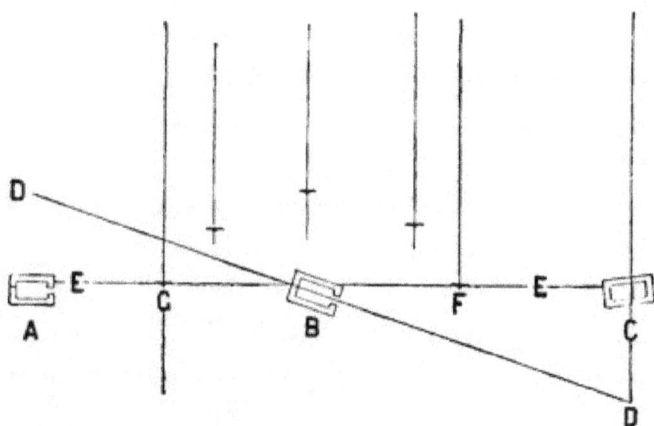

FIG. 6.

been due to this cause.   The diagram will perhaps explain what I mean.

The butts A, B, C, together with the rest of the row not shown, are all on the line E E—at right angles to the general direction of the drive.   Now the man in the butt B, though he will doubtless survey the position of his neighbours before the drive begins, will probably, after his attention has become riveted on a succession of approaching birds, begin instinctively to face the front wall of his butt. Being so used to finding his neighbours placed at right angles to the side walls of his butt, and on the same line as the front, that danger in this quarter has become a matter of instinct rather than observation, his brain will imagine them to be located on the line D D. This delusion may only last a moment or two while he is watching birds ; but it may lead him to shoot at a bird at the point F, and so seriously damage the man in the butt C, or on the other side to take a shot at the point G, imagining the bird to have passed the line, and so to injure the man in the butt A.

I have no evidence to prove that accidents have occurred from this cause, but they have occurred at drives where I have seen butts placed in this manner, and I have myself been so near shooting my neighbour under these circumstances that it cannot be wrong to point out the possible danger.

Let there be always plenty of butts on the moor, that you may be able to drive according to the wind. If in any drive you notice that two or three of the guns invariably get all the shooting, it is better to put two or possibly three in a second line behind them, being careful they are fully 200 yards off, any less distance not being safe for the eyes of your friends.

In the early part of the season it is better not to have too many drivers ; the birds which they pass by without flushing will be all young ones, precisely those required for breeding stock, and if they came on, as they would, at the end of the drive, singly and flying very slowly, they would all be massacred. If your moor is at the end of a spur of the greater range, you can always insure a good double drive by pushing them first to the end, next the cultivated land, and then bringing them back ; but in such a case your men had better sweep in some of the pastures below the end of the moor, on which there are sure to be birds. This formation of ground accounts partially for the certainty with which a large bag can be made on many moors, notably on Broomhead and Blubber-house.[1] In severe or bad breeding seasons the lower moors will suffer less than the higher, and as the former will be always fed, to a certain extent, by the latter, and have the advantage of them, it behoves the owner of moorland which is lower than his neighbours, and constitutes the end of a large ridge or stretch, not to be too hard upon the birds, especially late on in the season. Were he able to kill every

[1] Mr. Rimington Wilson's and Lord Walsingham's respectively.

P

bird upon his land, it would undoubtedly be re-stocked from the higher ground, and in the winter months, when mild weather prevails higher up, he is sure to have many more than his share upon his ground.

The counting and picking up of the dead birds is a subject for serious consideration. I well remember, twenty years ago in Yorkshire, amongst a few of us who met constantly and whose comparative form would have been difficult to handicap, every day's grouse driving might as well have been a valuable sweepstake or a series of matches for 100*l.* a side, so keen was the rivalry, the scoring, and the picking up. But I cannot say that it was a desirable state of things. The counting of what you have killed is no doubt necessary, but it might be done on the same principle as I have recommended for partridge driving, that is, keeping a score of the claims without putting them against any names. That which promotes keenness is good ; that which provokes jealousy is surely bad. The lines of pegs halfway between each butt, recommended by Sir R. Payne-Gallwey, were first adopted, I believe, upon a suggestion of mine at Broomhead some years ago, and Mr. Wilson has seen no reason to remove them since. To insure bagging all that have been knocked down, as well as in the interests of humanity, there should always be a professional 'picker up' in the person of a keeper with a brace or more of retrieving spaniels, who should hunt round the ine of butts after the guns have gathered all they can. An old pointer or setter is not bad for this work, but spaniels that will hunt close, if they are not too hard-mouthed, are better. Should you be a breeder of retrievers, here is a good opportunity for your dog man to do a little breaking in ; and if they are well under control, there is no doubt they are the best of all.

I well remember the first appearance of old John Young, Lord Londesborough's head man for over a quarter of a century, upon a West Riding moor in 1871. He was supposed never to have seen a grouse, though a veteran in years and in experience of field and covert. He brought with him three of the most useful-looking brown retrievers to pick up his master's birds. Clad as he was in a heavy green velveteen coat with brass buttons, a red waistcoat, thick cord breeches, and gaiters, and an enormous gold-laced hat, he appeared to radiate heat and light on all around, and was a sufficiently striking object on the heather on a sweltering September day. He had about eight grouse in each hand, and his dogs were still diligently hunting, when we came across him, far away from his master's butt. We chaffed him on the

P 2

fact that, though he was a novice to grouse, he seemed to be a pretty good hand at picking up. Laying down his birds, and raising the gold-laced beaver with an air peculiar to him, 'Never was on a moor before in my life, I can assure you, gentlemen,' he said, with perfect courtesy. Nevertheless, he had gathered about fifteen more birds than his master, always a most generous neighbour, had claimed ; and though he must have narrowly escaped an apoplectic fit, he and his dogs continued to work equally hard all day.

In laying out your lines of butts, bear in mind that there is no invariable necessity for your driving line to progress from a given base in a direct line to the centre of the butts. It frequently occurs that on a particular range of moor the birds will always fly in a great curve, or a complete ring, eventually getting back in this manner to the ground they were flushed upon. In this case you must also drive on a curve, and the first half of the beat may have to be driven by advancing almost at right angles to the direction desired, or, so to speak, across the face of the row of butts. As in this diagram, for instance, you may wish to drive your birds, mostly lying about A, to somewhere about the point D.

But for reasons connected with the nature of the ground, they will not fly from A to D direct, but in-

variably fly from A in the curves indicated, alighting
mostly at the points x x.   Now, make your formation
as shown here, follow their curve to the point x with

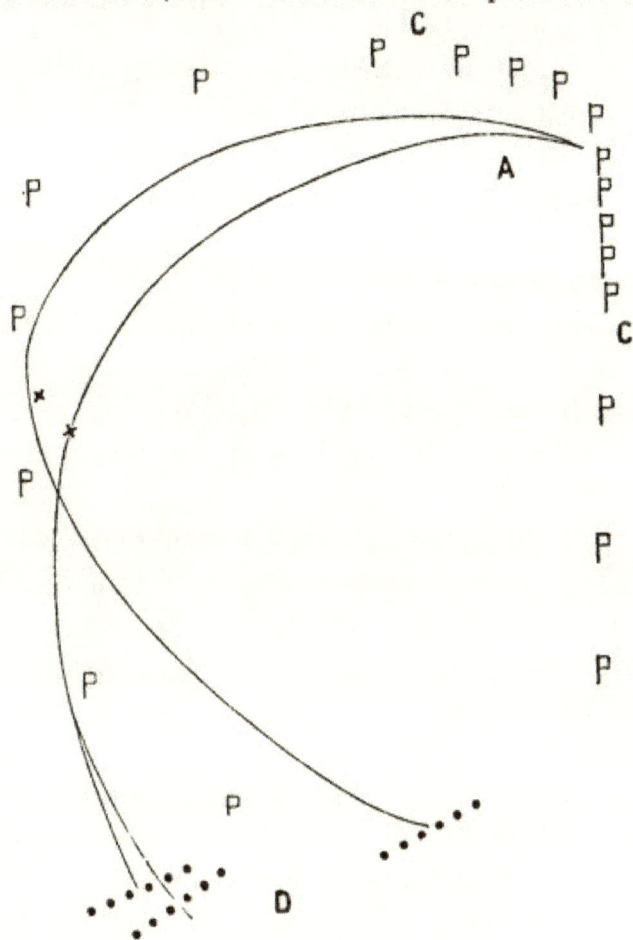

FIG. 7.

the main body of your men, and on flushing them
again at the points x x you will find they fly on to
one or other of the points about D, where I have indicated lines of butts.

To arrive at these things you must either be on
the moor as constantly as a keeper or a shepherd, or
have out a few men and make experimental drives,
letting your head man lie on a high point, whence he
can command a view of the whole manœuvre.

The endless varieties and possibilities of managing
grouse according to conditions of ground, wind, and
season, will afford you many interesting and pleasant
days between the intervals of your shooting parties,
while they will add immensely to your enjoyment of
the results.

For actual marksmanship I must refer my readers
to what I have endeavoured to make clear in the
volume on 'Partridge' of this series, and to the diagrams explaining the reasons for shooting over birds,
&c., repeating once more that it is impossible to teach
anyone how to shoot driven birds. With driven grouse
the necessity for shooting high is even more marked
than with partridges. You will get many more shots
on the level and below you, and in aiming at these you
must constantly bear in mind to avoid the tendency
to dwell or poke at the birds. This *always* results

more or less in your dropping the muzzle of the gun
and shooting underneath. You will often see very
bad practice made at grouse flying very low, creeping
as it were over the heather, and perhaps going slowly
against the wind. Here *all* the missing takes place
from shooting under them. The only way to avoid it
is to form the habit of firing the instant the gun is firm
on the shoulder, and of striking your aim high, almost
as though you would shoot just over the bird's back.

Many people think they miss these birds from
shooting *in front* of them. I fancy this is rarely
the case, but at any rate the matter can be easily
tested by firing one or two shots straight at them, and
watching the result. You will find that you kill low-
flying birds more easily when they are above you than
below, a fact which sufficiently proves that in aiming
at the latter it is the depression of the muzzle which
accounts for the missing. Keep the left arm well
forward, and lift it well, relying upon this member
entirely for the swing and support of your piece.
You have less to guide your eye in the way of station-
ary objects, such as trees, &c., in grouse driving, and
therefore you must make up your mind to rely more
than ever on calculation as to where to aim. The
principle, which I have before advocated, of rapidly
deciding in your mind where the spot is in the air at

which your shot will intercept the bird's flight, and
throwing your gun directly and quickly upon it, is
the only one by which you can compete with the
endless variety of angle, curve, elevation and pace,
which lends to the flight of driven grouse its undoubted fascination.   There can be no 'knack' in
excelling at a sport which presents this feature in the
highest degree of all.   The individual driven grouse
which comes straight at your nose on a still day is
easy enough, but these are the 'half-volleys' of grouse
driving, and to hit them does not necessarily make
you a good bat.   It is a very different matter to realise
the proper total from a succession of fine drives under
varying conditions of light, locality and wind ; and
when the day comes that you have achieved this, in
first-rate form from start to finish, you will sleep like
a public-school boy who has made 100 at Lord's, or
a Prime Minister who has carried a great measure
through the Commons by a triumphant majority, perhaps the two most enviable achievements known in
this country.

CHAPTER V

GROUND, STOCK, AND POACHING

It is beginning to be generally understood that a moor, whether English or Scotch, will not produce the stock of grouse demanded by modern ideas, or to satisfy appetites whetted by the experience of exceptional seasons and results, without due attention to the management of the ground, and to the nourishment of a healthy stock of birds. The old system of treating grouse entirely as *feræ naturæ*, and trusting them and the ground on which they breed to the development of nature, may leave you always a sprinkling of birds, but will not give you the stock you have a right to expect after paying the high value which such shooting now commands, nor satisfy the requirements of your friends. Further, it is found that however large the supply, the demand for these, the best of all game birds for the table, increases proportionately, and that it is possible to throw away a great deal of good money and food supply by allowing incompetence or want of care to decrease the productive powers of good moorland.

Again, as this demand increases and the subject is more and more widely ventilated, the ingenuity of the poacher, the pothunter, and the receiver of poached or illegally killed game becomes annually more formidable. The only saving clause is that the red grouse being universally known to be exclusively indigenous to the British Islands, we do not see the poulterer's shops in March, April, or May full of 'Siberian' or 'Norwegian' grouse stolen from British moors, as we undoubtedly should if the species were found in those foreign countries. I must refer my readers to my remarks in the volume on 'The Partridge' as to the illegally procured birds which come into the London markets on August 12 and September 1, and to the suggestions I there made, which I now wish to urge again. Owners and lessees of shootings seem for the most part not to have realised the extent of the illicit traffic in game, which applies to grouse almost more than any other kind ; and I venture again to express the hope that some one with more leisure and more influence than I have may found some Association to combat this evil in a businesslike manner. Those who are in London on August 12 may be quite certain that any grouse that is offered to them,

unless sent direct by a friend from his own moor, is
a poached, practically a stolen, bird. I remember
being served with one which was absolutely putrid on
the Twelfth, some years ago, at a well-known London
restaurant. An old friend, the late Lord Dupplin,
was dining near me, and had an equally bad one
served to him. We agreed to send them both away—
in fact, though the price was 14s. per bird, they
were uneatable—but the head waiter explained (?)
to us that this was the true flavour of the grouse, and
that we were ignorant. Poor Duppy! I can see his
face of mingled disgust and amusement now at the
idea of a crapulous Swiss waiter explaining to him and
me what a grouse ought to taste like.

But since the price that can be obtained for these
birds on the Twelfth will always be a temptation to
the evilly disposed, it behoves owners to look closely
after what happens in the moorland districts in the
week preceding that day. They cannot always be on
the spot at that time, but if an association or league,
such as I suggested in the former volume, were
formed, trained detectives could easily watch the
consignments passing through certain centres from
the moorland, and trace their origin and destination.
It has even come to this, that, as I am informed, silk
and other nets are actually provided by London

poulterers, and are supplied to their fellow-culprits
in this traffic, if not to the poachers direct; and no
questions are asked as long as they get the supply of
grouse for sale on the Twelfth. This is a disgraceful
state of things; and it should be remembered that,
without troubling Parliament with further legislation
(which, unhappily, in these days is beset with difficulties of all kinds), there is ample law to put a stop
to these practices **if** only trouble is taken to run the
offenders to ground.

It would be impossible to prevent the *sale* itself
of grouse at a distance from the moors, say in London
or elsewhere, but at least those who are fond of sport
may do something to check the demand. I would,
therefore, beg all good sportsmen who may **be** far
from the moors on the Twelfth to restrain their appetite for grouse, and refuse to purchase any **for a day**
or two at least. If this **were** universally done in
restaurants and clubs, it would go far towards check-
ing the evil, and those to whom I appeal would be
spared the indignation or gastronomic disappoint-
ment which they will probably experience on being
offered a grouse of a week old which purports to have
been killed that morning.

Grouse are poached in many ways, and one of the
most destructive **is** the recently introduced practice

of surrounding a moor with nets, which catch the
birds as they fly off it on to the neighbouring pastures. This has been carried to such a pitch in some
parts of Yorkshire, Westmoreland, and the other
northern counties, that the value of a moor becomes
seriously affected by it. A sort of blackmail is set
up, which obliges anyone taking the moor either to
hire all the adjoining pasture land as well, or to enter
into an agreement with certain parties not to net in
this manner—for either of which forms of protection
he is mulcted in proportion to the value of the netting on such ground, often amounting to nearly as
large a number of birds as he will get on the moor
proper by fair shooting. On one Yorkshire moor
that I know this lately became so serious, and the
stock was getting so much reduced, that the owner
purchased netting himself, which he set on the moor
edges in charge of his own men, so as to intercept
the birds before they reached the enemy's nets, those
taken being merely set at liberty again. Miles of
this netting these poachers have in some places, so
that the protecting nets of the owner and the constant watching become a serious consideration.

It is difficult to see how this can be prevented by
the operation of law, since where it is done on any
scale the net owners are careful to take out a game

licence, and to keep strictly to their own ground. But *a great deal of netting* is done illegally on other people's ground, both by night and day—pure poaching. in fact—and has become a very common and lucrative business.   This is due almost entirely to the supineness or ignorance of the owners of moors, who for the most part are not in the locality at the time when it is done, and who seem to me much too ready to accept the invariable excuse of ' disease ' or ' cold breeding season' for the low stock of birds on the ground.

As with partridges and other game, I have always observed that where there are really first-rate and honest keepers, there is always a pretty good stock of grouse.   Of course seasons will vary, and anyone used to the moors will know pretty well when to make the allowance for bad weather, &c.; but it is astonishing how lightly moors suffer from this cause or from disease when the keeper and his subordinates are thoroughly trustworthy.   The only remedy you have as an owner is to pay strictly by results.   The details must be left to your administrator, the keeper.   So long as you have a good show of birds, allowing for variation of seasons, your ground is well burnt, and all the other details well looked after, keep and reward him as much as you can.   But if the totals begin to fall gradually year by year, the heather remains long and old, the driving slack and listless, and you are puzzled to account for the deterioration of your moor, change your whole staff of keepers, tell your new ones that you expect certain results and mean to have them, and in a year or two you will probably be astonished to find how the grouse have taken to your ground again.

On high moors you are liable to lose a great many birds by their leaving the ground for lower ranges in severe weather. It is quite worth while to feed them a little at such times. It is chiefly when the snow is caked or frozen over with a very thin coating of ice, and they cannot scratch through it to get food, that they are most pinched and may leave the ground, never to come back. I remember Mr. Walter Stanhope[1] telling me that in the very hard winter of 1859–60 the grouse on his Dunford Bridge moors left the ground in hundreds ; many were killed in the fields in a half-starved state, and even one or two in the barrack square at Sheffield, some fifteen miles off. He then sent men up to the moor with long rakes, and

---

[1] Mr. Walter Spencer Stanhope, who for many years represented one of the divisions of the West Riding in Parliament. An admirable letter from his pen is given in the Badminton Library, *Shooting*, vol. ii. p. 11, describing some of the earliest methods and results of driving grouse.

as they raked the snow off the grouse followed them close, as gulls will follow the plough, or chickens the good-wife in the poultry yard, perfectly tame.

Your keepers should see to these methods of helping them to feed in severe weather, and not, as is too often the case, helplessly gape at the half-starved packs sitting on walls or scratching at the ground in the fields below the moorland, until, forced by hunger, they rise and fly clean away in search of milder conditions.

The same authority (Mr. Stanhope) always expressed himself in favour of plantations round and about the edges of the moors. Though they may attain no value as timber, they will prove a great protection to the grouse in a heavy snow. Then they will be able to creep under the boughs of the stunted larches or spruces, scratching and picking a bit when they cannot get at food or shelter on the open moor. Grouse, I believe, very rarely die of cold, excepting the devoted hens, which sometimes allow themselves to be frozen, or so pinched by the cold while sitting on their nests that they succumb within a short time. But they suffer severely from starvation in hard winters, and although their moving off the ground in large packs in search of food may, as Mr. Rimington Wilson has observed, serve to mingle the blood and improve the breeding stock on the ground they move to, it will hardly benefit you on the deserted high ground, as few of them, if any, are likely to return. Grouse travel much longer distances than is generally supposed, and I am firmly convinced that many a Scotch bird has been killed well on this side of the border. Lord Huntingfield is said to have seen a pack of grouse flying over his place in Norfolk. I have not his lordship's word for it, but have often heard it from friends of his, and certainly his authority would be indisputable, after the many hundreds his unerring aim has accounted for.[1]

Mr. Rimington Wilson, in an admirable letter to the ' Field' of September 10, 1892, gives four principal points to be attended to in the management of a moor :

   1. Heather burning.

   2. Driving *v.* shooting in other ways.

   3. Keeping down vermin.

   4. Sheep, &c.

To these I would add :

   5. Watchful protection against poachers.

   6. Feeding &c. in hard weather.

---

[1] I have only shot one week with Lord Huntingfield. His accuracy was marvellous, while never appearing to take a long shot. It was a very pretty lesson, and one which I am proud to have learnt.

7. Planting round and upon lower parts of your moor.

As regards burning, it is instructive to find Mr. Wilson, Lord Walsingham, and the Mackintosh (see p. 156) all agreed as to the necessity of this system in order to keep the heather in a healthy condition. Mr. Wilson believes in burning altogether any large tract of deep old heather, though as a general rule the moor should be burnt in strips. Where possible these should run parallel with your lines of butts. He remarks also on the splendid stretches of young heather following on an accidental fire. I have noticed the same myself, and fully agree with him that most moors are not severely enough burned. The old heather is always damp underneath, affords no healthy food for grouse or sheep, and is abominable to walk through. Artistically speaking, I regret that I must give my verdict in favour of systematic burning, while, practically, I must own that it is absolutely essential for the healthy condition of the grouse. On a moor that is exclusively 'dogged' it must be burnt in patches, so that the young birds, feeding on the very young shoots, may have close to them the resort of good cover in an older patch, and avoid being driven off their feed by the older birds, and that they may thus be more evenly distributed over the ground.

On driving *v.* shooting over dogs I have already delivered myself in other chapters of this volume, but must again quote Mr. Wilson : 'It is, perhaps, superfluous to remark that to make a moor as pro-ductive as possible shooting over dogs ought to be allowed to a very limited extent, if at all. *The candle should not be burnt at both ends.*'

A certain number of sheep will do no harm upon a moor, but too many will do a great deal; while cattle and horses will always cause the heather to deteriorate, and a coarse, rank kind of grass to spring up, which is not good for pasture and useless for grouse. Here, again, liberality and a kindly feeling to the shepherds will do more for your stock than anything. They have it in their hands to injure if not to cripple your sport altogether. Their dogs can destroy in an hour in the breeding season what would give you a good day's driving later on. But I have always found them a kindly and simple race of people, and if well treated they will see that their flocks do not trample on the nests or young birds, and that their dogs do not career wildly over the moor during the nesting period. They are really your best and most loyal grouse-keepers if you enlist them on your side; and besides so ordering their work on the hills as not to injure the grouse, they can render immense assistance to your keepers in the tracking of vermin, detection of poaching, and other such matters, besides sometimes lending willing and skilful aid to the management of your drives. Moral : above all things be kind and liberal to the shepherds and farmers.

Mr. Wilson omits to mention protection against poaching, though his moors lie in a country where it is well understood ; but I think I can account for this. I said above that good keepers always have a good show of game ; and certainly his head man, Ward, is an excellent example of this. A past master in the art of driving, his is also a name of terror to poachers, and in the security which so loyal a servant inspires, Mr. Wilson may well have forgotten how little his boundaries might be respected were they under less formidable protection.

In addition to feeding the birds and raking off the frozen snow in winter, I would endorse what the Mackintosh says as to the improvement of the water supply by puddling up the streams, and making many little reservoirs, so as to insure the birds plenty to drink in a very dry breeding season, such as we experienced last year (1893).

Vermin must be thoroughly kept down, and on Scotch moors, terminating as they mostly do in high rocky ground, it is no easy work to keep in check the depredations of foxes, crows, jackdaws, eagles, ravens, stoats, weasels, hawks of all kinds, and even occasionally wild cats, or cats which have become wild and taken to the rocks and ravines. I would never kill an eagle, but rather keep so grand a bird on the best my moor provided, nor would I, personally, shoot a peregrine; but the other species I have named, besides being less picturesque, are less rare, and must be 'attended to.' The anti-game-law party in Scotland lately started the cry that the destruction of hawks, owls &c. had subjected them to a plague of field voles (the common little brown mouse so often seen on the hills), and that these creatures were devouring their pastures, and impoverishing their stock ; but a perusal of the evidence before the Royal Commission on this subject will, I think, convince any reasonable person that the appearance of these animals in large numbers in particular localities has been of spasmodic recurrence from time immemorial, and that when they appear hawks and owls usually appear also in increased numbers to keep them in check. They seem to leave certain districts, or die off, as erratically and as rapidly as they appear, and the agitators failed altogether to connect their appearance with the destruction of vermin by gamekeepers.

Poaching, dishonesty, and disloyalty, encouraged

as they are by the unscrupulousness of the receivers
of stolen and illegally killed game in the large towns,
are after all the things most to be guarded against, and
I have endeavoured to indicate how I think they may
best be combated.   I have before me a working model
of the nets used in Yorkshire, with poles, clips &c.
complete, as well as a fair selection of specimens of
snares ; but I think that the accurate description of
how all such engines should be used is against the
interests of sport, and may serve only to encourage
poaching by diffusing the science of how to do it.
Wherever there is good moorland, well watered and
with plenty of sheltered places, there ought to be a
good stock of grouse.   Laziness is much more
common among hill keepers than where population
is more dense, while the climate of Scotch glens,
especially on the west coast, tends to enervate men.
The great antidote for this is to be constantly on the
high ground in the fresher air, as you will discover for
yourself during a long stay in Scotland.   Your head
man should, therefore, see that his assistants are constantly on the moor looking after the welfare of the
birds ; instead of giving way, as they often do, to the
temptation of merely gazing at it from below all day,
and leaving it to take care of itself all night.

The great and mysterious plague known as the

grouse disease is the most powerful enemy to be
fought against.   I cannot agree that it is due to
overcrowding—and here again I turn to the Mackintosh and Mr. Rimington Wilson for corroboration.
Mr. Wilson writes me : ' Since about 1870 there has
been no disease on these moors sufficiently severe to
prevent shooting ; previous to this date disease seems
to have recurred severely and regularly about every
seven years.   There is no doubt that driving has produced this healthier state of affairs.'   The Mackintosh
writes : ' On the Moy Hall moor there has been
practically no disease since 1873.   Driving was first
resorted to in 1869, and only then when birds were
too wild to sit to dogs ;' but he adds that it was not
seriously taken up until 1872.

In considering these two statements we must bear
in mind that the former is an undoubted authority on
Yorkshire driving of over twenty years' standing, on
whose moors all the English records have been
eclipsed ; and that the latter is the most successful
exponent of the adoption of the system in Scotland,
and holds the record for the latter country.   I might
add that to my certain knowledge, where good
management prevails, many other moors have yielded
a fair proportion of birds even in the years when
disease has been reported severe and prevalent over

both Scotland and England. What are we to think of those moors, which have been let to a variety of tenants for twenty years, and where nothing but the old-fashioned system of exclusive 'dogging' in the early part of the season has ever been practised, which are almost annually reported as having suffered severely from disease, and have produced gradually declining results? Is it too much to agree with authorities such as I have quoted, and to come to the conclusion that other causes besides disease have been at work on these unfortunate moors? I think not; and it will take a great deal to convince me that good grouse ground can deteriorate to this extent for no visible cause except the eternal cry of 'disease.' The birds on ill-preserved ground are never good specimens of the race. A deer-forest grouse is not, as a rule, to be compared, for weight, plumage, or flavour to one from Studley or Wemmergill. If the Scotch keeper on such ground does not learn by more direct channels, he will eventually discover by the depreciated value of the moor which he manages that he or his predecessors have killed the grouse with the golden eggs. A pound a brace or even more has been, and is still, paid by the unwary who rent certain Scotch shootings; but a Yorkshire moor which yields 3,000 brace, though very scarce in the market, will not fetch 3,000*l.* for the season. Those who take the average shooting, and wish for a moderate amount of sport at a moderate expense, should look more closely than they do into the records of the moor, should submit to no clauses in their lease which oblige them to keep on any particular keeper or nominee of the landlord, and should study more closely the methods which have been adopted on the moors where a really successful result is shown.

The exact nature of the grouse disease is very difficult to determine. Lord Walsingham, some years since, offered a considerable money prize for the best essay on the subject ; but the result was unsatisfactory, and no one, if I recollect rightly, offered a solution worthy to receive the reward. Dr. Cobbold's pamphlet still remains as the only scientific effort offering a tangible solution of the question. He ascribes it all to the *Strongylus pergracilis*, a little thread-like worm which breeds in the throat, and eventually in thousands in all the organs of the bird. It is further alleged that ponies and sheep had died on the moors during years when disease was prevalent from the attacks of the same parasite. But not even Dr. Cobbold can tell us whence or how the *Strongylus pergracilis* is produced, or whether it is the cause or effect of weakness in the larger body. I remember,

in 1874 or thereabouts, on the late Sir Charles
Forbes's moors at Dalradample, in Aberdeenshire,
we were all taking refuge on a wet stormy day in one
of the butts for luncheon. I sat on a seat in the
corner, made of sods cut from the moor, and when I
rose, found on my mackintosh and on the sod under
me a quantity of small thread-like worms, answering
exactly to Dr. Cobbold's description of the *Strongylus*.
On examination, I found many others under where
others of the party were lying or sitting, as though
the warmth of their bodies had drawn these creatures
to the surface. The particular growth they were in
was not heather, but the coarse grass, reddish at the
tips, so common on the moors and rough hill pastures. I put several of them carefully into a bottle
with bits of the grass, intending to send them to
Lord Walsingham, as one of our first entomologists,
for examination ; but, alas ! by next morning they
were all dried up and almost invisible—dead, and
shrivelled to nothing.

This seemed to show that they were produced,
supposing them to be identical with Cobbold's parasite, on certain ground, and prevalent, like the field
voles, at spasmodic intervals. I was much disappointed
at my failure to get a scientific opinion, but commend
this experience to those who would pursue the subject

seriously. I should add that the ground was very damp, and that the weather had been very wet for some weeks previously.

I believe that no remedy has ever been hit on or tried with any satisfactory result. Rock salt has been suggested ; but this does not appear to commend itself to the grouse. I have always thought that if it were practicable and not too expensive the heather might, as an experiment, be sown with salt, in case the parasite is really generated first upon the ground. I am sure that very little would suffice to kill worms such as I found on the occasion mentioned, and it might prove beneficial as against tapeworms in their young or embryo condition. So far as we know at present, we can only fight against the disease, or ward it off, by the common-sense practice of regular heather burning, and maintaining a vigorous race of birds by the methods and management I have mentioned above, aided by such suggestions as those who have long and practical experience of moors and moor-game can furnish in addition.

I have alluded above to accidental fires. These may do no harm, possibly some eventual good, when the ground is somewhat damp and the weather broken, as in spring ; but in very hot dry weather in the summer they may prove very serious. At such times take every precaution against casual fires being lighted, and request your guests to be careful with matches, and also to watch that sparks from the gun do not start a conflagration. I set my butt on fire three times in one day at Studley, and only extinguished it with considerable difficulty.

On these very moors, in 1872, the most disastrous moorland fire ever known took place. The fire destroyed 1,300 acres of the best of the ground, going eight or ten feet deep into the peat, and the smoke of it was perceptible for thirty or forty miles. I have not been on this ground lately, but can vouch for the fact that, ten years after the fire, the vast expanse of the 'burnt ground' on Studley moor remained black and barren, a warning of what the careless lighting of a match may do in hot weather.

CHAPTER VI

'THE FRINGE OF THE MOOR'

MR. JOHN GUILLE MILLAIS has in his delightful book, 'Game Birds and Shooting Sketches,' given a description of bird and animal life in the early morning on the lower edges of the moorland, and this, with many other passages in the work, I commend to those who love the poetry of nature. A son of the great painter whose tender and masterly touch alone seems able to grasp the realities and idealities, the romances or complexities, which go to make up the life of this age, he develops, as one of the first naturalists of to-day, a convincing admiration for nature and a brilliant power of drawing birds—inheritances of his father's talents.

From Sir John, my earliest master in outdoor painting,[1] I am not ashamed to have stolen the title of this chapter, in order to describe the picturesque

[1] I believe I may claim the honour of being the only pupil Sir J. Millais ever had—alas ! for too short a time.

and varied ground which, lying next to or forming part of the moorland proper, leads you by the pleasantest of transitions to the cultivated land. This is the Bohemia of shooting—the tract where we have all spent some of the pleasantest of our days in circumventing its distinctive denizens, or in making a mixed bag without the aid of the organisation of a regular shooting party. Here sits the capercailzie and lurks the roe ; here abides the blackcock and crouches the hare ; here stalks the pheasant and sleeps the woodcock ; while from above and below the grouse and the partridge meet on the heathery slopes and rushy bottoms of this debatable land, the fringe of the moor.

Driving the woods for black-game and anything else that may be in them provides the pleasantest of shooting days, liberally tinged with the element of surprise, which is as essentially an integral part of sport as it is admitted to be of wit. I quite agree with the late Mr. Bromley-Davenport, than whom no better sportsman ever rode, shot, or fished, that it is hateful to know exactly how much game there is in a covert, how many birds in a turnip field. All interest is gone the moment the element of uncertainty or surprise is removed. The great charm of the moor edge is its variety. The long plantation of larch or

BLACKCOCK FORWARD.

A. Thorburn.

fir, standing ankle-deep in yellow grass or breast-high
in bracken, breaks imperceptibly into a bed of heather,
dotted with young trees, which in turn gives way to
swampy hollows or rushy wastes, not infrequently
bordering a field or two of stubble or turnips before
the wood or moor begins again.   Small coverts, great
open brakes of fern, and deep ravines where the
heather can scarce cling to the steep sides between
the rocks, succeed each other in delightful confusion,
the whole forming an agglomeration of various sorts
of covert, which used to be called by the old keeper
at Drumlanrig [1] by the expressive term of 'what-
nots.'

Many charming days have I enjoyed in years
gone by among those 'what-nots,' where sometimes
twelve or thirteen varieties of game, from the fallow
deer to the jack-snipe, were killed in one day, and
great were the numbers of the black-game.   The two
distinct kinds of black-game driving are determined
by the nature of the ground.   In the one your company of well-organised drivers sweeps a succession of
so-called pastures, though the herbage on them is
not of the best, differing but little, except for the

---

[1] Drumlanrig Castle in Dumfriesshire, the principal seat of
the Duke of Buccleuch, which stands on an estate of 175,000
acres.

frequently intersecting stone walls and marked in-
closures, from the moor itself. In the other, sometimes with an imposing but casual array of beaters,
suggesting somewhat the levies of a pretender or
an outlaw, but more often with the unaided skill
of a half-dozen of keepers and gillies, the woods are
ranged towards you as you stand in carefully selected
spots, 'passes' where the blackcocks are sure to
cross, and where you are equally on the look-out for
a woodcock or a roebuck.

The former style of black-game driving has been
undoubtedly carried to the greatest perfection, and
with the best results, on the Duke of Buccleuch's
Dumfriesshire estates. Here, at Sanquhar or Wan-
lock Head, lie the great stretches of rough pasture—
part grass, part rushes, part heather—which favour a
great stock of these birds, and which, lying between
the oat stubbles and the luxuriant heather, afford
them the variety of food that this specie seem in
particular to affect. Here, ensconced behind a high
wall, after, perhaps, removing the topmost course
of stones to clear your view in front, having reached
your places in strictly enforced silence, and weighed
the consequences of any mistake, such as killing a
greyhen or showing yourself unduly, which may expose you to a fire of time-honoured chaff, you may

see a pack of a hundred or more blackcocks coming straight at your face, and on about the same level— a sight never to be forgotten, and one that makes your heart beat faster and your hand tremble lest you bring ridicule upon yourself by missing these great ponderous objects as they come by you so close that you could almost touch them. The missing is easier than you would think, and we all know who have tried it how simple it is to shoot behind a black-cock, looking as big as a turkey, and seeming to be going very slow, within fifteen or twenty yards. Nothing will avail you but absolute confidence in your own shooting powers and a complete disregard of the disturbing personality of the quarry. You must shoot as at a driven partridge, if anything a shade more forward, and with more rather than less accuracy. With these precautions you will strike the bird in the head and neck, and he will collapse as easily as the aforesaid partridge. Without them, or if you should vainly try to kill two or three at a shot, you will inevitably miss altogether, or see your bird flinch and disappear, as you think, 'cut to ribbons.' This means that he will fly half a mile, rise again about fifty yards in front of your dog, and gaily fly on, never to be seen again ; or wheel round and return contemptuously over your head, at the height

R

of the cross on St. Paul's Cathedral, to the ground whence he was first disturbed.

Black-game have wonderful turning power, and it is a sight to see them, when they are driven down a heavy wind and suspect or are sure of danger in front, wheel deliberately round and go up wind over the drivers in the teeth of half a gale.   For this reason it is necessary to observe silence as you move to your post and after you have reached it ; even smoking being in some places prohibited.   The great thing is to get the main body, the large pack or packs over the guns, scatter them to a certain extent, and at any rate utilise them for the next drive.

To insure this you must also be careful not to show yourself, bearing in mind that they are quite capable of turning completely round and going back when within a few yards of you, and that when they have accomplished this you have done with that particular lot for the day.

The first bird or two that comes by you should spare ; they will probably be greyhens, flushed by the drivers at the start ; but do not despise this warning, as should they come against a bright sky, or should you be unduly keen, you may find that you have incurred the penalty of error.   I suppose that no one who has shot black-game has not made this mistake

more than once; therefore, I advise you, always let
the first bird or two pass you before firing, as after
they get level with you it is easy to distinguish the
cock from the hen. Should you know that there is a
large lot of cocks between the guns and the drivers,
the first odd birds, whether cocks or hens, should
always be allowed to pass without a shot being fired, so
that the main body may come on without suspicion of
danger.

This applies when driving woods, but is seldom
likely to be rigorously followed, as you will then be
probably anxious to secure the mixed bag which
the coverts afford. But in driving on the open moor
or pastures it is absolutely essential, if you are going
for a bag of blackcocks exclusively, to follow these
tactics.

In grouse driving, especially on broken ground, I
am in favour of the beaters making some noise, for
birds seated in hollows or anywhere out of sight of the
flags, having heard the guns ahead and not being conscious of the presence of the drivers, may rise and
turn back. But for black-game driving I recommend
absolute silence, as if too much scared they will
get high up and leave the ground you are working,
often crossing a broad deep valley and alighting on
a far-off hill, clean off your day's ground. For black-

R 2

game driving no flags are necessary, or at the most one or two for men posted on the flank to prevent the birds taking some particular line away from the drive.

Driving them from the woods is almost entirely a question of judicious placing of the guns ; the keeper should know the points or 'passes' where they almost invariably break from a particular covert, and here the guns should be placed pretty close together. As this conduces to talking, silence must again be urged in waiting for these birds, the fact that they drive best up wind furnishing an additional reason for the exercise of caution and self-control.

Walking the woods and broken ground in line in late September or early October is a very pretty form of sport, though the line is very difficult to keep in proper formation. Here you get very unexpected and difficult shots, a blackcock rising with a great rattle out of a little ravine being a customer whom it requires some skill to stop. At this time of year the cocks are found singly, scattered about the woods, seeking the various berries and grasses which they like as a change from heather, and some of them will lie very close. But they are then mostly young cocks ; so that for the good of your breeding stock it is better not to pursue them too closely in this fashion. The same remark applies even more strongly to attacking the young broods during the last days of August. At this time the cockney sportsman, having noted in the almanac that on August 20 'Black-game shooting begins,' sallies forth, and decimates the immature pullets, none of which will fly far, while nearly all could be caught by the hand in the thick heather after the dog has ascertained their whereabouts. The old cock he probably never sees, or if he does he misses him, and the old hen most likely escapes also. Having done as much harm as it is possible to do in the day, he will return and indite an account of his prowess to the 'Field;' quaintly remarking that he '*had* 18½ brace of black-game' on the 20th. Since he clearly need not have shot the majority of them, and should be ashamed of himself if he did, the fact that he possessed them is perhaps all that need be recorded. But it may be added that a young blackcock whom you happen upon 'in the way of business' is, if you let him get far enough before putting shot into him, one of the most delicious of all birds for the table.

Stalking black-game, whether on the stooks of corn, or later on the open moor and pastures, is a very agreeable art, and one which will try your skill and sportsmanlike qualities to the utmost. Foul weather, when it is hardly fit to be out, is the best for this. You will then find the old cocks, which should always be the object of your pursuit, sitting on walls or mounds, and other bare dry places. The wind must be very carefully considered, and the stalk conducted with as much care as if you were after deer. If you alarm other birds or beasts, the blackcocks, like deer, will take alarm also, and though their sense of smell is not so keen as, their eyesight is undoubtedly superior to, that of the nobler animal. It is often a good plan to employ your man, always granted that you can trust his discretion, to move about at a distance, and in a different direction, so as to distract their wary eyes while you creep upon them. As chances are few at this sport, and it is important to kill these old stagers, who live to an immense age, long after they have become utterly useless for stud purposes, I would advise you never to spare a sitting shot.

Of capercailzie shooting there is not much to be said. It is no doubt a beautiful sight to see these magnificent birds sailing past you as you stand in a clearing of the wood, and a very satisfactory thing to bring them down stone dead, as you can do if you hit them well forward. But as their flight is not long, the drives are not exciting, and beautiful as the bird may be he is not fit to eat in any shape but soup. Whatever you may do, the capercailzie will leave your ground or remain on it as they list, selecting their favourite trees for residence, and being found perched there with monotonous regularity. They do not seem to acquire in Scotland (the only part of the British Islands where they can be found) even the wildness of habit which makes the pursuit of them so exciting in Germany and Austria. But as they—that is, the cocks only, for a hen is never shot—are only pursued in the latter countries in the breeding season, and are, in fact, slain in the act of carolling forth the song of love, I confess to but little sympathy for the sport.

But when you have to deal with one that is driven to you, be not deceived by his size or the comparatively slow beat of his wings. He is going fully as fast as a blackcock or a grouse, and unless you hit him in the head you need not trouble to fire. I once missed five old cocks in one drive, none of them more than thirty-five yards off, from misjudging their pace, and probably also in some degree their distance from me. All that can be said about them has been admirably put by Mr. Millais in his book[1] and by Lord Charles Kerr in the Badminton Library.[2]

Last, but not least, we must breathe the keen air and tread the summer snows of the high tops, while we attack the shy and graceful ptarmigan.

[1] *Game Birds and Shooting Sketches.*
[2] *Moor and Marsh,* p. 53.

The glorious scenery which surrounds the haunts of these beautiful birds makes the pursuit of them especially fascinating. The splendid air and brilliant light, the panoramic view, the shifting cloud and mist, the dizzy height and wondrous silence—these weird surroundings are so fine that we almost forget our wish to slay the creatures that inhabit them, and probably few men have descended from the ptarmigan hill in the evening without a pang of regret at having carried their predatory instinct into these picturesque solitudes.

At first you cannot see the birds against the stones, so closely do they resemble the pale grey rock, white spa, and speckled moss which form their background; but presently they move and run before you, seeming quite tame, but fifteen yards away. In another second they are all in the air together, their white wings flashing in the sun, they have doubled in a bunch along the hill, and now, well separated from one another, are sailing away at a terrific pace, while you sorrowfully eject your empty and profitless cartridge cases. You must advance upon them with the gun held ready, almost up to the shoulder, and as they all turn together, the killing moment, try and knock over a brace cleverly, though the second bird will take you all you know to stop.

'WHERE ARE THEY?'

A. Thorburn

They always rise all together and close to one another, and many people, otherwise scrupulous sportsmen, will, as they turn, shoot into the brown, or rather the 'white,' of the covey.   This I think horribly cruel and unfair, specially so in the case of ptarmigan, for a wounded bird who may fly across a valley which it would take you four hours of descent and ascent to cross, is more often than not never retrieved, but left to linger in a rift between the rocks, or fall a victim on the mossy slopes to the eagle, the raven, or the fox.

In beating a round hill, it is a good plan to separate and work round it in two parties, when you will send some beautiful rocketing shots from one to the other ; but your guns must be accurate, careful shots, or as you approach to meet again you may easily shoot one another.   The handling of the gun altogether demands experience and closer attention on ptarmigan ground than on any other.   The footing is often bad, and slips over loose stones are frequent, while the possibility of blinding one of the party by a ricochet off the rocks must always be borne in mind. The best way to carry the gun on such ground, *wherever possible*, is in the right hand only, thrown back, with the barrels resting on your right shoulder and the hand on the grip.   Then, should you fall, your piece

will fall forward as you extend your arm, and should a
jar discharge it, will probably do no harm. But when
there is anyone in front of you, it is obvious this
method of carrying the gun becomes the most unsafe,
and you must harden your heart and be prepared to
lose here and there a chance by carrying it at half-
cock carefully nursed over your left arm, while you
are clinging to the steep face or picking your way
among loose stones.

Ptarmigan can be driven, though to do it to a
profitable extent there should be a great stock of them,
and an elaborate organisation becomes necessary. The
ground they inhabit is so steep that the drivers must
usually be sent up by a different route from the guns,
and unless the whole thing is very carefully arranged
the drive is likely to fail of its result. There are
usually only a few broods on a particular hill, and I
think, if you are not too hard upon them (for on certain
days it is possible to kill almost every bird you see),
it is a better and pleasanter way to walk the ground
for them. Pointers or setters you will hardly require,
though here and there, especially for finding a wounded
bird, they will be useful. But the blue hares, which
are usually pretty well sprinkled over the ptarmigan
ground, are trying to your dogs, and you can be
pretty sure of finding the birds without them.

Ptarmigan, like all other birds, are much in-
fluenced by the wind, and should your march run
along the top of the hill it is useless to go out unless
the wind favours their lying on your side ; otherwise
every bird on the hill will be over the march, and
though you may get a splendid walk, you will make
but a poor bag of either birds or hares.

Where possible, separate into two parties, so as to
drive birds to one another, and in this way each party
is likely to be of service to the other in retrieving
wounded birds. The valleys, which they cross in a
few seconds and with consummate ease, are almost a
day's work for men to traverse ; and somehow the
idea of leaving these beautiful birds to a lingering
death in their own wild home is peculiarly repugnant
to the feelings of a good sportsman.

To revert to the lower ground, I think that
where you have, in addition to grouse, a large stock
of black-game, the interests of the farmers should be
borne in mind. There is no doubt that when the
corn is standing in stooks a large flock of these birds,
visiting the fields every night and morning, will
destroy a large amount of grain. You will find yourself all the more popular in the glen if you visit them
on off days when keen on this food, and a beautiful
afternoon's sport may be enjoyed by lying in wait for

them as they come from the moor to the corn-land.
Black-game if disturbed once or twice on their feed
will be chary of returning to the same place for a
space of time, and the farmer will be found very
grateful to you if, while enjoying a pleasant variety of
sport, you show some anxiety to protect his produce
from these voracious visitors.

I regret to have to record my opinion that the
decrease in the numbers of black-game in Scotland
is due entirely to illegal destruction of these birds.
They are easily poached, and since the poulterers
have been suffered to expose them for sale during the
spring and summer months as 'Norwegian,' the
diminution in the general stock has become very
marked.   No one should buy or eat black-game from
Christmas until the following August.   Whether they
come from Norway or not, they are not in season ;
they must have been destroyed during the period
when every animal but the lowest vermin should be
let alone, and have never been come by in the honest
ways of sport.

CHAPTER VII

RECORDS AND REMARKS

ALL the British shooting world now knows that a man can kill 500 brace of grouse to his own gun in one day—given the accuracy, the physique, the endurance, and the grouse necessary—since the feat has been performed by an Englishman on his own moor in Yorkshire. We also know that 1,000 brace and upwards to a party of well-selected shots is a performance we may always expect to hear of in a good grouse season, and that it has been done already several times in the same county. We further know that 500 brace can be killed in a day in Scotland, since it was done last year (1893) in Inverness-shire ; and in none of these cases are we sure that the limit of possibility has been reached.

To defend large bags is always a difficult task, since they must generally appear unnatural and un-sportsmanlike to persons who have no experience of well-organised and accurate shooting on strictly preserved ground ; and, be it observed, it is only from such as these that the attack ever comes. Such experience and study as I have been able to bring to bear on the subject convinces me that the more grouse there are on the moors, the more partridges in the fields, and the more pheasants in the coverts, the better for everybody in this struggling age. We ought to rejoice in the discovery that by good management the food-producing power of the moors, no less than their opportunities for healthy pleasure and exercise, can be increased to such a pitch. If the grouse are there, it is clear they must be killed to be utilised as food, and surely no one would advocate their being destroyed by means of nets or other engines in the wholesale manner of the poacher or poulterer. It is evident the results cannot be obtained by the old-fashioned methods, since where these have been abandoned the stock has so much increased that it would no longer be possible to deal with the birds except by organised driving.

I have never been one of those who have cavilled at Lord Walsingham's unique performance. Records must and will continue to be broken by Englishmen until the limit is reached, and it seems to me far better that everyone should know the extraordinary value and fecundity of well-preserved moors.

I append the account of Lord Walsingham's great day, copied from his own record, and signed by him for me at the time:

August 30, 1888.   (*First drive commenced at* 5.12 *a.m.*)

No. of birds in each drive	No. of minutes for each drive
49	33
64	38
59	16
79	18
71	24
58	18
56	19
53	20
42	20
61	16
16	17
21	30
32	25
91	21
39	28
93	21
52	20
33	24
23	21
30	20

Walk home } 14 concluding at 7.30 P.M.

———
1,036

From first shot to last, 14 hours 18 minutes.

Number of cartridges fired about 1,550, including forty signal shots not fired at birds.

Deducting the last fourteen birds (killed walking home), and adding 22 + 12 *picked up*, we have 1,056 killed in 449 minutes, or 2½ per minute in the actual time occupied in shooting in the twenty drives. Once I killed three birds at one shot, the only three in sight at the time, and three times I killed two at one shot, each time intentionally.

WALSINGHAM.

September 20, 1888.

Although the result has been published, I do not think any previous work contains this account of the details. The small pick-up, 34 birds out of a total of 1,056 only about 3 per cent., testifies to clean killing and humane and careful gathering of wounded ; while the hours occupied and proportion of kills to misses are sufficient to show that to produce the performance a man must be a first-rate sportsman and athlete.

Here is the account of two days at Mr. Rimington Wilson's, on the Broomhead moors near Sheffield, last year (1893). The first constitutes the record bag for one day's grouse shooting :

Nine guns { August 30 . . . 2,648 grouse
           { September 1 . . . 1,603 ,,

Remarks.—Six drives each day ; the first at 10.15 A.M., the last at 5 P.M.

The second day's driving was over the same batteries and the same ground as the first.

Both days fine and wind favourable.

1,910 grouse picked up by luncheon on the 30th.

Mr. Wilson also held the record previous to this day—viz. 2,626 grouse, killed at Broomhead on September 6, 1872, by thirteen guns, including the late Mr. J. W. Rimington Wilson, one of the finest shots and most accomplished men of his time, and his two sons, who took outside places all day. The most recent record, as given above, to nine guns, is of course by far the more remarkable of the two.

Here, again, are some of the results of the well-known Wemmergill moor, kindly furnished me by Lord Westbury, who has rented it almost ever since Sir Frederick Milbank gave it up. He says : ' For the last seven years this moor, which is under 12,000 acres, has yielded an *average* of over 6,000 birds a year ; this period includes two very bad seasons—viz. 1891, when only 1,826 birds were killed, and 1892, when there was *no shooting.*'

This average is 50 per cent higher than that of Sir Frederick Milbank during his twelve years' tenancy of the same moor, viz. 4,133 birds, although his period includes the exceptional total of 17,064 in 1872 ;[1] Lord Westbury's highest year being 9,797 in 1888. This looks as though the preservation of the birds and the ground had reached a more perfect and even condition.

[1] Badminton Library, *Moor and Marsh*, p. 37.

s

I append the best day in each season during Lord Westbury's tenancy :

Year	Date	Grouse	Guns
1887	August 23	1,287	7
1888	,, 23	1,596	7
1889	,, 21	2,053	8
1890	,, 20	1,324	9
1891	A very bad year ; no large bags.		
1892	No shooting, owing to severe frost in May, which destroyed most of the eggs.		
1893	September 6	1,807	8

On the adjoining moor of High Force enormous totals have also been reached, the record of 1872, during the Duke of Beaufort's tenancy, showing 15,484 birds for nineteen days' shooting. On this moor, as the guest of the late Mr. Clare Vyner, I took part in a wonderful week, averaging over 1,200 birds each day for four days, to only six guns. I had the best drive I have ever seen, picking up 115 birds in the single drive. I had knocked down 145, but owing to pressure of time and much thick bracken near my butt, which in the heat of an August day gave the dogs no chance, I had to leave thirty birds on the ground, most of which, however, came into the pick-up announced next day.

It is curious that Lord de Grey should have also

had his biggest drive, 128 birds, later on the same day, especially since we have both taken part in larger bags than the total of that particular occasion.

Lord de Grey, who is admittedly the best game shot of our generation, and who has of course immense experience, has killed to his own gun 575 grouse in one day, shooting as one of a party of seven guns on the Studley Royal moors. Sir Frederick Milbank's performance[1] exceeds this in numbers, and will probably, as the performance of an individual making one of a party of guns, never be surpassed. Lord de Grey's view is that, without disparagement of any such feat as this or Lord Walsingham's, which is only possible to a first-rate man, there is a great deal of luck as to whether the chance ever presents itself to perform it, and that the general shooting throughout a succession of days *under every variety of condition* is the test which the most experienced will apply to a man's form.

It is necessary to notice an exceptional performance, and to recognise it as such. It is rarely achieved but by the first-rate man, and does not alter the general conditions which govern the sport in

---

[1] Badminton Library, *Moor and Marsh*, p. 37.

question. We can all remember how when Mr. W.
G. Grace produced a series of scores such as had
never been dreamt of in the cricket field, people
began to talk of altering the rules to assist the
bowlers ; of adding a stump, or narrowing the pro-
portions of the bat, in order to restore the balance of
the game. But these scores, like those named above,
now remain recorded as the meteors or comets in the
celestial field of great reputations, of rare and spasmodic recurrence, and valuable only as a standard of
possibility to stimulate minor constellations to greater
brilliancy.

The first-rate performer, as before remarked, is
good under all circumstances. I have met those who
have seen W. G. Grace in a rustic cricket match, or
John Roberts on a country house table, just as I have
seen De Grey walking for an ordinary bag of partridges,
or pursuing the occasional snipe or rabbit. The performance shows the same excellence under all these
circumstances, and the quality which excites merely
pleasure and admiration under the average conditions
should not produce jealousy or carping criticism when
reproduced on the rare opportunity which admits of
the execution of a sensational feat.

There is no danger of the frequent recurrence of
Lord Walsingham's 500 brace in a day, of Lord de

Grey's 240 partridges in one drive,[1] of John Robert's
spot-barred break of 1,300 odd, or of Dr. Grace's
hundreds in an innings. The first-rate form which
gradually builds up a great reputation is sure on some
rare occasion, when all conditions are favourable, to
produce an exceptional or startling feat ; but there is
no reason on this account to imagine that all the
ordinary rules of the sport in question are to be sub-
versed by this meteoric performance, or to deplore the
fact that the result exceeds what had been foreseen.
These isolated achievements, properly considered, do
no harm, but on the contrary merely serve to raise
the general standard of excellence in all outdoor
amusements which it has always been the pride of the
Englishman to maintain before the world. Some
fifty years ago Colonel Campbell of Monzie made
bags to his own gun over dogs which have never been
surpassed, excepting perhaps on one occasion by the
late Maharajah Duleep Singh.[2] I do not think any

[1] This is, no doubt, the record for an individual performance in a partridge drive ; the feat, which I give on Lord de
Grey's own authority, was performed by him last year, 1893,
at Baron de Hirsch's in Hungary.

[2] Colonel Campbell killed in one day in 1843, 184½ brace
of grouse ; in 1846, 191 brace; and on the authority of 'Hark-
away' is said on another day to have killed 222½ brace.
The Maharajah Duleep Singh in 1872 bagged 220 brace in
a day.

bad consequences have followed these rare feats.   If they have, as is probably the case, stimulated others to improve their shooting and the management of their moors, they have done more good than harm, and merely resulted in an increase in the supply of grouse available as food or sport for those who own moor-land estates.

As remarked before, the best black-game ground is undoubtedly to be found on the Duke of Buc-cleuch's large estates in Dumfriesshire, while on other ground in the border counties, as well as in Perth-shire and Aberdeenshire, they have been killed in considerable numbers.

The Duke of Buccleuch kindly furnishes me with the following totals of the five best years on his Drumlanrig Castle property :

1861	.	.	.	.	. 1,586
1865	.	.	.	.	. 1,530
1869	.	.	.	.	. 1,508 }Black-game
1870	.	.	.		. 1,486
1871	.	.	.		. 1,429

These are diminishing totals, as will be observed, and I regret to say that his Grace adds that the numbers are still growing less, though there is little or no poaching on his ground.   But I must recur to the subject of illegally killed game, and have no

ON THE WALL.

hesitation in putting down the diminished numbers
to the account of the poulterers in London and
elsewhere. Perhaps some one well acquainted with
Norway will tell us from what part of that country
the large supplies with which it is credited come to
our markets !

Here is the best bag ever made on the Duke's
ground :

SANQUHAR, DUMFRIESSHIRE

Grouse	. . .	5
Black-game	. .	247
Partridges .	.	21
Pheasant . .	.	1
Hares . .	.	40
Rabbits .	.	2
Total	.	316

the guns including H.R.H. Prince Christian, the late
Duke of Buccleuch, and eight others. Of the 247
black-game over 100 brace were cocks, and I fancy
this constitutes the record bag of these birds.

In 1874, at Newlands near Langholm, another of
the Duke's estates on the Border, the present Duke
and Colonel Francis Cust bagged 98 black-game, 81
cocks and 17 greyhens, in one day, starting late and
having only one gun each. The Duke informs me that
if they had begun earlier and had taken two guns each

they could easily have killed 60 brace or more.   This, especially considering the date, October 9, is the best day I ever heard of for two guns.

Of capercailzie, probably no greater quantity has ever been killed than on the day mentioned by Mr. Millais, 70 in one day, on the Dowager Duchess of Athole's ground near Dunkeld ; while the 35 cocks shot at Ballinling by a party of whom Mr. Millais was one, is seldom, if ever, likely to be equalled.

These birds having many years ago become extinct in this country, were, as is well known, re-introduced by the second Marquess of Breadalbane at Taymouth, and have spread over most of the lowland counties of Scotland.   So far as I have seen they keep very much to themselves, and I should say without doubt contrive to drive away black-game from their especial haunts, though they remain on fairly friendly terms with pheasants, woodcocks, and other game. They have never been found yet on the English side of the Border, though black-game have been killed in nearly every county in England and Wales, some-times within a short distance of London itself.   Mr. Millais mentions the curious instance of a black-cock and a hansom cab coming within the range of his acute vision at the same time in the neighbourhood of Aldershot.   There is only one way to ' transplant these birds into a new country—by procuring the eggs and putting them into pheasant or partridge nests, the former, of course, for choice. But they go where they list ; they will not stay if the country does not suit them, but will travel for miles until they find congenial cover and food, even as they have led me in this little work far away from their recognised home and companions, the heather and the grouse.

COOKERY OF THE GROUSE

BY

GEORGE SAINTSBURY

I HAVE always regretted (but never so much as since I undertook the duty of these chapters) that I did not preserve a French book on game and its cookery which passed through my hands some years ago. The author frankly admitted that grouse do not live in France, though black-game of course are found there. But he wished to be complete, and moreover, as he very justly observed, some of his French readers might have one or more brace of grouse sent him by an English friend, and then what was he to do? So he gave with great pride what he was pleased to call a receipt for 'Grouse à la Dundy.' Dundy, I remember, he defined as being not only the gamiest, *la plus giboyeuse*, city of Scotland, but also renowned for every variety of refinement of taste and luxury—superior in short to Peebles itself. And the way that they cooked grouse in Dundy was—but that is exactly what I have forgotten. To the best of my memory it was like

most French fashions of cooking game—a sufficiently
ingenious method of making the best of any natural
flavour that the bird might have, and imbuing it with
a good many others, not at all disagreeable, but super-
added rather than evolved or assisted, a method useful
enough for old birds or indifferent birds, but improper
for others.

This process could nowhere be more a counsel of
imperfection than in the case of grouse ; which, I venture to think, has of all game birds the most distinct
and the least surpassable flavour. There are those,
of course, who will put in claims for others, and this
is not the place to fight the matter out. I shall only
say that while nearly all game birds are good, and
some eminently good, grouse seems to me to be the
best, to possess the fullest and at the same time the
least violent flavour—to have the best consistency of
flesh and to present the greatest variety of attractions
in different parts. It has become almost an affectation
to speak of the excellence of his back ; let us rather
say that he is all good—back and breast, legs and
wings.

Black-game, capercailzie, and ptarmigan are but
varieties of grouse, and almost everything that applies
to the red grouse applies to them. Indeed, the excellent Baron Brisse characteristically includes both

black-game and capercailzie in saying that there are
two kinds of *coq de bruyère*, the one about the size of
a peacock, the other about the size of a pheasant.
All three birds, it is scarcely necessary to say, have,
owing to their habitat and food, a much stronger
flavour than the red grouse ; and it depends very much
on the predominance or moderation of this flavour
whether they are intolerable, tolerable, or excellent.
Moreover, in the case of two of them at least, English
estimation of them is wont to be injuriously affected
by the importation of vast numbers of ptarmigan
and capercailzie from the North of Europe, without
the slightest regard to their fitness for food.   I have
seen it stated, indeed, that most of the Norwegian
capercailzie which are sold in English shops are
poached by illegal and unsportsmanlike processes,
at the very time when they are most out of season.
Ptarmigan soup, however, is quite excellent, and I am
not sure that even grouse at its best can give points
to a roast greyhen in good condition.   But partly
because of the strong nature of their food—whereof
pine and juniper shoots and seeds are the chief parts—
and partly because they are stronger flying birds, and
therefore tougher than the red grouse, black-game
require even more keeping than that 'estimable vola-
tile.'   The whole tribe, indeed, will bear this process

as no other birds will. It was the custom of a hospitable friend of mine in Scotland, who was equally good with rod and gun, to keep a supply of grouse hanging till he could accompany them with salmon caught in a river which was by no means a very early opening one, and I never found birds taste better. The less regarded members of the grouse tribe will, as I have said, bear much longer keeping. Indeed, the best if not the only really good capercailzie that I ever tasted had been subjected to the indignity of being forgotten. He was imported into the Channel Islands by an enterprising game dealer ; I bought him, and as the house in which I was living had no good larder, I asked the man to keep him on his own premises till he and we were ready. We promptly forgot all about him, and it was several weeks before the shamefaced dealer, who was equally oblivious, said one day, ' I'm afraid, sir, that capercailzie . . . !' Nevertheless we had him sent home. It was necessary to amputate and discard a considerable part of him, but the rest was altogether admirable.

With all these birds, but especially with ptarmigan, dryness is the great thing to be feared when roasting them ; and this must be guarded against by liberal basting, by jackets of bacon, and in other well-known ways, especially, perhaps, by the German method of marinading and larding given below.   Except in soup, old birds of all the three kinds are very nearly hopeless, and should not be attempted.   And though in the abstract most, if not all, of the methods of what may be called applied grouse-cookery are applicable to them, it is well to remember that the extremely strong flavour above referred to marries itself but awkwardly to miscellaneous additions, and is almost impossible simply to disguise with them.   Indeed, it is noteworthy that even French cookery books do not as a rule meddle much with the *coq de bruyère*, but prefer him plain.   Nor does any of the tribe make a very good devil.   'Tickler,' indeed, in the *Noctes Ambrosianæ*, avoucheth that even eagle's thigh is good devilled ; but the context does not inspire complete confidence in the good faith of the sage of Southside at that moment. On the whole, it may be laid down that black-game and capercailzie (the latter when young and in very good condition) are best roasted, ptarmigan stewed or converted into soup.   But I must own that I have eaten roast ptarmigan which left the room (at least the bones did) without a stain on their character— which were 'white birds' as much metaphorically as literally.

With these preliminary remarks and cautions as to the outlying varieties we may turn to the cooking

T

of grouse proper. For very obvious reasons the anti-
quarian part of the matter needs but little attention.
Until railway-and-steamboat-time grouse were anything but common in London and exceedingly uncommon in Paris, and the *chef* of literary tendencies
was not likely to trouble himself much about them.
Their rarity in the former place is exemplified in the
well-known though doubtless apocryphal legend of the
Highland chieftain who ordered 'grouse and salmon'
for his domestics at a London hotel. And the books
said very little about them. For instance, a lady had
the great kindness to examine for me a country-house
collection of cookery books, English, Scotch, French,
and American, extending to some score of volumes,
and all printed between 1790 and 1830. They yielded
practically nothing but the direction 'Roast moor-game
half an hour : serve with fried bread crumbs, bread
sauce, and sliced raw onions in a little water in the
same boat,' and the still more general advice to 'dress
them like partridges and send them up with currant
jelly and fried bread crumbs.' It is somewhat interesting to notice that the onion sauce (or rather salad) here
suggested is neither more nor less than a degraded
and barbarous survival of the onion *purée* which, as
was noted in the volume on the Partridge in this series,
Gervase Markham had prescribed for that bird some

two centuries earlier. As for the currant jelly I think it hardly survives now, but for people who like currant jelly with flesh or fowl it is not bad with grouse, while as usual cranberry or rowan-berry jelly is better still. German and American cooks also sometimes recommend *plum*-sauce. But in connection with the general direction to 'cook them like partridges' I am tempted to add two receipts for dressing that bird which I did not know at the time of writing on it, but which seem admirably adapted to grouse also, and which come from the collection referred to above. They appear in *La Cuisine de Santé*, an elaborate work in three volumes written by M. Jourdain Le Cointe, and revised in the year 1790 by a medical practitioner of Montpellier. This latter man of art, by the way, seems during that stirring time to have been as unpolitically engaged as his brother *savant* who was indifferent to the Revolution because he had an unprecedented number of irregular verbs all nicely conjugated and written out in his desk.

The first of these receipts is called *à la Sultane*, and is described as one of the favourite dishes of Venetian cookery ; the other, also asserted to be Italian in origin, is *à la cendre*.

For birds *à la Sultane* you take four, and sacrifice the least promising of the quartette to make a *farce* for the other three, with the usual accompaniment of mushrooms, anchovies, &c. You then, having stuffed the others, lard them not merely with bacon but with anchovies and truffles, and roast them before a not too fierce fire, basting them till they are two-thirds done with good *consommé*. 'Il unit l'agrément et la salubrité,' says of this dish M. Jourdain le Comte or the Montpellier doctor, evidently leaning back in his chair with a sense of satisfaction after writing the words. It would be interesting to try this receipt with grouse, and I think it would answer, though I should be disposed to omit the anchovies. The other manner, *à la cendre*, contains a slight puzzle to me. It is directed that the birds, jacketed in bacon and stuffed with the usual *farce* made of one of their number, shall each be wrapped with extreme care, so that no part is uncovered, in a large sheet of white paper strewed with sliced truffles. Each packet being carefully tied up with packthread is buried in hot ashes, turning it if necessary till cooked. Our authority says that this way of cooking is very popular in Italy, but to his thinking dries the birds too much and deprives them of their *qualité restaurante*. That, I should say, would depend on the stuffing and jacketting. But what sort of paper is it that will stand the heat of ashes hot enough to cook a partridge through? Burnt-paper ash is not the nicest

of condiments, and, moreover, the phrase 'sortez-les
du papier' at the end of the article implies that the
wrapping is *ex hypothesi* intact. Perhaps somebody who
has a hearth and wood-ashes at his or her disposal
will try the method.

Turning to modern and straightforward cookery, I
observe that some critics, while speaking very amiably of
my efforts in alien art on the partridge, have been pleased
to speak compassionately of my preference of plain roast
bird as 'very English.' I hope that nothing worse will
ever be said of any taste of mine; and that, as according to a famous axiom, 'it is permissible to Dorians to
speak Doric,' so it may be permissible to Englishmen to
eat English food. At any rate, though I have just given
some and shall hope to give several other receipts for
more elaborate dealing, I must repeat and emphasise
the same preference here. A plainly and perfectly
roasted grouse, with the accompaniments above referred to (or others, such as chipped or ribboned
potatoes), is so good that he can in no other way be
improved, though of course he may be varied. Some
extreme grouse-eaters even declare that you ought to
eat nothing at all but grouse at the same meal ; and
though I cannot go with them there, I am thoroughly
of the mind of a certain wise and gracious hostess who
once said to me, 'I have given you very few things

for dinner to-day ; for there is grouse, and I think grouse *is* a dinner.' Certainly it is rather wicked to eat a mere snippet of it at the end of a dinner of soup, fish, half a dozen entrées, and very likely a solid *relevé*. The soup and the fish and one entrée ought to be ample when grouse in sufficient quantity forms the roast. Also grouse forms a better 'solid' than anything else that I know to finish a fish dinner with— there is some subtle and peculiar appropriateness in its specially earthy and dry savour as a contrast to the fishinesses. For accompanying vegetables nothing can equal French beans, which Nature supplies at the right time exactly, and for drinking to match, nothing can even approach claret, good, but not too good. Not 'forty thousand college councils' shall ever persuade me but that it is something of a solecism and something of a sin to drink the *very* best Bordeaux with any solid food whatever. That should be drunk with a *recueillement* which is impossible to the palate when it is simultaneously called to deal with the grosser act of eating. Let, therefore, the host, however fortunate and liberal, keep the First Three and also his best Léovilles and Rauzans, Moutons and Pichon Longuevilles, for the time when the grouse has vanished ; but let him accompany it while it is being discussed with anything up to Palmer or Lagrange, or even

such second growths as Cos Destournel or Durfort.
Not that Burgundy (again just short of the very best)
goes ill with grouse, but that claret goes better. Alexis
Soyer, who, though I have heard good judges declare
him to have been a very overrated cook, said some
excellent things, soon to be quoted, about grouse, re-
commends a 'little sweet champagne' with grouse. It
was spoken like a Frenchman.

The accompaniments of roast grouse, besides those
already mentioned, are not very numerous. The liver
of the birds cooked separately, pounded and spread
upon the toast on which they are served, with
butter, salt, and cayenne, is often recommended.
Most people are unhappy without gravy ; for myself
I think if the grouse is properly done, not too much
and not too dry, it is better without any. The favourite,
and to the general taste indispensable, bread crumbs
are often horribly ill cooked, and unless very well
cooked are the reverse of appetising. Soyer, as above
reported by a good Scotch writer on cookery, who
calls herself 'Jenny Wren,' liked to eat grouse, which
he justly declared to vary inexplicably in flavour from
year to year, 'absolutely by themselves with nothing
but a crust of bread,' and this shows a purity of taste
which makes one almost forgive him his sweet champagne therewith. Watercress is as good with grouse

as with most roasted birds, and salad almost as good as with any ; though perhaps the brown-fleshed birds do not so imperatively call for this adjunct as the white. I seem to have heard that there were times and places where grouse were eaten with melted butter ; but it is well known that there were times and seasons when there was hardly anything to which Britons did not add that unlovely trimming. It must be confessed that the thing is still done (the trimming being actually poured over the birds) in Scotland, where they certainly understand cookery, and where they ought to understand that of grouse in particular. But it seems to me an abomination, and it must be remembered that if Scottish cookery, admirable as it is, has a tendency to sin, that tendency is in the direction of what is delicately called ' richness,' and that this may be an instance. No doubt the counter tendency of the grouse to the other original sin of dryness has also to be considered.

There is a good deal more dispute as to the time, or in other words the degree, to which grouse ought to be roasted than in regard to most other gam. birds. Nobody—not, I should suppose, even an ogre or a cannibal—likes underdone pheasant ; and I never heard of anybody who liked underdone partridge. On the other hand, only very unfortunately constituted persons

(who should not eat wild- or water-fowl at all) like wild
duck or widgeon, or anything of that kind, from solan
geese to plovers, otherwise than distinctly underdone.
But in regard to grouse it is impossible to say that
there is a distinctly orthodox or a distinctly heterodox
school in this respect.   The ambiguity of general
opinion is shown by the variation in time—from twenty
minutes to half an hour—usually allotted for the roasting of an average-sized young bird (I have even
seen three-quarters advised, but this is utterly pre-
posterous).   This amounts to the difference between
a distinct redness close to the bone and 'cooking
through.'   There is even a school who would have
grouse decidedly underdone.   I think they are wrong,
and that there should be nothing in the very least
saignant about a grouse when he is carved, but that,
if possible, he should be taken away from the fire the
very minute that the last possibility of such a trace
has disappeared.

The other two simple ways of cooking grouse (I
suppose men do boil them, just as they boiled Lord
Soulis, but I never knew a case) are broiling and con-
version into soup.   A broiled or 'brandered' grouse
is quite admirable, but must of course be quite young,
plentifully buttered (or oiled), and fairly peppered.
When successfully done it is like all broiled birds, one

of the very best things that it is possible to eat, and can be accompanied by an almost unlimited variety of sauces or gravies, from the plainest to the most elaborate. The same hyperbole may be used of grouse soup when it is what grouse soup should be. There are considerable variations in the methods of preparing it; and, as in most cases, it is necessary to look to the end or object. Philosophically considered, the whole subject of soup may be divided into three parts. There is soup more or less clear, such as is probably at the present moment chiefly in favour as being most restorative in effect and most elegant in consumption. There is a *purée* of creamy texture, thick, but not containing any positive solids. And lastly there is the old-fashioned broth with solids in it, which is more an *olla* or stew than a soup strictly speaking, and which, though a little robust and massive for our modern dinners, is one of the most satisfactory varieties of food for reasonably hungry people. The first of these forms is that in which grouse soup is least commonly presented, and to which perhaps this bird lends itself least characteristically. It is, however, good in its way, and I never saw a better receipt for it than that which is given by Mrs. Henry Reeve. You take old, but quite fresh birds, which may be either grouse or black-game, or (I should add) ptarmigan. You add water at the rate

COOKERY OF THE GROUSE

of three pints to the brace of birds, and keep it sim-
mering as slowly as possible for hours, adding peppercorns and a little onion and carrot.   Some time before
serving you take the best pieces of the breast out
(the birds of course have been cut up at first), press
them and cut them up in little bits to add to the
strained soup.

Purée of grouse is much more in request and—for
those who can consume thick soups—much better.
The apparent variety of receipts for it is great; the
real, smaller. All can be reduced, with little difficulty,
to a common form.   The birds are roasted, but not
so long as if they were going to be simply eaten—a
quarter of an hour is generally held to be enough. All
or most of the meat is then removed from the bones,
which are put into a sufficient quantity of ready-
made clear stock or *consommé*, with vegetables and
seasonings to taste.   This is allowed to simmer from
one to three hours, the longer the better.   Meanwhile,
the meat which was taken off is pounded in a mortar
and pressed through a sieve, some adding butter and
grated biscuit or toasted bread, others ground rice,
others nothing but seasoning.   This paste is then
stirred into the strained soup till it attains the required
thickness.   Celery in moderation is an important ingredient in *purée* of grouse, and some send lemon

with it to table ; but lemon is one of those good things
which are liable to abuse in cookery, in regard to meats
and fowls.   It is more at home with fish and sweets.

Of the ruder and more national form (which is
also, I think, the best) of grouse soup, the celebrated
stew whereof Meg Merrilies made Dominie Sampson
partake was probably a variety, though the authority
saith that moor-game were not the only ingredient of
that soup or broth or stew.   The beginning is the
same as for *purée*, and indeed *purée* and this sort of
soup melt into each other by imperceptible gradations.
For you may either roast the birds as in the former
case, cut off the best of the meat, break up and
slightly pound the rest, fry it with butter, some ham
and vegetables, and then stew it with good stock, in
quantity sufficient (some say a quart to a bird), and
after straining put the best pieces of meat in at the
last moment, to warm up with a glass of claret.   Or
you may cut up the birds into joints to begin with,
fry them in butter, and then add the stock, the vegetables and the etceteras, proceeding in ordinary soup
fashion till the thing is done.   Some in this last stage
advocate the adding of a young cabbage in pieces,
with wine or not, as liked.   And as the birds have,
in this case, no ordinary cooking but the slight fry,
and no pounding or other mollification, it is necessary

to 'simmer till tender,' which in the case of an old
grouse or black-cock may be a considerable time.
For the really hungry man this is, no doubt, the best
way of all ; but as a dinner dish it is perhaps, as has
been hinted, too solid for the mere overture to which
we have now reduced soup. In the days of the
ancestors, they ate it late instead of early in the order
of dishes ; and I am not certain that they were wrong.

There are few things more engaging about grouse
than the excellent appearance that it makes in cold
cookery, whether by itself, in salads, or in pies.
Chaudfroid of grouse (it is quite useless for purists to
warn us that the word has nothing to do with *chaud*
and nothing with *froid*, that its being *chaud* is an accident, and that its creator was one Chauffroix) is excellent. So are grouse potted whole (baked, with wine
and butter, and afterwards stowed singly into pots with
clarified butter poured over), or in joints, or in pounded
paste. So is the cold roast bird in the severest
simplicity, especially if he has not been cut into when
hot. So is grouse salad, of which a savoury, but rather
violent, if not even slightly vulgar, variety assigned to
Soyer is to be found in all the books with more or
fewer changes. The general principle is that, the joints
of not too much roasted grouse being laid on a bed
of salad and fenced round with garnishings of hard-

boiled egg, gherkins, beetroot, &c., a dressing of what the French would call an unusually *corsé* kind is poured over and if possible slightly iced. In the most aggressive prescription I have seen for this, no less than two table-spoonfuls of chopped shallots and as much of tarragon and chervil figure. But anybody who can make a salad at all can, of course, adjust the dressing to his or her fancy, and the garnishing likewise.

Grouse pie is of a higher order than these, although the odd changes of fashion have banished it from the chief meal of the day to breakfast, luncheon, and supper, at neither of which does anything better often appear. I do not know that anybody eats grouse pie hot, though I can conceive no particular or valid reason against it. It may be made, of course, in all the gradations of pies—the homely old variety with edible crust, the 'raised pie,' whereof the crust is not intended to be eaten, though persons of unsophisticated habits and healthy appetite may be observed some-times to attempt the feat—and the pie in which there is no pretence of crust at all, but which is concocted in a more or less ornamental case of fireproof china. (It was this last, perhaps, of which the poet of the Lakes, where there is much moor-game, wrote 'celestial with *terrine*' though his foolish printers usually spell it 'terrene.') And so the complexity of the materials and methods observes similar gradations, which by connection or accident very often adjust themselves to the three varieties of casing just mentioned. The simplest form of grouse pie merely requires the birds (jointed, halved, or sometimes whole), a proportion (a pound to a brace is usual) of rump steak cut into knobs, seasoning, crust, and a sufficiency of good gravy (which may or may not be touched up with lemon juice and claret) to fill up and moisten the mixture. To this, of course, the usual enrichments of hard eggs (whether of the domestic fowl or, as the youthful heir of Glenroy in *Destiny* suggests, plovers' eggs), mush-rooms, truffles, forcemeat balls, and so forth, may be added. These additions may further be said to be customary in the raised grouse pie, and invariable in that which is made in a *terrine*. These latter forms merge themselves very much in the general 'game pie,' an excellent thing in its way no doubt. But I do not know that it is so good as the simple grouse pie with nothing added but steak, seasoning, an alliaceous touch of some sort, and a few eggs and mushrooms.

And so we come at last to the more elaborate varieties of cooking this noble animal. In that utter-ance of Soyer's above quoted he is made to confess that 'his art cannot improve grouse,' that in good

years the flavour is such as to baffle more ornamental
treatment, while in others there is nothing particular
to be done with the fowl. Nevertheless, people will
do things with it ; and some of the things they do
must be told with the general caution, or at least
opinion, that they are vanity. In the first place there
is a way of pressing grouse which, since the initial
process is to boil or stew the bird to rags, must be
specially applicable, and should be chiefly or only
applied, to the very oldest specimens. Having inflicted
this fiery and watery torment on them you pull the
meat off the bones, season it pretty freely, and clothe
it with jelly (either with ordinary aspic or by fortifying
the liquor in which it was boiled with gelatine), adding
eggs, truffles, and anything else you please before
letting it get solid in a mould or dish. It stands to
reason that this is only a way—though not at all a
bad way—of using birds not otherwise eatable.

Salmis of grouse stands much higher—indeed, it
is probably the best of its kind, except that made of
wild duck ; and inasmuch as there must always be
remnants of roast birds, it is almost a necessary supplement to simpler cookery, besides being extremely
good of itself. But it is necessary to remember several
things about a salmis. The first is, that though the
birds are always cooked first, it is indispensable that

the sauce or gravy, or whatever you choose to call it, should have a thorough flavour of them, which is not to be attained by merely warming the pieces of game in it. This may be given, of course, in various ways, either by stewing the bones, skin, trimmings, and less worthy pieces of the grouse in the stock used, or by adding some *purée* or 'essence of game;' but it must be attained somehow. The next thing to remember is that this gravy or sauce when finished should never be a mere bath or slop. Madame Lebour-Fawssett says it should be 'of the consistency of well-made melted butter,' and I agree with her. Lastly, remember that there must always be wine in a salmis; and that it is of great importance what wine it is. English books *will* recommend port or sherry. which, in my humble judgment, are extremely bad wines for all savoury cooking purposes. Pale dry sherry is, for that end, mostly quite useless, though I own that if I were rich I should try the experiment of boiling a ham in Manzanilla. The now despised, though in its way gorgeous, 'old brown' is apt to overpower every other flavour, and is too sweet, objections which apply still more strongly to port and even to Madeira, which is sometimes recommended, and which is certainly preferable to either port or sherry. Besides, all these wines, and still more the brown 'cooking' brandy, which it is whispered is sometimes used, provoke undue thirst and general discomfort. A sound red Bordeaux with flavour and some body for brown meats, and a good (not an acid or wiry) Chablis or Pouilly for white, are probably the best things for the purpose. And I must again praise the French lady above cited for recommending equal parts of stock and wine as the main body of salmis sauce. The mixture is added to a foundation of well-warmed and browned butter and flour, plenty of seasoning, including herbs, some shallot rather than onion, and at the last a little lemon juice, remembering the warnings above given. Nothing more but patience, careful watching, and still greater care when the game has been put in the mixture never to let it boil, is required to make a good salmis. But all this is required, and without it the thing cannot be a success.

There is no perceptible difference between the better class of receipts for hashing grouse and those for a salmis of it. If there is any, it is that the hash gravy may be a little thinner ; but that is a matter of taste, and it is not uncommon to find cookery books in which the titles of the receipts for the two processes might be changed and little or no harm done. The fact is that 'salmis' (a term of which even the great

Littré did not know the origin, but which I venture
to think a mere abbreviation of ' salmigondis ') is /
neither more nor less than a hash or *ragoût* of *game*
or wild birds, which has had its name extended without strict propriety to the tame duck, but no farther.

Stewed grouse, which is, or was, common in Scotland, is a sort of application of the process of hashing
to birds not previously cooked, and presumably old.
You cut them up, fry them with butter and shallot, or
garlic, take out the latter and then simmer them gently
for half an hour with equal but not large quantities
of stock and wine. There should be a good deal of
pepper.

Grouse can of course be made into *quenelles*, *kro-
meskis*, *croquettes*, *salpicons*, *bouchées*, and all the other
varieties of rissoles in which pounded or minced meat
is conveyed into fanciful and easily consumed shapes
of small size. They might be made into a *pain* or
quenelle on a great scale ; they can be soufflèd, and
are very good so. It is further obvious and easy to
stuff them in roasting or accompany them in pieces
with all kinds of forcemeat, from the simplest to the
most complicated, from the plain liver-and-bread-
crumb to compounds *à la financière* and *à la Lucullus*,
in which truffles and cockscombs and the like figure.
Grouse cutlets—the birds being usually halved, partly

boned, fried, and then simmered in espagnole or some similar sauce—are well enough, and can be sophisticated before being served up by having truffles and other associations stuck on them. It is also sometimes recommended that they should be prepared in ·this way before being made into a pie.

Most of the books contain a receipt usually stated (conscientiously) to be German, for marinading grouse, which might be useful either in the case of birds accidentally kept too long or in that of very aged ones, or, as observed above, to tame the wildness of the rougher members of the tribe. Otherwise I cannot conceive it to be necessary to treat good red grouse in this way, however useful something of the same kind may be to make pork taste like wild boar, rabbit like hare, and very dry roe-venison like the flesh of a hart of grease. You take (the particulars never vary) a quarter of a pint of vinegar, a score of juniper berries, some peppercorns, and two or three bay leaves. You steep the birds in this for three days, frequently turning them and spooning the marinade over them. You then stuff them with turkey stuffing, lard the breasts, roast and serve.

But after this and the other things the mind returns from these excesses to the elegance of a good roast grouse simple of himself, with some such a feeling as

that which 'Neville Temple and Edward Trevor'
attributed long ago to Tannhäuser when

> a dewy sense
> Of innocent worship stole

over his heated brain and sense as he contemplated
the Princess after his return from the Venusberg. It
is true that the ingenious wickedness of some may
draw a bad moral in favour of variety even from this
comparison ; but on their heads be it.

PRINTED BY
SPOTTISWOODE AND CO., NEW-STREET SQUARE
LONDON

MESSRS. LONGMANS, GREEN, & CO.'S
CLASSIFIED CATALOGUE

OF

WORKS IN GENERAL LITERATURE.

History, Politics, Polity, and Political Memoirs.

Abbott.—A HISTORY OF GREECE. By EVELYN ABBOTT, M.A., LL.D. Part I.—From the Earliest Times to the Ionian Revolt. Crown 8vo., 10s. 6d. Part II.—500-445 B.C. Cr. 8vo., 10s. 6d.

Acland and Ransome.—A HANDBOOK IN OUTLINE OF THE POLITICAL HISTORY OF ENGLAND TO 1890. Chronologically Arranged. By the Right Hon. A. H. DYKE ACLAND, M.P., and CYRIL RANSOME, M.A. Crown 8vo., 6s.

ANNUAL REGISTER (THE). A Review of Public Events at Home and Abroad, for the year 1892. 8vo., 18s.

Volumes of the ANNUAL REGISTER for the years 1863-1891 can still be had. 18s. each.

Armstrong.—ELIZABETH FARNESE ; The Termagant of Spain. By EDWARD ARMSTRONG, M.A., Fellow of Queen's College, Oxford. 8vo., 16s.

Arnold.—Works by T. ARNOLD, D.D., formerly Head Master of Rugby School.

INTRODUCTORY LECTURES ON MODERN HISTORY. 8vo., 7s. 6d.

MISCELLANEOUS WORKS. 8vo., 7s. 6d.

Bagwell.—IRELAND UNDER THE TUDORS. By RICHARD BAGWELL, LL.D. 3 vols. Vols. I. and II. From the first Invasion of the Northmen to the year 1578. 8vo., 32s. Vol. III. 1578-1603. 8vo., 18s.

Ball.—HISTORICAL REVIEW OF THE LEGISLATIVE SYSTEMS OPERATIVE IN IRELAND, from the Invasion of Henry the Second to the Union (1172-1800). By the Rt. Hon. J. T. BALL. 8vo., 6s.

Besant.—THE HISTORY OF LONDON. By WALTER BESANT. With 74 Illustrations. Crown 8vo. School Reading-book Edition, 1s. 9d.; Prize-book Edition, 2s. 6d.

Buckle.—HISTORY OF CIVILISATION IN ENGLAND AND FRANCE, SPAIN AND SCOTLAND. By HENRY THOMAS BUCKLE. 3 vols. Crown 8vo., 24s.

Creighton.—HISTORY OF THE PAPACY DURING THE REFORMATION. By MANDELL CREIGHTON, D.D., LL.D., Bishop of Peterborough. 8vo. Vols. I. and II. 1378-1464. 32s. Vols. III. and IV. 1464-1518. 24s. Vol. V. 1517-1527. 15s.

Crump.—A SHORT INQUIRY INTO THE FORMATION OF POLITICAL OPINION, from the reign of the Great Families to the advent of Democracy. By ARTHUR CRUMP. 8vo., 7s. 6d.

De Tocqueville. — DEMOCRACY IN AMERICA. By ALEXIS DE TOCQUEVILLE. 2 vols. Crown 8vo., 16s.

Fitzpatrick.—SECRET SERVICE UNDER PITT. By W. J FITZPATRICK, F.S.A., Author of 'Correspondence of Daniel O'Connell'. 8vo., 7s. 6d.

Freeman.—THE HISTORICAL GEOGRAPHY OF EUROPE. By EDWARD A. FREEMAN, D.C.L., LL.D. With 65 Maps. 2 vols. 8vo., 31s. 6d.

History, Politics, Polity, and Political Memoirs—*continued.*

Froude.—Works by JAMES A. FROUDE, Regius Professor of Modern History in the University of Oxford.

THE HISTORY OF ENGLAND, from the Fall of Wolsey to the Defeat of the Spanish Armada.
Popular Edition. 12 vols. Crown 8vo., 3s. 6d. each.
Silver Library Edition. 12 vols. Crown 8vo., 3s. 6d. each.

THE DIVORCE OF CATHERINE OF ARAGON : the Story as told by the Imperial Ambassadors resident at the Court of Henry VIII. Crown 8vo., 6s.

THE SPANISH STORY OF THE ARMADA, and other Essays, Historical and Descriptive. Crown 8vo., 6s.

THE ENGLISH IN IRELAND IN THE EIGHTEENTH CENTURY. 3 vols. Cr. 8vo., 18s.

SHORT STUDIES ON GREAT SUBJECTS. 4 vols. Cr. 8vo., 3s. 6d. each.

CÆSAR : a Sketch. Cr. 8vo., 3s. 6d.

Gardiner.—Works by SAMUEL RAWSON GARDINER, M.A., Hon. LL.D., Edinburgh, Fellow of Merton College, Oxford.

HISTORY OF ENGLAND, from the Accession of James I. to the Outbreak of the Civil War, 1603-1642. 10 vols. Crown 8vo., 6s. each.

A HISTORY OF THE GREAT CIVIL WAR, 1642-1649. 4 vols. Cr. 8vo., 6s. each.

THE STUDENT'S HISTORY OF ENGLAND. With 378 Illustrations. Cr. 8vo., 12s.

Also in Three Volumes.
Vol. I. B.C. 55—A.D. 1509. With 173 Illustrations. Crown 8vo. 4s.
Vol. II. 1509-1689. With 96 Illustrations. Crown 8vo. 4s.
Vol. III. 1689-1885. With 109 Illustrations. Crown 8vo. 4s.

Granville.—THE LETTERS OF HARRIET COUNTESS GRANVILLE, 1810-1845. Edited by her Son, the Hon. F. LEVESON GOWER. 2 vols. 8vo., 32s.

Greville.—A JOURNAL OF THE REIGNS OF KING GEORGE IV., KING WILLIAM IV., AND QUEEN VICTORIA. By CHARLES C. F GREVILLE, formerly Clerk of the Council. 8 vols. Crown 8vo., 6s. each.

Hart.—PRACTICAL ESSAYS IN AMERICAN GOVERNMENT. By ALBERT BUSHNELL HART, Ph.D., &c. Cr 8vo., 6s

Hearn.—THE GOVERNMENT OF ENGLAND : its Structure and its Development By W. EDWARD HEARN. 8vo., 16s.

Historic Towns.—Edited by E. A. FREEMAN, D.C.L., and Rev. WILLIAM HUNT, M.A. With Maps and Plans. Crown 8vo., 3s. 6d. each.

BRISTOL. By the Rev. W. HUNT.

CARLISLE. By MANDELL CREIGHTON, D.D., Bishop of Peterborough.

CINQUE PORTS. By MONTAGU BURROWS.

COLCHESTER. By Rev. E. L. CUTTS.

EXETER. By E. A. FREEMAN.

LONDON. By Rev. W. J. LOFTIE.

OXFORD. By Rev. C. W. BOASE.

WINCHESTER. By Rev. G. W. KITCHIN, D.D.

YORK. By Rev. JAMES RAINE.

NEW YORK. By THEODORE ROOSEVELT.

BOSTON (U.S.) By HENRY CABOT LODGE.

Horley.—SEFTON : A DESCRIPTIVE AND HISTORICAL ACCOUNT. Comprising the Collected Notes and Researches of the late Rev. ENGELBERT HORLEY, M.A., Rector 1871-1883. By W. D. CARÖE, M.A. (Cantab.), Fellow of the Royal Institute of British Architects, and E. J. A. GORDON. With 17 Plates and 32 Illustrations in the Text. Royal 8vo., 31s. 6d.

Joyce.—A SHORT HISTORY OF IRELAND, from the Earliest Times to 1608. By P W. JOYCE, LL.D. Crown 8vo., 10s. 6d.

Lang.—ST. ANDREWS. By ANDREW LANG. With 8 Plates and 24 Illustrations in the Text, by T HODGE. 8vo., 15s. net.

Lecky.—Works by WILLIAM EDWARD HARTPOLE LECKY.

HISTORY OF ENGLAND IN THE EIGHTEENTH CENTURY.
Library Edition. 8 vols. 8vo., £7 4s.
Cabinet Edition. ENGLAND. 7 vols. Cr. 8vo., 6s. each. IRELAND. 5 vols. Crown 8vo., 6s. each.

HISTORY OF EUROPEAN MORALS FROM AUGUSTUS TO CHARLEMAGNE. 2 vols. Crown 8vo., 16s.

HISTORY OF THE RISE AND INFLUENCE OF THE SPIRIT OF RATIONALISM IN EUROPE. 2 vols. Crown 8vo., 16s.

History, Politics, Polity, and Political Memoirs—*continued.*

Macaulay.—Works by LORD MAC-AULAY.

COMPLETE WORKS.

Cabinet Ed. 16 vols. Pt. 8vo., £4 16s.
Library Edition. 8 vols. 8vo., £5 5s.

HISTORY OF ENGLAND FROM THE AC-CESSION OF JAMES THE SECOND.

Popular Edition. 2 vols. Cr. 8vo., 5s.
Student's Edition. 2 vols. Cr. 8vo., 12s.
People's Edition. 4 vols. Cr. 8vo., 16s.
Cabinet Edition. 8 vols. Pt. 8vo., 48s.
Library Edition. 5 vols. 8vo., £4.

CRITICAL AND HISTORICAL ESSAYS, WITH LAYS OF ANCIENT ROME, in 1 volume.

Popular Edition. Crown 8vo., 2s. 6d.
Authorised Edition. Crown 8vo., 2s. 6d., or 3s. 6d., gilt edges.

Silver Library Edition. Crown 8vo., 3s. 6d.

CRITICAL AND HISTORICAL ESSAYS.

Student's Edition. 1 vol. Cr. 8vo., 6s.
People's Edition. 2 vols. Cr. 8vo., 8s.
Trevelyan Edition. 2 vols. Cr. 8vo., 9s.
Cabinet Edition. 4 vols. Post 8vo., 24s.
Library Edition. 3 vols. 8vo., 36s.

ESSAYS which may be had separately price 6d. each sewed, 1s. each cloth.

Frederick the Great.
Lord Bacon.
Addison and Wal-pole.
Croker's Boswell's Johnson.
Hallam's Constitu-tional History.
Warren Hastings (3d. swd., 6d. cl.).

Lord Clive.
The Earl of Chat-ham(Two Essays).
Ranke and Glad-stone.
Milton and Machia-velli.
Lord Byron,and The Comic Dramatists of the Restoration.

SPEECHES. Crown 8vo., 3s. 6d.

MISCELLANEOUS WRITINGS.

People's Ed. 1 vol. Cr. 8vo., 4s. 6d.
Library Edition. 2 vols. 8vo., 21s.

MISCELLANEOUS WRITINGS AND SPEECHES.

Popular Edition. Cr. 8vo., 2s. 6d.
Student's Edition. Crown 8vo., 6s.

Cabinet Edition. Including Indian Penal Code, Lays of Ancient Rome, and Miscellaneous Poems. 4 vols. Post 8vo., 24s.

Macaulay.—Works by LORD MAC-AULAY.—*continued.*

SELECTIONS FROM THE WRITINGS OF LORD MACAULAY. Edited, with Occasional Notes, by the Right Hon. Sir G. O. Trevelyan, Bart. Crown 8vo., 6s.

May.—THE CONSTITUTIONAL HISTORY OF ENGLAND since the Accession of George III. 1760-1870. By Sir THOMAS ERSKINE MAY, K.C.B. (Lord Farn-borough). 3 vols. Crown 8vo., 18s.

Merivale.—Works by the Very Rev. CHARLES MERIVALE, late Dean of Ely.

HISTORY OF THE ROMANS UNDER THE EMPIRE.
Cabinet Edition. 8 vols. Cr. 8vo., 48s.
Silver Library Edition. 8 vols. Cr. 8vo., 3s. 6d. each.

THE FALL OF THE ROMAN REPUBLIC: a Short History of the Last Century of the Commonwealth. 12mo., 7s. 6d.

Parkes.—FIFTY YEARS IN THE MAKING OF AUSTRALIAN HISTORY. By Sir HENRY PARKES, G.C.M.G. With 2 Portraits (1854 and 1892). 2 vols. 8vo., 32s.

Prendergast.—IRELAND FROM THE RESTORATION TO THE REVOLUTION, 1660-1690. By JOHN P. PRENDERGAST, Author of 'The Cromwellian Settlement in Ireland'. 8vo., 5s.

Round.—GEOFFREY DE MANDEVILLE: a Study of the Anarchy. By J. H. ROUND, M.A. 8vo., 16s.

Seebohm.—THE ENGLISH VILLAGE COMMUNITY Examined in its Relations to the Manorial and Tribal Systems, &c. By FREDERIC SEEBOHM. With 13 Maps and Plates. 8vo., 16s.

Smith.—CARTHAGE AND THE CARTHA-GINIANS. By R. BOSWORTH SMITH, M.A. With Maps, &c. Cr. 8vo., 3s. 6d.

Stephens.—PAROCHIAL SELF-GOVERN-MENT IN RURAL DISTRICTS: Argument and Plan. By HENRY C. STEPHENS, M.P. 4to., 12s. 6d. Popular Edition. Cr. 8vo., 1s.

Stephens.—A HISTORY OF THE FRENCH REVOLUTION. By H. MORSE STEPHENS, Balliol College, Oxford. 3 vols. 8vo. Vols. I. and II. 18s. each.

History, Politics, Polity, and Political Memoirs—*continued.*

Stubbs.—HISTORY OF THE UNIVERSITY OF DUBLIN, from its Foundation to the End of the Eighteenth Century. By J. W. STUBBS. 8vo., 12s. 6d.

Sutherland.—THE HISTORY OF AUSTRALIA AND NEW ZEALAND, from 1606 to 1890. By ALEXANDER SUTHERLAND, M.A., and GEORGE SUTHERLAND, M.A. Crown 8vo., 2s. 6d.

Thompson.—POLITICS IN A DEMOCRACY: an Essay. By DANIEL GREENLEAF THOMPSON. Cr. 8vo., 5s.

Todd.—PARLIAMENTARY GOVERNMENT IN THE COLONIES. By ALPHEUS TODD, LL.D. 8vo., 30s. net.

Tupper. — OUR INDIAN PROTECTORATE: an Introduction to the Study of the Relations between the British Government and its Indian Feudatories. By CHARLES LEWIS TUPPER, Indian Civil Service. Royal 8vo., 16s.

Wakeman and Hassall.—ESSAYS INTRODUCTORY TO THE STUDY OF ENGLISH CONSTITUTIONAL HISTORY. By Resident Members of the University of Oxford. Edited by HENRY OFFLEY WAKEMAN, M.A., and ARTHUR HASSALL, M.A. Crown 8vo., 6s.

Walpole.—Works by SPENCER WALPOLE.

HISTORY OF ENGLAND FROM THE CONCLUSION OF THE GREAT WAR IN 1815 TO 1858. 6 vols. Crown 8vo., 6s. each.

THE LAND OF HOME RULE: being an Account of the History and Institutions of the Isle of Man. Cr. 8vo., 6s.

Wylie.—HISTORY OF ENGLAND UNDER HENRY IV. By JAMES HAMILTON WYLIE, M.A., one of H. M. Inspectors of Schools. 3 vols. Crown 8vo. Vol. I. 10s. 6d. Vol. II. 15s. Vol. III.
[In preparation.

Biography, Personal Memoirs, &c.

Armstrong.—THE LIFE AND LETTERS OF EDMUND J. ARMSTRONG. Edited by G. F. ARMSTRONG. Fcp. 8vo., 7s. 6d.

Bacon.—LETTERS AND LIFE, INCLUDING ALL HIS OCCASIONAL WORKS. Edited by J. SPEDDING. 7 vols. 8vo., £4 4s.

Bagehot.—BIOGRAPHICAL STUDIES. By WALTER BAGEHOT. 8vo., 12s.

Boyd.—TWENTY-FIVE YEARS OF ST. ANDREWS, 1865-1890. By A. K. H. BOYD, D.D., Author of 'Recreations of a Country Parson,' &c. 2 vols. 8vo. Vol. I., 12s. Vol. II., 15s.

Carlyle.—THOMAS CARLYLE: a History of his Life. By J. A. FROUDE. 1795-1835. 2 vols. Crown 8vo., 7s. 1834-1881. 2 vols. Crown 8vo., 7s.

Fabert.—ABRAHAM FABERT: Governor of Sedan and Marshal of France. His Life and Times, 1599-1662. By GEORGE HOOPER, Author of 'Waterloo,' 'Wellington,' &c. With a Portrait. 8vo., 10s. 6d.

Fox.—THE EARLY HISTORY OF CHARLES JAMES FOX. By the Right Hon. Sir G. O. TREVELYAN, Bart.

Library Edition. 8vo., 18s.
Cabinet Edition. Crown 8vo., 6s.

Hamilton.—LIFE OF SIR WILLIAM HAMILTON. By R. P. GRAVES. 3 vols. 15s. each.

ADDENDUM TO THE LIFE OF SIR WM. ROWAN HAMILTON, LL.D., D.C.L., 8vo., 6d. sewed.

Hassall.—THE NARRATIVE OF A BUSY LIFE: an Autobiography. By ARTHUR HILL HASSALL, M.D. 8vo., 5s.

Havelock.—MEMOIRS OF SIR HENRY HAVELOCK, K.C.B. By JOHN CLARK MARSHMAN. Crown 8vo., 3s. 6d.

Macaulay.—THE LIFE AND LETTERS OF LORD MACAULAY. By the Right Hon. Sir G. O. TREVELYAN, Bart.
Popular Edition. 1 vol. Cr. 8vo., 2s. 6d.
Student's Edition. 1 vol. Cr. 8vo., 6s.
Cabinet Edition. 2 vols. Post 8vo., 12s.
Library Edition. 2 vols. 8vo., 36s.

Marbot.—THE MEMOIRS OF THE BARON DE MARBOT. Translated from the French by ARTHUR JOHN BUTLER, M.A. Crown 8vo., 7s. 6d.

Montrose.—DEEDS OF MONTROSE: THE MEMOIRS OF JAMES, MARQUIS OF MONTROSE, 1639-1650. By the Rev. GEORGE WISHART, D.D. (Bishop of Edinburgh, 1662-1671). Translated, with Introduction, Notes, &c., and the original Latin, by the Rev. ALEXANDER MURDOCH, F.S.A. (Scot.), and H. F. MORELAND SIMPSON, M.A. (Cantab.). 4to., 36s. net.

Biography, Personal Memoirs, &c.—*continued*.

Seebohm.—The Oxford Reformers —John Colet, Erasmus and Thomas More : a History of their Fellow-Work. By Frederic Seebohm. 8vo., 14s.

Shakespeare.—Outlines of the Life of Shakespeare. By J. O. Halliwell-Phillipps. With numerous Illustrations and Fac-similes. 2 vols. Royal 8vo., £1 1s.

Shakespeare's True Life. By Jas. Walter. With 500 Illustrations by Gerald E. Moira. Imp. 8vo., 21s.

Sherbrooke.—Life and Letters of the Right Hon. Robert Lowe, Viscount Sherbrooke, G.C.B., together with a Memoir of his Kinsman, Sir John Coape Sherbrooke, G.C.B. By A. Patchett Martin. With 5 Portraits. 2 vols. 8vo., 36s.

Stephen.—Essays in Ecclesiastical Biography. By Sir James Stephen. Crown 8vo., 7s. 6d.

Verney.—Memoirs of the Verney Family during the Civil War. Compiled from the Letters and Illustrated by the Portraits at Claydon House, Bucks. By Frances Parthenope Verney. With a Preface by S. R. Gardiner, M.A., LL.D. With 38 Portraits, Woodcuts and Fac-simile. 2 vols. Royal 8vo., 42s.

Wagner.—Wagner as I Knew Him. By Ferdinand Praeger. Crown 8vo., 7s. 6d.

Walford.—Twelve English Authoresses. By L. B. Walford, Author of 'Mischief of Monica,' &c. With Portrait of Hannah More. Crown 8vo., 4s. 6d.

Wellington.—Life of the Duke of Wellington. By the Rev. G. R. Gleig, M.A. Crown 8vo., 3s. 6d.

Wordsworth.—Works by Charles Wordsworth, D.C.L., late Bishop of St. Andrews.

Annals of My Early Life, 1806-1846. 8vo., 15s.

Annals of My Life, 1847-1856. 8vo., 10s. 6d.

Travel and Adventure.

Arnold.—Seas and Lands. By Sir Edwin Arnold, K.C.I.E. With 71 Illustrations. Cr. 8vo., 7s. 6d.

AUSTRALIA AS IT IS; or, Facts and Features, Sketches and Incidents of Australia and Australian Life, with Notices of New Zealand. By A Clergyman. Crown 8vo., 5s.

Baker.—Works by Sir Samuel White Baker.

Eight Years in Ceylon. With 6 Illustrations. Crown 8vo., 3s. 6d.

The Rifle and the Hound in Ceylon. 6 Illustrations. Cr. 8vo., 3s. 6d.

Bent.—Works by J. Theodore Bent, F.S.A., F.R.G.S.

The Ruined Cities of Mashonaland : being a Record of Excavation and Exploration in 1891. With Map, 13 Plates, and 104 Illustrations in the Text. Cr. 8vo., 7s. 6d.

The Sacred City of the Ethiopians: being a Record of Travel and Research in Abyssinia in 1893. With 8 Plates and 65 Illustrations in the Text. 8vo., 18s

Brassey.—Works by Lady Brassey.

A Voyage in the 'Sunbeam'; Our Home on the Ocean for Eleven Months.

Library Edition. With 8 Maps and Charts, and 118 Illustrations. 8vo., 21s.

Cabinet Edition. With Map and 66 Illustrations. Crown 8vo., 7s. 6d.

Silver Library Edition. With 66 Illustrations. Crown 8vo., 3s. 6d.

Popular Edition. With 60 Illustrations. 4to., 6d. sewed, 1s. cloth.

School Edition. With 37 Illustrations. Fcp., 2s. cloth, or 3s. white parchment.

Sunshine and Storm in the East.

Library Edition. With 2 Maps and 141 Illustrations. 8vo., 21s.

Cabinet Edition. With 2 Maps and 114 Illustrations. Crown 8vo., 7s. 6d

Popular Edition. With 103 Illustrations. 4to., 6d. sewed, 1s. cloth.

Travel and Adventure—*continued.*

Brassey.—Works by LADY BRASSEY—*continued.*

IN THE TRADES, THE TROPICS, AND THE 'ROARING FORTIES'. Cabinet Edition. With Map and 220 Illustrations. Crown 8vo., 7s. 6d. Popular Edition. With 183 Illustrations. 4to., 6d. sewed, 1s. cloth.

THREE VOYAGES IN THE 'SUNBEAM'. Popular Edition. With 346 Illustrations. 4to., 2s. 6d.

THE LAST VOYAGE TO INDIA AND AUSTRALIA IN THE 'SUNBEAM'. With Charts and Maps, and 40 Illustrations in Monotone (20 full-page), and nearly 200 Illustrations in the Text from Drawings by R. T. PRITCHETT. 8vo., 21s.

Curzon.—PERSIA AND THE PERSIAN QUESTION. With 9 Maps, 96 Illustrations, Appendices, and an Index. By the Hon. GEORGE N. CURZON, M.P., late Fellow of All Souls' College, Oxford. 2 vols. 8vo., 42s.

Froude.—Works by JAMES A. FROUDE.

OCEANA : or England and her Colonies. With 9 Illustrations. Crown 8vo., 2s. boards, 2s. 6d. cloth.

THE ENGLISH IN THE WEST INDIES : or the Bow of Ulysses. With 9 Illustrations. Cr. 8vo., 2s. bds., 2s. 6d. cl.

Howard.—LIFE WITH TRANS-SIBERIAN SAVAGES. By B. DOUGLAS HOWARD, M.A. Crown 8vo., 6s.

Howitt.—VISITS TO REMARKABLE PLACES, Old Halls, Battle-Fields, Scenes illustrative of Striking Passages in English History and Poetry. By WILLIAM HOWITT. With 80 Illustrations. Crown 8vo., 3s. 6d.

Knight.—Works by E. F. KNIGHT, Author of the Cruise of the 'Falcon'.

THE CRUISE OF THE 'ALERTE': the Narrative of a Search for Treasure on the Desert Island of Trinidad. With 2 Maps and 23 Illustrations. Crown 8vo., 3s. 6d.

WHERE THREE EMPIRES MEET: a Narrative of Recent Travel in Kashmir, Western Tibet, Baltistan, Ladak, Gilgit, and the adjoining Countries. With a Map and 54 Illustrations. Cr. 8vo., 7s. 6d.

Lees and Clutterbuck.—B. C. 1887: A RAMBLE IN BRITISH COLUMBIA. By J. A. LEES and W. J. CLUTTERBUCK, Authors of 'Three in Norway'. With Map and 75 Illustrations. Cr. 8vo., 3s. 6d.

Montague.—TALES OF A NOMAD ; or, Sport and Strife. By CHARLES MONTAGUE. Crown 8vo., 6s.

Nansen.—Works by Dr. FRIDTJOF NANSEN.

THE FIRST CROSSING OF GREENLAND. With numerous Illustrations and a Map. Crown 8vo., 7s. 6d.

ESKIMO LIFE. Translated by WILLIAM ARCHER. With 16 Plates and 15 Illustrations in the Text. 8vo., 16s.

Riley.—ATHOS : or the Mountain of the Monks. By ATHELSTAN RILEY, M.A. With Map and 29 Illustrations. 8vo., 21s.

Rockhill.—THE LAND OF THE LAMAS : Notes of a Journey through China, Mongolia, and Tibet. By WILLIAM WOODVILLE ROCKHILL. With 2 Maps and 61 Illustrations. 8vo., 15s.

Stephens.—MADOC: An Essay on the Discovery of America, by MADOC AP OWEN GWYNEDD, in the Twelfth Century. By THOMAS STEPHENS. Edited by LLYWARCH REYNOLDS, B.A. Oxon. 8vo., 7s. 6d.

THREE IN NORWAY. By Two of Them. With a Map and 59 Illustrations. Cr. 8vo., 2s. boards, 2s. 6d. cloth.

Von Hohnel.—DISCOVERY OF LAKES RUDOLF AND STEFANIE: Account of Count SAMUEL TELEKI'S Exploring and Hunting Expedition in Eastern Equatorial Africa in 1887 and 1888. By Lieutenant LUDWIG VON HOHNEL. With 179 Illustrations and 6 Maps. 2 vols. 8vo., 42s.

Whishaw.—OUT OF DOORS IN TSAR LAND; a Record of the Seeings and Doings of a Wanderer in Russia. By FRED. J. WHISHAW. Cr. 8vo., 7s. 6d.

Wolff.—Works by HENRY W. WOLFF.

RAMBLES IN THE BLACK FOREST. Crown 8vo., 7s. 6d.

THE WATERING PLACES OF THE VOSGES. Crown 8vo., 4s. 6d.

THE COUNTRY OF THE VOSGES. With a Map. 8vo., 12s.

Sport and Pastime.

THE BADMINTON LIBRARY.

Edited by the DUKE OF BEAUFORT, K.G., assisted by ALFRED E. T. WATSON.

ATHLETICS AND FOOTBALL. By MONTAGUE SHEARMAN. With 51 Illustrations. Crown 8vo., 10s. 6d.

BIG GAME SHOOTING. By C. PHILLIPPS-WOLLEY, F. C. SELOUS, ST. GEORGE LITTLEDALE, &c. With 150 Illustrations. 2 vols., 10s. 6d. each.

BOATING. By W. B. WOODGATE. With 49 Illustrations. Cr. 8vo., 10s. 6d.

COURSING AND FALCONRY. By HARDING COX and the Hon. GERALD LASCELLES. With 76 Illustrations. Crown 8vo., 10s. 6d.

CRICKET. By A. G. STEEL and the Hon. R. H. LYTTELTON. With Contributions by ANDREW LANG, R. A. H. MITCHELL, W. G. GRACE, and F. GALE. With 63 Illustrations. Cr. 8vo., 10s. 6d.

CYCLING. By VISCOUNT BURY (Earl of Albemarle), K.C.M.G., and G. LACY HILLIER. With 89 Illustrations. Crown 8vo., 10s. 6d.

DRIVING. By the DUKE OF BEAUFORT. With 65 Illustrations. Cr. 8vo., 10s. 6d.

FENCING, BOXING, AND WRESTLING. By WALTER H. POLLOCK, F. C. GROVE, C. PREVOST, E. B. MITCHELL, and WALTER ARMSTRONG. With 42 Illustrations. Crown 8vo., 10s. 6d.

FISHING. By H. CHOLMONDELEY-PENNELL. With Contributions by the MARQUIS OF EXETER, HENRY R. FRANCIS, R. B. MARSTON, &c.

Vol. I. Salmon, Trout, and Grayling. With 158 Illustrations. Crown 8vo., 10s. 6d.

Vol. II. Pike and other Coarse Fish. With 133 Illustrations. Crown 8vo., 10s. 6d.

GOLF. By HORACE G. HUTCHINSON, the Rt. Hon. A. J. BALFOUR, M.P., Sir W. G. SIMPSON, Bart., ANDREW LANG, and other Writers. With 91 Illustrations. Cr. 8vo., 10s. 6d.

HUNTING. By the DUKE OF BEAUFORT, K.G., and MOWBRAY MORRIS. With Contributions by the EARL OF SUFFOLK AND BERKSHIRE, Rev. E. W. L. DAVIES. With 53 Illustrations. Crown 8vo., 10s. 6d.

MOUNTAINEERING. By C. T. DENT, Sir F. POLLOCK, Bart., W. M. CONWAY, DOUGLAS FRESHFIELD, C. E. MATHEWS, C. PILKINGTON. With 108 Illustrations. Cr. 8vo., 10s. 6d.

RACING AND STEEPLE-CHASING. Racing: By the EARL OF SUFFOLK AND BERKSHIRE and W. G. CRAVEN. With a Contribution by the Hon. F. LAWLEY. Steeple-chasing: By ARTHUR COVENTRY and ALFRED E. T. WATSON. With 58 Illusts. Cr. 8vo., 10s. 6d.

RIDING AND POLO. By Captain ROBERT WEIR, J. MORAY BROWN, the DUKE OF BEAUFORT, K.G., the EARL of SUFFOLK AND BERKSHIRE, &c. With 59 Illustrations. Cr. 8vo., 10s. 6d.

SHOOTING. By Lord WALSINGHAM and Sir RALPH PAYNE-GALLWEY, Bart. With Contributions by LORD LOVAT, A. J. STUART-WORTLEY, &c.
Vol. I. Field and Covert. With 105 Illustrations. Crown 8vo., 10s. 6d.
Vol. II. Moor and Marsh. With 65 Illustrations. Cr. 8vo., 10s. 6d.

SKATING, CURLING, TOBOGANING, AND OTHER ICE SPORTS. By JN. M. HEATHCOTE, C. G. TEBBUTT, T. MAXWELL WITHAM, &c. With 284 Illustrations. Cr. 8vo., 10s. 6d.

SWIMMING. By ARCHIBALD SINCLAIR and WILLIAM HENRY, Hon. Secs. of the Life Saving Society. With 119 Illustrations. Cr. 8vo., 10s. 6d.

TENNIS, LAWN TENNIS, RACQUETS, AND FIVES. By J. M. and C. G. HEATHCOTE, E. O. PLEYDELL-BOUVERIE and A. C. AINGER. With Contributions by the Hon. A. LYTTELTON, W. C. MARSHALL, Miss L. DOD, H. W. W. WILBERFORCE, H. F. LAWFORD, &c. With 79 Illustrations. Crown 8vo., 10s. 6d.

YACHTING. By the EARL OF PEMBROKE, R. T. PRITCHETT, the MARQUIS OF DUFFERIN AND AVA, the EARL OF ONSLOW, LORD BRASSEY, Lieut.-Col. BUCKNILL, LEWIS HERRESHOFF, G. L. WATSON, E. F. KNIGHT, etc. With Illustrations by R. T. PRITCHETT, and from Photographs. 2 vols. 10s. 6d., each.

Sport and Pastime—continued.
FUR AND FEATHER SERIES.
Edited by A. E. T. WATSON.

THE PARTRIDGE. Natural History, by the Rev. H. A. MACPHERSON; Shooting, by A. J. STUART-WORTLEY; Cookery, by GEORGE SAINTSBURY. With 11 full-page Illustrations and Vignette by A. THORBURN, A. J STUART-WORTLEY, and C. WHYMPER, and 15 Diagrams in the Text by A. J. STUART-WORTLEY. Crown 8vo., 5s.

THE GROUSE. By A. J. STUART-WORTLEY, the Rev. H. A. MACPHERSON, and GEORGE SAINTSBURY. [In preparation.

THE PHEASANT By A. J STUART-WORTLEY, the Rev. H. A. MACPHERSON, and A. J. INNES SHAND. [In preparation.

THE HARE AND THE RABBIT. By the Hon. GERALD LASCELLES, &c. [In preparation.

WILDFOWL. By the Hon. JOHN SCOTT-MONTAGU, M.P., &c. Illustrated by A. J STUART WORTLEY, A. THORBURN, and others. [In preparation.

Campbell-Walker.—THE CORRECT CARD: or, How to Play at Whist; a Whist Catechism. By Major A. CAMPBELL-WALKER. Fcp. 8vo., 2s. 6d.

DEAD SHOT (THE): or, Sportsman's Complete Guide. Being a Treatise on the Use of the Gun, with Rudimentary and Finishing Lessons on the Art of Shooting Game of all kinds. By MARKSMAN. Crown 8vo., 10s. 6d.

Falkener.—GAMES, ANCIENT AND ORIENTAL, AND HOW TO PLAY THEM. By EDWARD FALKENER. With numerous Photographs, Diagrams, &c. 8vo., 21s.

Ford.—THE THEORY AND PRACTICE OF ARCHERY. By HORACE FORD. New Edition, thoroughly Revised and Rewritten by W. BUTT, M.A. With a Preface by C. J. LONGMAN, M.A. 8vo., 14s.

Fowler.—RECOLLECTIONS OF OLD COUNTRY LIFE. By J. K. FOWLER ("Rusticus"), formerly of Aylesbury. With Portraits, &c. 8vo., 10s. 6d.

Francis.—A BOOK ON ANGLING: or, Treatise on the Art of Fishing in every Branch; including full Illustrated List of Salmon Flies. By FRANCIS FRANCIS. With Coloured Plates. Cr. 8vo., 15s.

Hawker.—THE DIARY OF COLONEL PETER HAWKER, author of "Instructions to Young Sportsmen". With an Introduction by Sir RALPH PAYNE-GALLWEY, Bart. 2 vols. 8vo., 32s.

Hopkins.—FISHING REMINISCENCES. By Major E. P. HOPKINS. With Illustrations. Crown 8vo., 6s. 6d.

Lang.—ANGLING SKETCHES. By ANDREW LANG. With 20 Illustrations. Crown 8vo., 7s. 6d.

Longman.—CHESS OPENINGS. By FRED. W. LONGMAN. Fcp. 8vo., 2s. 6d.

Maskelyne.—SHARPS AND FLATS: a Complete Revelation of the Secrets of Cheating at Games of Chance and Skill. By JOHN NEVIL MASKELYNE. With 62 Illustrations and Diagrams. Crown 8vo., 6s.

Payne-Gallwey.—Works by Sir RALPH PAYNE-GALLWEY, Bart.

LETTERS TO YOUNG SHOOTERS (First Series). On the Choice and Use of a Gun. With 41 Illustrations. Cr. 8vo., 7s. 6d.

LETTERS TO YOUNG SHOOTERS. (Second Series). On the Production, Preservation, and Killing of Game. With Directions in Shooting Wood-Pigeons and Breaking-in Retrievers. With 103 Illustrations. Crown 8vo., 12s. 6d.

Pole.—THE THEORY OF THE MODERN SCIENTIFIC GAME OF WHIST. By W. POLE, F.R.S. Fcp. 8vo., 2s. 6d.

Proctor.—Works by RICHARD A. PROCTOR.

HOW TO PLAY WHIST: WITH THE LAWS AND ETIQUETTE OF WHIST. Crown 8vo., 3s. 6d.

HOME WHIST: an Easy Guide to Correct Play. 16mo., 1s.

Ronalds.—THE FLY-FISHER'S ENTOMOLOGY. By ALFRED RONALDS. With 20 Coloured Plates. 8vo., 14s.

Wilcocks. THE SEA FISHERMAN: Comprising the Chief Methods of Hook and Line Fishing in the British and other Seas, and Remarks on Nets, Boats, and Boating. By J. C. WILCOCKS. Illustrated. Crown 8vo., 6s.

Mental, Moral, and Political Philosophy.
LOGIC, RHETORIC, PSYCHOLOGY, ETC.

Abbott.—THE ELEMENTS OF LOGIC. By T. K. ABBOTT, B.D. 12mo., 3s.

Aristotle.—Works by.

THE POLITICS: G. Bekker's Greek Text of Books I., III., IV. (VII.), with an English Translation by W. E. BOLLAND, M.A., and short Introductory Essays by A. LANG, M.A. Crown 8vo., 7s. 6d.

THE POLITICS: Introductory Essays. By ANDREW LANG (from Bolland and Lang's 'Politics'). Cr. 8vo., 2s. 6d.

THE ETHICS: Greek Text, Illustrated with Essay and Notes. By Sir ALEXANDER GRANT, Bart. 2 vols. 8vo., 32s.

THE NICOMACHEAN ETHICS: Newly Translated into English. By ROBERT WILLIAMS. Crown 8vo., 7s. 6d.

AN INTRODUCTION TO ARISTOTLE'S ETHICS. Books I.-IV. (Book X. c. vi.-ix. in an Appendix.) With a continuous Analysis and Notes. Intended for the use of Beginners and Junior Students. By the Rev. EDWARD MOORE, D.D., Principal of St. Edmund Hall, and late Fellow and Tutor of Queen's College, Oxford. Crown 8vo., 10s. 6d.

Bacon.—Works by.

COMPLETE WORKS. Edited by R. L. ELLIS, J. SPEDDING, and D. D. HEATH. 7 vols. 8vo., £3 13s. 6d.

THE ESSAYS: with Annotations. By RICHARD WHATELY, D.D. 8vo. 10s. 6d.

Bain.—Works by ALEXANDER BAIN, LL.D.

MENTAL SCIENCE. Crown 8vo., 6s. 6d.

MORAL SCIENCE. Crown 8vo., 4s. 6d.

The two works as above can be had in one volume, price 10s. 6d.

SENSES AND THE INTELLECT. 8vo., 15s.

EMOTIONS AND THE WILL. 8vo., 15s.

LOGIC, DEDUCTIVE AND INDUCTIVE. Part I., 4s. Part II., 6s. 6d.

PRACTICAL ESSAYS. Crown 8vo., 2s.

Bray.—Works by CHARLES BRAY.

THE PHILOSOPHY OF NECESSITY: or Law in Mind as in Matter. Cr. 8vo., 5s.

THE EDUCATION OF THE FEELINGS: a Moral System for Schools. Crown 8vo., 2s. 6d.

Bray.—ELEMENTS OF MORALITY, in Easy Lessons for Home and School Teaching. By Mrs. CHARLES BRAY. Cr. 8vo., 1s. 6d.

Crozier.—CIVILISATION AND PROGRESS. By JOHN BEATTIE CROZIER, M.D. With New Preface, more fully explaining the nature of the New Organon used in the solution of its problems. 8vo., 14s.

Davidson.—THE LOGIC OF DEFINITION, Explained and Applied. By WILLIAM L. DAVIDSON, M.A. Crown 8vo., 6s.

Green.—THE WORKS OF THOMAS HILL GREEN. Edited by R. L. NETTLESHIP.

Vols. I. and II. Philosophical Works. 8vo., 16s. each.

Vol. III. Miscellanies. With Index to the three Volumes, and Memoir. 8vo., 21s.

Hearn.—THE ARYAN HOUSEHOLD: its Structure and its Development. An Introduction to Comparative Jurisprudence. By W. EDWARD HEARN. 8vo., 16s.

Hodgson.—Works by SHADWORTH H. HODGSON.

TIME AND SPACE: a Metaphysical Essay. 8vo., 16s.

THE THEORY OF PRACTICE: an Ethical Inquiry. 2 vols. 8vo., 24s.

THE PHILOSOPHY OF REFLECTION. 2 vols. 8vo., 21s.

Hume.—THE PHILOSOPHICAL WORKS OF DAVID HUME. Edited by T. H. GREEN and T. H. GROSE. 4 vols. 8vo., 56s. Or separately, Essays. 2 vols. 28s. Treatise of Human Nature. 2 vols. 28s.

Mental, Moral and Political Philosophy—*continued.*

Johnstone.—A SHORT INTRODUCTION TO THE STUDY OF LOGIC. By LAURENCE JOHNSTONE. With Questions. Cr. 8vo., 2s. 6d.

Jones.—AN INTRODUCTION TO GENERAL LOGIC. By E. E. CONSTANCE JONES, Author of ' Elements of Logic as a Science of Propositions'. Cr. 8vo., 4s. 6d.

Justinian.—THE INSTITUTES OF JUSTINIAN : Latin Text, chiefly that of Huschke, with English Introduction, Translation, Notes, and Summary. By THOMAS C. SANDARS, M.A. 8vo. 18s.

Kant.—Works by IMMANUEL KANT.

CRITIQUE OF PRACTICAL REASON, AND OTHER WORKS ON THE THEORY OF ETHICS. Translated by T. K. ABBOTT, B.D. With Memoir. 8vo., 12s. 6d.

INTRODUCTION TO LOGIC, AND HIS ESSAY ON THE MISTAKEN SUBTILTY OF THE FOUR FIGURES. Translated by T. K. ABBOTT, and with Notes by S. T. COLERIDGE. 8vo., 6s.

Killick.—HANDBOOK TO MILL'S SYSTEM OF LOGIC. By Rev. A. H. KILLICK, M.A. Crown 8vo., 3s. 6d.

Ladd.—Works by GEORGE TURNBULL LADD.

ELEMENTS OF PHYSIOLOGICAL PSYCHOLOGY. 8vo., 21s.

OUTLINES OF PHYSIOLOGICAL PSYCHOLOGY. A Text-Book of Mental Science for Academies and Colleges. 8vo., 12s.

PSYCHOLOGY, DESCRIPTIVE AND EXPLANATORY : a Treatise of the Phenomena, Laws, and Development of Human Mental Life. 8vo., 21s.

Lewes.—THE HISTORY OF PHILOSOPHY, from Thales to Comte. By GEORGE HENRY LEWES. 2 vols. 8vo., 32s.

Max Müller.—Works by F. MAX MÜLLER.

THE SCIENCE OF THOUGHT. 8vo., 21s.

THREE INTRODUCTORY LECTURES ON THE SCIENCE OF THOUGHT. 8vo., 2s. 6d.

Mill.—ANALYSIS OF THE PHENOMENA OF THE HUMAN MIND. By JAMES MILL. 2 vols. 8vo., 28s.

Mill.—Works by JOHN STUART MILL.

A SYSTEM OF LOGIC. Cr. 8vo., 3s. 6d.

ON LIBERTY. Cr. 8vo., 1s. 4d.

ON REPRESENTATIVE GOVERNMENT. Crown 8vo., 2s.

UTILITARIANISM. 8vo., 5s.

EXAMINATION OF SIR WILLIAM HAMILTON'S PHILOSOPHY. 8vo., 16s.

NATURE, THE UTILITY OF RELIGION, AND THEISM. Three Essays. 8vo., 5s.

Monck.—INTRODUCTION TO LOGIC. By H. S. MONCK. Crown 8vo., 5s.

Ribot.—THE PSYCHOLOGY OF ATTENTION. By TH. RIBOT. Cr. 8vo., 3s.

Sidgwick.—DISTINCTION : and the Criticism of Belief. By ALFRED SIDGWICK. Crown 8vo., 6s.

Stock.—DEDUCTIVE LOGIC. By ST. GEORGE STOCK. Fcp. 8vo., 3s. 6d.

Sully.—Works by JAMES SULLY, Grote Professor of Mind and Logic at University College, London.

THE HUMAN MIND : a Text-book of Psychology. 2 vols. 8vo., 21s.

OUTLINES OF PSYCHOLOGY. 8vo., 9s.

THE TEACHER'S HANDBOOK OF PSYCHOLOGY. Crown 8vo., 5s.

Swinburne.—PICTURE LOGIC : an Attempt to Popularise the Science of Reasoning. By ALFRED JAMES SWINBURNE, M.A. With 23 Woodcuts. Post 8vo., 5s.

Thompson.—Works by DANIEL GREENLEAF THOMPSON.

A SYSTEM OF PSYCHOLOGY. 2 vols. 8vo., 36s.

THE RELIGIOUS SENTIMENTS OF THE HUMAN MIND. 8vo., 7s. 6d.

THE PROBLEM OF EVIL : an Introduction to the Practical Sciences. 8vo., 10s. 6d.

Mental, Moral and Political **Philosophy**—*continued.*

Thompson. — Works by DANIEL GREENLEAF THOMPSON—*continued.*

SOCIAL PROGRESS. 8vo., 7s. 6d.

THE PHILOSOPHY OF FICTION IN LITERATURE. Crown 8vo., 6s.

Thomson.—OUTLINES OF THE NECESSARY LAWS OF THOUGHT: a Treatise on Pure and Applied Logic. By WILLIAM THOMSON, D.D., formerly Lord Archbishop of York. Post 8vo., 6s.

Webb.—THE VEIL OF ISIS: a Series of Essays on Idealism. By T. E. WEBB. 8vo., 10s. 6d.

Whately.—Works by R. WHATELY, formerly Archbishop of Dublin.

BACON'S ESSAYS. With Annotation. By R. WHATELY. 8vo., 10s. 6d.

ELEMENTS OF LOGIC. Cr. 8vo., 4s. 6d.

ELEMENTS OF RHETORIC. Cr. 8vo., 4s. 6d.

LESSONS ON REASONING. Fcp. 8vo., 1s. 6d.

Zeller.—Works by Dr. EDWARD ZELLER, Professor in the University of Berlin.

HISTORY OF ECLECTICISM IN GREEK PHILOSOPHY. Translated by SARAH F. ALLEYNE. Cr. 8vo., 10s. 6d.

THE STOICS, EPICUREANS, AND SCEPTICS. Translated by the Rev. O. J. REICHEL, M.A. Crown 8vo., 15s.

OUTLINES OF THE HISTORY OF GREEK PHILOSOPHY. Translated by SARAH F. ALLEYNE and EVELYN ABBOTT. Crown 8vo., 10s. 6d.

PLATO AND THE OLDER ACADEMY. Translated by SARAH F. ALLEYNE and ALFRED GOODWIN, B.A. Crown 8vo., 18s.

SOCRATES AND THE SOCRATIC SCHOOLS. Translated by the Rev. O. J. REICHEL, M.A. Crown 8vo., 10s. 6d.

THE PRE-SOCRATIC SCHOOLS: a History of Greek Philosophy from the Earliest Period to the time of Socrates. Translated by SARAH F. ALLEYNE. 2 vols. Crown 8vo., 30s.

MANUALS OF CATHOLIC PHILOSOPHY.
(Stonyhurst Series.)

A MANUAL OF POLITICAL ECONOMY. By C. S. DEVAS, M.A. Cr. 8vo., 6s. 6d.

FIRST PRINCIPLES OF KNOWLEDGE. By JOHN RICKABY, S.J. Crown 8vo., 5s.

GENERAL METAPHYSICS. By JOHN RICKABY, S.J. Crown 8vo., 5s.

LOGIC. By RICHARD F. CLARKE, S.J. Crown 8vo., 5s.

MORAL PHILOSOPHY (ETHICS AND NATURAL LAW). By JOSEPH RICKABY, S.J. Crown 8vo., 5s.

NATURAL THEOLOGY. By BERNARD BOEDDER, S.J. Crown 8vo., 6s. 6d.

PSYCHOLOGY. By MICHAEL MAHER, S.J. Crown 8vo., 6s. 6d.

History and Science of Language, &c.

Davidson.—LEADING AND IMPORTANT ENGLISH WORDS: Explained and Exemplified. By WILLIAM L. DAVIDSON, M.A. Fcp. 8vo., 3s. 6d.

Farrar.—LANGUAGE AND LANGUAGES: By F. W. FARRAR, D.D., F.R.S., Cr. 8vo., 6s.

Graham.—ENGLISH SYNONYMS. Classified and Explained: with Practical Exercises. By G. F. GRAHAM. Fcp. 8vo., 6s.

History and Science of Language, &c.—*continued.*

Max Müller.—Works by F. MAX MÜLLER.

SELECTED ESSAYS ON LANGUAGE, MYTHOLOGY, AND RELIGION. 2 vols. Crown 8vo., 16s.

THE SCIENCE OF LANGUAGE, Founded on Lectures delivered at the Royal Institution in 1861 and 1863. 2 vols. Crown 8vo., 21s.

BIOGRAPHIES OF WORDS, AND THE HOME OF THE ARYAS. Crown 8vo., 7s. 6d.

THREE LECTURES ON THE SCIENCE OF LANGUAGE, AND ITS PLACE IN GENERAL EDUCATION, delivered at Oxford, 1889. Crown 8vo., 3s.

Roget.—THESAURUS OF ENGLISH WORDS AND PHRASES. Classified and Arranged so as to Facilitate the Expression of Ideas and assist in Literary Composition. By PETER MARK ROGET, M.D., F.R.S. Recomposed throughout, enlarged and improved, partly from the Author's Notes, and with a full Index. by the Author's Son, JOHN LEWIS ROGET. Crown 8vo., 10s. 6d.

Whately.—ENGLISH SYNONYMS. By E. JANE WHATELY. Fcp. 8vo., 3s.

Political Economy and Economics.

Ashley.—ENGLISH ECONOMIC HISTORY AND THEORY. By W. J. ASHLEY, M.A. Crown 8vo., Part I., 5s. Part II., 10s. 6d.

Bagehot.—ECONOMIC STUDIES. By WALTER BAGEHOT. 8vo., 10s. 6d.

Crump.—AN INVESTIGATION INTO THE CAUSES OF THE GREAT FALL IN PRICES which took place coincidently with the Demonetisation of Silver by Germany. By ARTHUR CRUMP. 8vo., 6s.

Devas.—A MANUAL OF POLITICAL ECONOMY. By C. S. DEVAS, M.A. Crown 8vo., 6s. 6d. (*Manuals of Catholic Philosophy.*)

Dowell.—A HISTORY OF TAXATION AND TAXES IN ENGLAND, from the Earliest Times to the Year 1885. By STEPHEN DOWELL (4 vols. 8vo.) Vols. I. and II. The History of Taxation. 21s. Vols. III. and IV. The History of Taxes, 21s.

Jordan.—THE STANDARD OF VALUE. By WILLIAM LEIGHTON JORDAN. 8vo., 6s.

Leslie.—ESSAYS IN POLITICAL ECONOMY. By T. E. CLIFFE LESLIE. 8vo., 10s. 6d.

Macleod.—Works by HENRY DUNNING MACLEOD, M.A.

THE ELEMENTS OF BANKING. Crown 8vo., 3s. 6d.

THE THEORY AND PRACTICE OF BANKING. Vol. I. 8vo., 12s. Vol. II. 14s.

THE THEORY OF CREDIT. 8vo. Vol. I. 10s. net. Vol. II., Part I., 4s. 6d. Vol. II. Part II., 10s. 6d.

Meath.—PROSPERITY OR PAUPERISM? Physical, Industrial, and Technical Training. By the EARL OF MEATH. 8vo., 5s.

Mill.—POLITICAL ECONOMY. By JOHN STUART MILL.

Library Edition. 2 vols. 8vo., 30s.

Popular Edition. Crown 8vo., 3s. 6d.

Shirres.—AN ANALYSIS OF THE IDEAS OF ECONOMICS. By L. P. SHIRRES, B.A., sometime Finance Under Secretary of the Government of Bengal. Crown 8vo., 6s.

Political Economy and Economics—*continued.*

Symes.—POLITICAL ECONOMY: a Short Text-book of Political Economy. With Problems for Solution, and Hints for Supplementary Reading. By J. E. SYMES, M.A., of University College, Nottingham. Crown 8vo., 2s. 6d.

Toynbee.—LECTURES ON THE INDUSTRIAL REVOLUTION OF THE 18th CENTURY IN ENGLAND. By ARNOLD TOYNBEE. 8vo., 10s. 6d.

Webb.—THE HISTORY OF TRADE UNIONISM. By SIDNEY and BEATRICE WEBB. 8vo., 18s.

Wilson.—Works by A. J. WILSON. Chiefly reprinted from *The Investors' Review.*

PRACTICAL HINTS TO SMALL INVESTORS. Crown 8vo., 1s.

PLAIN ADVICE ABOUT LIFE INSURANCE. Crown 8vo., 1s.

Wolff.—PEOPLE'S BANKS: a Record of Social and Economic Success. By HENRY W. WOLFF. 8vo., 7s. 6d.

Evolution, Anthropology, &c.

Clodd.—THE STORY OF CREATION: a Plain Account of Evolution. By EDWARD CLODD. With 77 Illustrations. Crown 8vo., 3s. 6d.

Huth.—THE MARRIAGE OF NEAR KIN, considered with Respect to the Law of Nations, the Result of Experience, and the Teachings of Biology. By ALFRED HENRY HUTH. Royal 8vo., 7s. 6d.

Lang.—CUSTOM AND MYTH: Studies of Early Usage and Belief. By ANDREW LANG, M.A. With 15 Illustrations. Crown 8vo., 3s. 6d.

Lubbock.—THE ORIGIN OF CIVILISATION and the Primitive Condition of Man. By Sir J. LUBBOCK, Bart., M.P. With 5 Plates and 20 Illustrations in the Text. 8vo. 18s.

Romanes.—Works by GEORGE JOHN ROMANES, M.A., LL.D., F.R.S.

DARWIN, AND AFTER DARWIN: an Exposition of the Darwinian Theory, and a Discussion on Post-Darwinian Questions. Part I. The Darwinian Theory. With Portrait of Darwin and 125 Illustrations. Crown 8vo., 10s. 6d.

AN EXAMINATION OF WEISMANNISM. Crown 8vo., 6s.

Classical Literature.

Abbott.—HELLENICA. A Collection of Essays on Greek Poetry, Philosophy, History, and Religion. Edited by EVELYN ABBOTT, M.A., LL.D. 8vo., 16s.

Æschylus.—EUMENIDES OF ÆSCHYLUS. With Metrical English Translation. By J. F. DAVIES. 8vo., 7s.

Aristophanes.—The ACHARNIANS OF ARISTOPHANES, translated into English Verse. By R. Y. TYRRELL. Crown 8vo., 1s.

Becker.—Works by Professor BECKER.

GALLUS: or, Roman Scenes in the Time of Augustus. Illustrated. Post 8vo., 7s. 6d.

CHARICLES: or, Illustrations of the Private Life of the Ancient Greeks. Illustrated. Post 8vo., 7s. 6d.

Cicero.—CICERO'S CORRESPONDENCE. By R. Y. TYRRELL. Vols. I., II., III. 8vo., each 12s.

Clerke.—FAMILIAR STUDIES IN HOMER. By AGNES M. CLERKE. Cr. 8vo., 7s. 6d.

Farnell.—GREEK LYRIC POETRY: a Complete Collection of the Surviving Passages from the Greek Song-Writing. Arranged with Prefatory Articles, Introductory Matter and Commentary. By GEORGE S. FARNELL, M.A. With 5 Plates. 8vo., 16s.

Harrison.—MYTHS OF THE ODYSSEY. IN ART AND LITERATURE. By JANE E. HARRISON. Illustrated with Outline Drawings. 8vo., 18s.

Lang.—HOMER AND THE EPIC. By ANDREW LANG. Crown 8vo., 9s. net.

Classical Literature—*continued*.

Mackail.—SELECT EPIGRAMS FROM THE GREEK ANTHOLOGY. By J. W. MACKAIL, Fellow of Balliol College, Oxford. Edited with a Revised Text, Introduction, Translation, and Notes. 8vo., 16s.

Plato.—PARMENIDES OF PLATO, Text, with Introduction, Analysis, &c. By T. MAGUIRE. 8vo., 7s. 6d.

Rich.—A DICTIONARY OF ROMAN AND GREEK ANTIQUITIES. By A. RICH, B.A. With 2000 Woodcuts. Crown 8vo., 7s. 6d.

Sophocles.—Translated into English Verse. By ROBERT WHITELAW, M.A., Assistant Master in Rugby School: late Fellow of Trinity College, Cambridge. Crown 8vo., 8s. 6d.

Theocritus.—THE IDYLLS OF THEOCRITUS. Translated into English Verse. By JAMES HENRY HALLARD, M.A Oxon. 8vo., 6s. 6d.

Tyrrell.—TRANSLATIONS INTO GREEK AND LATIN VERSE. Edited by R. Y. TYRRELL. 8vo., 6s.

Virgil.—THE ÆNEID OF VIRGIL. Translated into English Verse by JOHN CONINGTON. Crown 8vo., 6s.

THE POEMS OF VIRGIL. Translated into English Prose by JOHN CONINGTON. Crown 8vo., 6s.

THE ÆNEID OF VIRGIL, freely translated into English Blank Verse. By W. J. THORNHILL. Crown 8vo., 7s. 6d.

THE ÆNEID OF VIRGIL. Books I. to VI. Translated into English Verse by JAMES RHOADES. Crown 8vo., 5s.

Wilkins.—THE GROWTH OF THE HOMERIC POEMS. By G. WILKINS. 8vo. 6s.

Poetry and the Drama.

Allingham.—Works by WILLIAM ALLINGHAM.

IRISH SONGS AND POEMS. With Frontispiece of the Waterfall of Asaroe. Fcp. 8vo., 6s.

LAURENCE BLOOMFIELD. With Portrait of the Author. Fcp. 8vo., 3s. 6d.

FLOWER PIECES; DAY AND NIGHT SONGS; BALLADS. With 2 Designs by D. G. ROSSETTI. Fcp. 8vo., 6s.; large paper edition, 12s.

LIFE AND PHANTASY: with Frontispiece by Sir J. E. MILLAIS, Bart., and Design by ARTHUR HUGHES. Fcp. 8vo., 6s.; large paper edition, 12s.

THOUGHT AND WORD, AND ASHBY MANOR: a Play. With Portrait of the Author (1865), and four Theatrical Scenes drawn by Mr. Allingham. Fcp. 8vo., 6s.; large paper edition, 12s.

BLACKBERRIES. Imperial 16mo., 6s.

Sets of the above 6 vols. may be had in uniform half-parchment binding, price 30s.

Armstrong.—Works by G. F. SAVAGE-ARMSTRONG.

POEMS: Lyrical and Dramatic. Fcp. 8vo., 6s.

KING SAUL. (The Tragedy of Israel, Part I.) Fcp. 8vo. 5s.

KING DAVID. (The Tragedy of Israel, Part II.) Fcp. 8vo., 6s.

KING SOLOMON. (The Tragedy of Israel, Part III.) Fcp. 8vo., 6s.

UGONE: a Tragedy. Fcp. 8vo., 6s.

A GARLAND FROM GREECE: Poems. Fcp. 8vo., 7s. 6d.

STORIES OF WICKLOW: Poems. Fcp. 8vo., 7s. 6d.

MEPHISTOPHELES IN BROADCLOTH: a Satire. Fcp. 8vo., 4s.

ONE IN THE INFINITE: a Poem. Cr. 8vo., 7s. 6d.

Armstrong.—THE POETICAL WORKS OF EDMUND J. ARMSTRONG. Fcp. 8vo., 5s.

Poetry and the Drama—*continued.*

Arnold.—Works by Sir EDWIN ARNOLD, K.C.I.E., Author of 'The Light of Asia,' &c.

THE LIGHT OF THE WORLD: or, the Great Consummation. A Poem. Crown 8vo., 7s. 6d. net.

Presentation Edition. With 14 Illustrations by W. HOLMAN HUNT, &c., 4to., 20s. net.

POTIPHAR'S WIFE, and other Poems. Crown 8vo., 5s. net.

ADZUMA : or, the Japanese Wife. A Play. Crown 8vo., 6s. 6d. net.

Barrow.—THE SEVEN CITIES OF THE DEAD, and other Poems. By Sir JOHN CROKER BARROW, Bart. Fcp. 8vo., 5s.

Bell.—Works by Mrs. HUGH BELL.

CHAMBER COMEDIES : a Collection of Plays and Monologues for the Drawing Room. Crown 8vo., 6s.

NURSERY COMEDIES : Twelve Tiny Plays for Children. Fcp. 8vo., 1s. 6d.

Björnsen.—Works by BJÖRNSTJERNE BJÖRNSEN.

PASTOR SANG: a Play. Translated by WILLIAM WILSON. Cr. 8vo., 5s.

A GAUNTLET. a Drama. Translated into English by OSMAN EDWARDS. With Portrait of the Author. Crown 8vo., 5s.

Cochrane.—THE KESTREL'S NEST, and other Verses. By ALFRED COCHRANE. Fcp. 8vo., 3s. 6d.

Dante.—LA COMMEDIA DI DANTE. A New Text, carefully revised with the aid of the most recent Editions and Collations. Small 8vo., 6s.

Goethe.

FAUST, Part I., the German Text, with Introduction and Notes. By ALBERT M. SELSS, Ph.D., M.A. Cr. 8vo., 5s.

FAUST. Translated, with Notes. By T. E. WEBB. 8vo., 12s. 6d.

FAUST. The First Part. A New Translation, chiefly in Blank Verse ; with Introduction and Notes. By JAMES ADEY BIRDS. Cr. 8vo., 6s.

FAUST The Second Part. A New Translation in Verse. By JAMES ADEY BIRDS. Crown 8vo., 6s.

Ingelow.—Works by JEAN INGELOW.

POETICAL WORKS. 2 vols. Fcp. 8vo., 12s.

LYRICAL AND OTHER POEMS. Selected from the Writings of JEAN INGELOW. Fcp. 8vo., 2s. 6d. cloth plain, 3s. cloth gilt.

Lang.—Works by ANDREW LANG.

BAN AND ARRIÈRE BAN. A Rally of Fugitive Rhymes. Fcp. 8vo., 5s. net.

GRASS OF PARNASSUS. Fcp. 8vo., 2s. 6d. net.

BALLADS OF BOOKS. Edited by ANDREW LANG. Fcp. 8vo., 6s.

THE BLUE POETRY BOOK. Edited by ANDREW LANG. With 12 Plates and 88 Illustrations in the Text. Crown 8vo., 6s.

Special Edition, printed on Indian paper. With Notes, but without Illustrations. Crown 8vo., 7s. 6d.

Lecky.—POEMS. By W. E. H. LECKY. Fcp. 8vo., 5s.

Leyton.—Works by FRANK LEYTON.

THE SHADOWS OF THE LAKE, and other Poems. Crown 8vo., 7s. 6d. Cheap Edition. Crown 8vo., 3s. 6d.

SKELETON LEAVES : Poems. Crown 8vo., 6s.

Lytton.—Works by THE EARL OF LYTTON (OWEN MEREDITH).

KING POPPY : a Fantasia. With 1 Plate and Design on Title-Page by Sir ED. BURNE-JONES, A.R.A. Crown 8vo., 10s. 6d.

MARAH. Fcp. 8vo., 6s. 6d.

THE WANDERER. Cr. 8vo., 10s. 6d.

LUCILE. Crown 8vo., 10s. 6d.

SELECTED POEMS. Cr. 8vo., 10s. 6d.

Macaulay.—LAYS OF ANCIENT ROME, &c. By Lord MACAULAY.

Illustrated by G. SCHARF. Fcp. 4to., 10s. 6d.

———————— Bijou Edition. 18mo., 2s. 6d., gilt top.

———————— Popular Edition. Fcp. 4to., 6d. sewed, 1s. cloth.

Illustrated by J. R. WEGUELIN. Crown 8vo., 3s. 6d.

Annotated Edition. Fcp. 8vo., 1s. sewed, 1s. 6d. cloth.

Nesbit.—LAYS AND LEGENDS. by E. NESBIT (Mrs. HUBERT BLAND). First Series. Crown 8vo., 3s. 6d. Second Series, with Portrait. Crown 8vo., 5s.

Piatt.—AN ENCHANTED CASTLE, AND OTHER POEMS : Pictures, Portraits and People in Ireland. By SARAH PIATT. Crown 8vo., 3s. 6d.

Poetry and the Drama—*continued.*

Piatt.—Works by JOHN JAMES PIATT.

IDYLS AND LYRICS OF THE OHIO VALLEY. Crown 8vo., 5s.

LITTLE NEW WORLD IDYLS. Cr. 8vo., 5s.

Rhoades.—TERESA AND OTHER POEMS. By JAMES RHOADES. Crown 8vo., 3s. 6d.

Riley.—Works by JAMES WHITCOMB RILEY.

POEMS HERE AT HOME. Fcap. 8vo., 6s. net.

OLD FASHIONED ROSES : Poems. 12mo., 5s.

Roberts. — SONGS OF THE COMMON DAY, AND AVE : an Ode for the Shelley Centenary. By CHARLES G. D. ROBERTS. Crown 8vo., 3s. 6d.

Shakespeare.—BOWDLER'S FAMILY SHAKESPEARE. With 36 Woodcuts. 1 vol. 8vo., 14s. Or in 6 vols. Fcp. 8vo., 21s.

THE SHAKESPEARE BIRTHDAY BOOK. By MARY F. DUNBAR. 32mo., 1s. 6d. Drawing-Room Edition, with Photographs. Fcp. 8vo., 10s. 6d.

Stevenson.—A CHILD'S GARDEN OF VERSES. By ROBERT LOUIS STEVENSON. Small fcp. 8vo., 5s.

Works of Fiction, Humour, &c.

Anstey.—Works by F. ANSTEY, Author of 'Vice Versâ'.

THE BLACK POODLE, and other Stories. Crown 8vo., 2s. boards, 2s. 6d. cloth.

VOCES POPULI. Reprinted from 'Punch'. With Illustrations by J. BERNARD PARTRIDGE. First Series. Fcp. 4to., 5s. Second Series. Fcp. 4to., 6s.

THE TRAVELLING COMPANIONS. Reprinted from 'Punch'. With Illustrations by J. BERNARD PARTRIDGE. Post 4to., 5s.

THE MAN FROM BLANKLEY'S: a Story in Scenes, and other Sketches. With 24 Illustrations by J. BERNARD PARTRIDGE. Fcp. 4to., 6s.

ATELIER (THE) DU LYS: or, an Art Student in the Reign of Terror. Crown 8vo., 2s. 6d.

BY THE SAME AUTHOR.

MADEMOISELLE MORI: a Tale of Modern Rome. Crown 8vo., 2s. 6d.

BY THE SAME AUTHOR—*continued.*

THAT CHILD. Illustrated by GORDON BROWNE. Crown 8vo., 2s. 6d.

UNDER A CLOUD. Cr. 8vo., 2s. 6d.

THE FIDDLER OF LUGAU. With Illustrations by W. RALSTON. Crown 8vo., 2s. 6d.

A CHILD OF THE REVOLUTION. With Illustrations by C. J. STANILAND. Crown 8vo., 2s. 6d.

HESTER'S VENTURE: a Novel. Crown 8vo., 2s. 6d.

IN THE OLDEN TIME: a Tale of the Peasant War in Germany. Crown 8vo., 2s. 6d.

THE YOUNGER SISTER: a Tale. Cr. 8vo., 2s. 6d.

Baker.—BY THE WESTERN SEA. By JAMES BAKER, Author of ' John Westacott'. Crown 8vo., 3s. 6d.

Works of Fiction, Humour, &c.—continued.

Beaconsfield.—Works by the Earl of BEACONSFIELD.

NOVELS AND TALES. Cheap Edition. Complete in 11 vols. Cr. 8vo., 1s. 6d. each.

Vivian Grey.	Contarini Fleming,
The Young Duke,	&c.
&c.	Venetia. Tancred.
Alroy, Ixion, &c.	Coningsby. Sybil.
Henrietta Temple.	Lothair. Endymion.

NOVELS AND TALES. The Hughenden Edition. With 2 Portraits and 11 Vignettes. 11 vols. Cr. 8vo., 42s.

Comyn.—ATHERSTONE PRIORY: a Tale. By L. N. COMYN. Crown 8vo., 2s. 6d.

Deland.—Works by MARGARET DELAND, Author of 'John Ward'.

THE STORY OF A CHILD. Cr. 8vo., 5s.

MR. TOMMY DOVE, and other Stories. Crown 8vo., 6s.

Dougall.—Works by L. DOUGALL.

BEGGARS ALL. Crown 8vo., 3s. 6d.

WHAT NECESSITY KNOWS. Crown 8vo., 6s.

Doyle.—Works by A. CONAN DOYLE.

MICAH CLARKE: a Tale of Monmouth's Rebellion. With Frontispiece and Vignette. Cr. 8vo., 3s. 6d.

THE CAPTAIN OF THE POLESTAR, and other Tales. Cr. 8vo., 3s. 6d.

THE REFUGEES: a Tale of Two Continents. Cr. 8vo., 6s.

Farrar.—DARKNESS AND DAWN: or, Scenes in the Days of Nero. An Historic Tale. By Archdeacon FARRAR. Cr. 8vo., 7s. 6d.

Froude.—THE TWO CHIEFS OF DUNBOY: an Irish Romance of the Last Century. By J. A. FROUDE. Cr. 8vo., 3s. 6d.

Haggard.—Works by H. RIDER HAGGARD.

SHE. With 32 Illustrations by M. GREIFFENHAGEN and C. H. M. KERR. Cr. 8vo., 3s. 6d.

ALLAN QUATERMAIN. With 31 Illustrations by C. H. M. KERR. Cr. 8vo., 3s. 6d.

MAIWA'S REVENGE; or, The War of the Little Hand. Cr. 8vo., 1s. boards, 1s. 6d. cloth.

COLONEL QUARITCH, V.C. Cr. 8vo., 3s. 6d.

Haggard.—Works by H. RIDER HAGGARD—continued.

CLEOPATRA. With 29 Full-page Illustrations by M. GREIFFENHAGEN and R. CATON WOODVILLE. Cr. 8vo., 3s. 6d.

BEATRICE. Cr. 8vo., 3s. 6d.

ERIC BRIGHTEYES. With 17 Plates and 34 Illustrations in the Text by LANCELOT SPEED. Cr. 8vo., 3s. 6d.

NADA THE LILY. With 23 Illustrations by C. H. M. KERR. Cr. 8vo., 6s.

MONTEZUMA'S DAUGHTER. With 24 Illustrations by M. GREIFFENHAGEN. Cr. 8vo., 6s.

Haggard and Lang.—THE WORLD'S DESIRE. By H. RIDER HAGGARD and ANDREW LANG. Cr. 8vo., 6s.

Harte.— IN THE CARQUINEZ WOODS, and other Stories. By BRET HARTE. Cr. 8vo., 3s. 6d.

KEITH DERAMORE: a Novel. By the Author of 'Miss Molly'. Cr. 8vo., 6s.

Lyall.—THE AUTOBIOGRAPHY OF A SLANDER. By EDNA LYALL, Author of 'Donovan,' &c. Fcp. 8vo., 1s. sewed. Presentation Edition. With 20 Illustrations by LANCELOT SPEED. Cr. 8vo., 5s.

Melville.—Works by G. J. WHYTE MELVILLE.

The Gladiators.	Holmby House.
The Interpreter.	Kate Coventry.
Good for Nothing.	Digby Grand.
The Queen's Maries.	General Bounce.

Cr. 8vo., 1s. 6d. each.

Oliphant.—Works by Mrs. OLIPHANT.

MADAM. Cr. 8vo., 1s. 6d.

IN TRUST. Cr. 8vo., 1s. 6d.

Parr.—CAN THIS BE LOVE? By Mrs. PARR, Author of 'Dorothy Fox'. Cr. 8vo., 6s.

Payn.—Works by JAMES PAYN.

THE LUCK OF THE DARRELLS. Cr. 8vo., 1s. 6d.

THICKER THAN WATER. Cr. 8vo., 1s. 6d.

Phillipps-Wolley.—SNAP a Legend of the Lone Mountain. By C. PHILLIPPS-WOLLEY. With 13 Illustrations by H. G. WILLINK. Cr. 8vo., 3s. 6d.

Robertson.—THE KIDNAPPED SQUATTER, and other Australian Tales. By A. ROBERTSON. Cr. 8vo., 6s.

Works of Fiction, Humour, &c.—*continued.*

Sewell.—Works by ELIZABETH M. SEWELL.

A Glimpse of the World. | Amy Herbert.
Laneton Parsonage. | Cleve Hall.
Margaret Percival. | Gertrude.
Katharine Ashton. | Home Life.
The Earl's Daughter. | After Life.
The Experience of Life. | Ursula. Ivors.
· Cr. 8vo., 1s. 6d. each cloth plain. 2s. 6d. each cloth extra, gilt edges.

Stevenson.—Works by ROBERT LOUIS STEVENSON.

STRANGE CASE OF DR. JEKYLL AND MR. HYDE. Fcp. 8vo., 1s. sewed. 1s. 6d. cloth.

THE DYNAMITER. Fcp. 8vo., 1s. sewed, 1s. 6d. cloth.

Stevenson and Osbourne.—THE WRONG BOX. By ROBERT LOUIS STEVENSON and LLOYD OSBOURNE. Cr. 8vo., 3s. 6d.

Sturgis.—AFTER TWENTY YEARS, and other Stories. By JULIAN STURGIS. Cr. 8vo., 6s.

Suttner.—LAY DOWN YOUR ARMS *Die Waffen Nieder:* The Autobiography of Martha Tilling By BERTHA VON SUTTNER. Translated by T. HOLMES. Cr. 8vo., 1s. 6d.

Thompson.—A MORAL DILEMMA By ANNIE THOMPSON. Cr. 8vo., 6s.

Tirebuck.—Works by WILLIAM TIREBUCK.

DORRIE. Crown 8vo., 6s.

SWEETHEART GWEN. Cr. 8vo., 6s.

Trollope.—Works by ANTHONY TROLLOPE.

THE WARDEN. Cr. 8vo., 1s. 6d.

BARCHESTER TOWERS. Cr. 8vo., 1s. 6d.

TRUE, A, RELATION OF THE TRAVELS AND PERILOUS ADVENTURES OF MATHEW DUDGEON, Gentleman: Wherein is truly set down the Manner of his Taking, the Long Time of his Slavery in Algiers, and Means of his Delivery. Crown 8vo., 5s.

Walford.—Works by L. B. WALFORD.

THE MISCHIEF OF MONICA: a Novel. Cr. 8vo., 2s. 6d.

THE ONE GOOD GUEST: a Story. Cr. 8vo, 2s. 6d.

West.—HALF-HOURS WITH THE MILLIONAIRES: Showing how much harder it is to spend a million than to make it. Edited by B. B. WEST. Cr. 8vo., 6s.

Weyman.—Works by STANLEY J. WEYMAN.

THE HOUSE OF THE WOLF: a Romance. Cr. 8vo., 3s. 6d.

A GENTLEMAN OF FRANCE.. Cr. 8vo. 6s.

Popular Science (Natural History, &c.).

Butler.—OUR HOUSEHOLD INSECTS. By E. A. BUTLER. With 7 Plates and 113 Illustrations in the Text. Crown 8vo., 6s.

Furneaux.—THE OUTDOOR WORLD; or, The Young Collector's Handbook. By W. FURNEAUX, F.R.G.S. With 16 Coloured Plates, 2 Plain Plates, and 549 Illustrations in the Text. Crown 8vo., 7s. 6d.

Hartwig.—Works by Dr. GEORGE HARTWIG.

THE SEA AND ITS LIVING WONDERS. With 12 Plates and 303 Woodcuts. 8vo., 7s. net.

THE TROPICAL WORLD. With 8 Plates and 172 Woodcuts. 8vo., 7s. net.

THE POLAR WORLD. With 3 Maps, 8 Plates and 85 Woodcuts. 8vo., 7s net.

Hartwig.—Works by Dr. GEORGE HARTWIG—*continued.*

THE SUBTERRANEAN WORLD. With 3 Maps and 80 Woodcuts. 8vo., 7s. net.

THE AERIAL WORLD. With Map, 8 Plates and 60 Woodcuts. 8vo., 7s. net.

HEROES OF THE POLAR WORLD. 19 Illustrations. Crown 8vo., 2s.

WONDERS OF THE TROPICAL FORESTS. 40 Illustrations. Crown 8vo., 2s.

WORKERS UNDER THE GROUND. 29 Illustrations. Crown 8vo., 2s.

MARVELS OVER OUR HEADS. 29 Illustrations. Crown 8vo., 2s.

SEA MONSTERS AND SEA BIRDS. 75 Illustrations. Crown 8vo., 2s. 6d.

Popular Science (Natural History, &c.).

Hartwig.—Works by Dr. GEORGE HARTWIG—*continued.*

DENIZENS OF THE DEEP. 117 Illustrations. Crown 8vo., 2*s*. 6*d*.

VOLCANOES AND EARTHQUAKES. 30 Illustrations. Crown 8vo., 2*s*. 6*d*.

WILD ANIMALS OF THE TROPICS. 66 Illustrations. Crown 8vo., 3*s*. 6*d*.

Helmholtz.—POPULAR LECTURES ON SCIENTIFIC SUBJECTS. By HERMANN VON HELMHOLTZ. With 68 Woodcuts. 2 vols. Crown 8vo., 3*s*. 6*d*. each.

Lydekker.—PHASES OF ANIMAL LIFE, PAST AND PRESENT. By R. LYDEKKER, B.A. With 82 Illustrations. Crown 8vo., 6*s*.

Proctor.—Works by RICHARD A. PROCTOR.

And see Messrs. Longmans & Co.'s Catalogue of Scientific Works.

LIGHT SCIENCE FOR LEISURE HOURS. Familiar Essays on Scientific Subjects. 3 vols. Crown 8vo., 5*s*. each.

CHANCE AND LUCK: a Discussion of the Laws of Luck, Coincidence, Wagers, Lotteries and the Fallacies of Gambling, &c. Cr. 8vo., 2*s*. boards, 2*s*. 6*d*. cloth.

ROUGH WAYS MADE SMOOTH. Familiar Essays on Scientific Subjects. Silver Library Edition. Crown 8vo., 3*s*. 6*d*.

PLEASANT WAYS IN SCIENCE. Cr. 8vo., 5*s*. Silver Library Edition. Crown 8vo., 3*s*. 6*d*.

THE GREAT PYRAMID, OBSERVATORY, TOMB AND TEMPLE. With Illustrations. Crown 8vo., 5*s*.

NATURE STUDIES. By R. A. PROCTOR, GRANT ALLEN, A. WILSON, T. FOSTER and E. CLODD. Crown 8vo., 5*s*. Silver Library Edition. Crown 8vo., 3*s*. 6*d*.

LEISURE READINGS. By R. A. PROCTOR, E. CLODD, A. WILSON, T. FOSTER, and A. C. RANYARD. Cr. 8vo., 5*s*.

Stanley.—A FAMILIAR HISTORY OF BIRDS. By E. STANLEY, D.D., formerly Bishop of Norwich. With Illustrations. Cr. 8vo., 3*s*. 6*d*.

Wood.—Works by the Rev. J. G. WOOD.

HOMES WITHOUT HANDS: a Description of the Habitation of Animals, classed according to the Principle of Construction. With 140 Illustrations. 8vo., 7*s*. net.

INSECTS AT HOME: a Popular Account of British Insects, their Structure, Habits and Transformations. With 700 Illustrations. 8vo., 7*s*. net.

INSECTS ABROAD: a Popular Account of Foreign Insects, their Structure, Habits and Transformations. With 600 Illustrations. 8vo., 7*s*. net.

BIBLE ANIMALS: a Description of every Living Creature mentioned in the Scriptures. With 112 Illustrations. 8vo., 7*s*. net.

PETLAND REVISITED. With 33 Illustrations. Cr. 8vo., 3*s*. 6*d*.

OUT OF DOORS; a Selection of Original Articles on Practical Natural History. With 11 Illustrations. Cr. 8vo., 3*s*. 6*d*.

STRANGE DWELLINGS: a Description of the Habitations of Animals, abridged from 'Homes without Hands'. With 60 Illustrations. Cr. 8vo., 3*s*. 6*d*.

BIRD LIFE OF THE BIBLE. 32 Illustrations. Cr. 8vo., 3*s*. 6*d*.

WONDERFUL NESTS. 30 Illustrations. Cr. 8vo , 3*s*. 6*d*.

HOMES UNDER THE GROUND. 28 Illustrations. Cr. 8vo., 3*s*. 6*d*.

WILD ANIMALS OF THE BIBLE. 29 Illustrations. Cr. 8vo., 3*s*. 6*d*.

DOMESTIC ANIMALS OF THE BIBLE. 23 Illustrations. Cr. 8vo., 3*s*. 6*d*.

THE BRANCH BUILDERS. 28 Illustrations. Cr. 8vo., 2*s*. 6*d*.

SOCIAL HABITATIONS AND PARASITIC NESTS. 18 Illustrations. Cr. 8vo., 2*s*.

Works of Reference.

Maunder's (Samuel) Treasuries.

BIOGRAPHICAL TREASURY. With Supplement brought down to 1889. By Rev. JAMES WOOD. Fcp. 8vo., 6s.

TREASURY OF NATURAL HISTORY: or, Popular Dictionary of Zoology. With 900 Woodcuts. Fcp. 8vo., 6s.

TREASURY OF GEOGRAPHY, Physical, Historical, Descriptive, and Political. With 7 Maps and 16 Plates. Fcp. 8vo., 6s.

THE TREASURY OF BIBLE KNOWLEDGE. By the Rev. J. AYRE, M.A. With 5 Maps, 15 plates, and 300 Woodcuts. Fcp. 8vo., 6s.

HISTORICAL TREASURY: Outlines of Universal History, Separate Histories of all Nations. Fcp. 8vo., 6s.

TREASURY OF KNOWLEDGE AND LIBRARY OF REFERENCE. Comprising an English Dictionary and Grammar, Universal Gazeteer, Classical Dictionary, Chronology, Law Dictionary, &c. Fcp. 8vo., 6s.

Maunder's (Samuel) Treasuries —continued.

SCIENTIFIC AND LITERARY TREASURY. Fcp. 8vo., 6s.

THE TREASURY OF BOTANY. Edited by J. LINDLEY, F.R.S., and T. MOORE, F.L.S. With 274 Woodcuts and 20 Steel Plates. 2 vols. Fcp. 8vo., 12s.

Roget.—THESAURUS OF ENGLISH WORDS AND PHRASES. Classified and Arranged so as to Facilitate the Expression of Ideas and assist in Literary Composition. By PETER MARK ROGET, M.D., F.R.S. Recomposed throughout, enlarged and improved, partly from the Author's Notes, and with a full Index, by the Author's Son, JOHN LEWIS ROGET. Crown 8vo., 10s. 6d.

Willich.—POPULAR TABLES for giving information for ascertaining the value of Lifehold, Leasehold, and Church Property, the Public Funds, &c. By CHARLES M. WILLICH. Edited by H. BENCE JONES. Crown 8vo., 10s. 6d.

Children's Books.

Crake.—Works by Rev. A. D. CRAKE.

EDWY THE FAIR; or, the First Chronicle of Æscendune. Crown 8vo., 2s. 6d.

ALFGAR THE DANE: or, the Second Chronicle of Æscendune. Cr. 8vo., 2s. 6d.

THE RIVAL HEIRS: being the Third and Last Chronicle of Æscendune. Cr. 8vo., 2s. 6d.

THE HOUSE OF WALDERNE. A Tale of the Cloister and the Forest in the Days of the Barons' Wars. Crown 8vo., 2s. 6d.

BRIAN FITZ-COUNT. A Story of Wallingford Castle and Dorchester Abbey. Cr. 8vo., 2s. 6d.

Ingelow.—VERY YOUNG, AND QUITE ANOTHER STORY. Two Stories. By JEAN INGELOW. Crown 8vo., 2s. 6d.

Lang.—Works edited by ANDREW LANG.

THE BLUE FAIRY BOOK. With 8 Plates and 130 Illustrations in the Text by H. J. FORD and G. P. JACOMB HOOD. Crown 8vo., 6s.

Lang.—Works edited by ANDREW LANG —continued.

THE RED FAIRY BOOK. With 4 Plates and 96 Illustrations in the Text by H. J. FORD and LANCELOT SPEED. Crown 8vo., 6s.

THE GREEN FAIRY BOOK. With 11 Plates and 88 Illustrations in the Text by H. J. FORD and L. BOGLE. Cr. 8vo., 6s.

THE BLUE POETRY BOOK. With 12 Plates and 88 Illustrations in the Text by H. J. FORD and LANCELOT SPEED. Crown 8vo., 6s.

THE BLUE POETRY BOOK. School Edition, without Illustrations. Fcp. 8vo., 2s. 6d.

THE TRUE STORY BOOK. With 8 Plates and 58 Illustrations in the Text, by C. H. KERR, H. J. FORD, LANCELOT SPEED, and L. BOGLE. Crown 8vo., 6s.

Children's Books—*continued.*

Meade.—Works by L. T. MEADE.
DEB AND THE DUCHESS. Illustrated. Crown 8vo., 3s. 6d.
THE BERESFORD PRIZE. Illustrated. Cr. 8vo., 5s.
DADDY'S BOY. Illustrated. Crown 8vo., 3s. 6d.

Molesworth.—Works by Mrs. MOLESWORTH.
SILVERTHORNS. Illustrated. Cr. 8vo., 5s.
THE PALACE IN THE GARDEN. Illustrated. Crown 8vo., 5s.
THE THIRD MISS ST. QUENTIN. Cr. 8vo., 2s. 6d.
NEIGHBOURS. Illustrated. Cr. 8vo., 6s.
THE STORY OF A SPRING MORNING, &c. Illustrated. Crown 8vo., 2s. 6d.

Reader.—VOICES FROM FLOWERLAND: a Birthday Book and Language of Flowers. By EMILY E. READER. Illustrated by ADA BROOKE. Royal 16mo., cloth, 2s. 6d.; vegetable vellum, 3s. 6d.

Stevenson.—Works by ROBERT LOUIS STEVENSON.

A CHILD'S GARDEN OF VERSES. Small fcp. 8vo., 5s.

A CHILD'S GARLAND OF SONGS. Gathered from 'A Child's Garden of Verses'. Set to Music by C. VILLIERS STANFORD, Mus. Doc. 4to., 2s. sewed; 3s. 6d., cloth gilt.

The Silver Library.

CROWN 8vo. 3s. 6d. EACH VOLUME.

Baker's (Sir S. W.) Eight Years in Ceylon. With 6 Illustrations. 3s. 6d.
Baker's (Sir S. W.) Rifle and Hound in Ceylon. With 6 Illustrations. 3s. 6d.
Baring-Gould's (Rev. S.) Curious Myths of the Middle Ages. 3s. 6d.
Baring-Gould's (Rev. S.) Origin and Development of Religious Belief. 2 vols. 3s. 6d. each.
Brassey's (Lady) A Voyage in the 'Sunbeam'. With 66 Illustrations. 3s. 6d.
Clodd's (E.) Story of Creation: a Plain Account of Evolution. With 77 Illustrations. 3s. 6d.
Conybeare (Rev. W. J.) and Howson's (Very Rev. J. S.) Life and Epistles of St. Paul. 46 Illustrations. 3s. 6d.
Dougall's (L.) Beggars All; a Novel. 3s. 6d.
Doyle's (A. Conan) Micah Clarke: a Tale of Monmouth's Rebellion. 3s. 6d.
Doyle's (A. Conan) The Captain of the Polestar, and other Tales. 3s. 6d.
Froude's (J. A.) Short Studies on Great Subjects. 4 vols. 3s. 6d. each.
Froude's (J. A.) Cæsar: a Sketch. 3s. 6d.
Froude's (J. A.) Thomas Carlyle: a History of his Life. 1795-1835. 2 vols. 7s. 1834-1881. 2 vols. 7s.
Froude's (J. A.) The Two Chiefs of Dunboy. 3s. 6d.
Froude's (J. A.) The History of England, from the Fall of Wolsey to the Defeat of the Spanish Armada. 12 vols. 3s. 6d. each.

Gleig's (Rev. G. R.) Life of the Duke of Wellington. With Portrait. 3s. 6d.
Haggard's (H. R.) She: A History of Adventure. 32 Illustrations. 3s. 6d.
Haggard's (H. R.) Allan Quatermain. With 20 Illustrations. 3s. 6d.
Haggard's (H. R.) Colonel Quaritch, V.C.: a Tale of Country Life. 3s. 6d.
Haggard's (H. R.) Cleopatra. With 29 Full-page Illustrations. 3s. 6d.
Haggard's (H. R.) Eric Brighteyes. With 51 Illustrations. 3s. 6d.
Haggard's (H. R.) Beatrice. 3s. 6d.
Harte's (Bret) In the Carquinez Woods, and other Stories. 3s. 6d.
Helmholtz's (Hermann von) Popular Lectures on Scientific Subjects. With 68 Woodcuts. 2 vols. 3s. 6d. each.
Howitt's (W.) Visits to Remarkable Places. 80 Illustrations. 3s. 6d.
Jefferies' (R.) The Story of My Heart: My Autobiography. With Portrait. 3s. 6d.
Jefferies' (R.) Field and Hedgerow. With Portrait. 3s. 6d.
Jefferies' (R.) Red Deer. With 17 Illustrations. 3s. 6d.
Jefferies' (R.) Wood Magic: a Fable. 3s. 6d.
Jefferies' (R.) The Toilers of the Field. With Portrait from the Bust in Salisbury Cathedral. 3s. 6d.

The Silver Library—*continued.*

Knight's (E. F.) The Cruise of the 'Alerte': the Narrative of a Search for Treasure on the Desert Island of Trinidad. With 2 Maps and 23 Illustrations. 3s. 6d.

Lang's (A.) Custom and Myth: Studies of Early Usage and Belief. 3s. 6d.

Lees (J. A.) and Clutterbuck's (W. J.) B.C. 1887, A Ramble in British Columbia. With Maps and 75 Illustrations. 3s. 6d.

Macaulay's (Lord) Essays and Lays of Ancient Rome. 3s. 6d.

Macleod (H. D.) The Elements of Banking. 3s. 6d.

Marshman's (J. C.) Memoirs of Sir Henry Havelock. 3s. 6d.

Max Müller's (F.) India, what can it teach us ? 3s. 6d.

Max Müller's (F.) Introduction to the Science of Religion. 3s. 6d.

Merivale's (Dean) History of the Romans under the Empire. 8 vols. 3s. 6d. ea.

Mill's (J. S.) Political Economy. 3s. 6d.

Mill's (J. S.) System of Logic. 3s. 6d.

Milner's (Geo.) Country Pleasures. 3s. 6d.

Newman's (Cardinal) Apologia Pro Vita Sua. 3s. 6d.

Newman's (Cardinal) Historical Sketches. 3 vols. 3s. 6d. each.

Newman's (Cardinal) Callista: a Tale of the Third Century. 3s. 6d.

Newman's (Cardinal) Loss and Gain: a Tale. 3s. 6d.

Newman's (Cardinal) Essays, Critical and Historical. 2 vols. 7s.

Newman's (Cardinal) The Development of Christian Doctrine. 3s. 6d.

Newman's (Cardinal) The Arians of the Fourth Century. 3s. 6d.

Newman's (Cardinal) Verses on Various Occasions. 3s. 6d.

Newman's (Cardinal) The Present Position of Catholics in England. 3s. 6d.

Newman's (Cardinal) Parochial and Plain Sermons. 8 vols. 3s. 6d. each.

Newman's (Cardinal) Selection from the 'Parochial and Plain Sermons' 3s 6d.

Newman's (Cardinal) Sermons bearing upon Subjects of the Day. 3s. 6d.

Newman's (Cardinal) Difficulties felt by Anglicans in Catholic Teaching Considered. 2 vols. 3s. 6d. each,

Newman's (Cardinal) The Idea of a University. 3s. 6d.

Newman's (Cardinal) Biblical and Ecclesiastical Miracles. 3s. 6d.

Newman's (Cardinal) Discussions and Arguments. 3s. 6d.

Newman's (Cardinal) Grammar of Assent. 3s. 6d.

Newman's (Cardinal) Fifteen Sermons Preached before the University of Oxford. 3s. 6d.

Newman's (Cardinal) Lectures on the Doctrine of Justification. 3s. 6d.

Newman's (Cardinal) Sermons on Various Occasions. 3s. 6d.

Newman's (Cardinal) Via Media of the Anglican Church, in Lectures, &c. 2 vols. 3s. 6d. each.

Newman's (Cardinal) Discourses to Mixed Congregations. 3s. 6d.

Phillipps-Wolley's (C.) Snap: a Legend of the Lone Mountain. With 13 Illustrations. 3s. 6d.

Proctor's (R. A.) Other Worlds than Ours. 3s. 6d.

Proctor's (R. A.) Rough Ways made Smooth. 3s. 6d.

Proctor's (R. A.) Pleasant Ways in Science. 3s. 6d.

Proctor's (R. A.) The Orbs Around Us. 3s. 6d.

Proctor's (R. A.) The Expanse of Heaven. 3s. 6d.

Proctor's (R. A.) Myths and Marvels of Astronomy. 3s. 6d.

Proctor's (R. A.) Nature Studies. 3s. 6d.

Smith's (R. Bosworth) Carthage and the Carthaginians. 3s. 6d.

Stanley's (Bishop) Familiar History of Birds. 160 Illustrations. 3s. 6d.

Stevenson (Robert Louis) and Osbourne's (Lloyd) The Wrong Box. 3s. 6d.

Weyman's (Stanley J.) The House of the Wolf: a Romance. 3s. 6d.

Wood's (Rev. J. G.) Petland Revisited. With 33 Illustrations. 3s. 6d.

Wood's (Rev. J. G.) Strange Dwellings. With 60 Illustrations. 3s. 6d.

Wood's (Rev. J. G.) Out of Doors. 11 Illustrations. 3s. 6d.

Cookery, Domestic Management, &c.

Acton.—MODERN COOKERY. By ELIZA ACTON. With 150 Woodcuts. Fcp. 8vo., 4s. 6d.

Bull.—Works by THOMAS BULL, M.D.

HINTS TO MOTHERS ON THE MANAGE-MENT OF THEIR HEALTH DURING THE PERIOD OF PREGNANCY. Fcp. 8vo., 1s. 6d.

THE MATERNAL MANAGEMENT OF CHILDREN IN HEALTH AND DISEASE. Fcp. 8vo., 1s. 6d.

Cookery, Domestic Management, &c.—*continued.*

De Salis.—Works by Mrs. DE SALIS.

CAKES AND CONFECTIONS À LA MODE. Fcp. 8vo., 1s. 6d.

DOGS: a Manual for Amateurs. Fcp. 8vo., 1s. 6d.

DRESSED GAME AND POULTRY À LA MODE. Fcp. 8vo., 1s. 6d.

DRESSED VEGETABLES À LA MODE. Fcp. 8vo., 1s. 6d.

DRINKS À LA MODE. Fcp. 8vo., 1s. 6d.

ENTRÉES À LA MODE. Fcp. 8vo., 1s. 6d.

OYSTERS À LA MODE. Fcp. 8vo., 1s. 6d.

PUDDINGS AND PASTRY À LA MODE. Fcp. 8vo., 1s. 6d.

SAVOURIES À LA MODE. Fcp. 8vo., 1s. 6d.

SOUPS AND DRESSED FISH À LA MODE. Fcp. 8vo., 1s. 6d.

SWEETS AND SUPPER DISHES À LA MODE. Fcp. 8vo., 1s. 6d.

TEMPTING DISHES FOR SMALL INCOMES. Fcp. 8vo., 1s. 6d.

De Salis.—Works by Mrs. DE SALIS—*continued.*

FLORAL DECORATIONS. Suggestions and Descriptions. Fcp. 8vo., 1s. 6d.

NEW-LAID EGGS: Hints for Amateur Poultry Rearers. Fcp. 8vo., 1s. 6d.

WRINKLES AND NOTIONS FOR EVERY HOUSEHOLD. Cr. 8vo., 1s. 6d.

Harrison.—COOKERY FOR BUSY LIVES AND SMALL INCOMES. By MARY HARRISON. Cr. 8vo., 1s.

Lear.—MAIGRE COOKERY. By H. L. SIDNEY LEAR. 16mo., 2s.

Poole.—COOKERY FOR THE DIABETIC. By W. H. and Mrs. POOLE. With Preface by Dr. PAVY. Fcp. 8vo., 2s. 6d.

Walker.—A HANDBOOK FOR MOTHERS: being Simple Hints to Women on the Management of their Health during Pregnancy and Confinement, together with Plain Directions as to the Care of Infants. By JANE H. WALKER, L.R.C.P. and L.M. L.R.C.S. and M.D. (Brux.). With 13 Illustrations. Cr. 8vo., 2s. 6d.

Miscellaneous and Critical Works.

Allingham.—VARIETIES IN PROSE. By WILLIAM ALLINGHAM. 3 vols. Cr. 8vo., 18s. (Vols. 1 and 2, Rambles, by PATRICIUS WALKER. Vol. 3, Irish Sketches, etc.)

Armstrong.—ESSAYS AND SKETCHES. By EDMUND J. ARMSTRONG. Fcp. 8vo., 5s.

Bagehot.—LITERARY STUDIES. By WALTER BAGEHOT. 2 vols. 8vo., 28s.

Baines.—SHAKESPEARE STUDIES, AND OTHER ESSAYS. By THOMAS SPENCER BAINES, LL.D. With a biographical Preface by Prof. LEWIS CAMPBELL. Crown 8vo., 7s. 6d.

Baring-Gould.—CURIOUS MYTHS OF THE MIDDLE AGES. By Rev. S. BARING-GOULD. Crown 8vo., 3s. 6d.

Battye.—PICTURES IN PROSE OF NATURE, WILD SPORT, AND HUMBLE LIFE. By AUBYN TREVOR BATTYE, B.A. Crown 8vo., 6s.

Boyd ('A. K. H. B.').—Works by A. K. H. BOYD, D.D.

AUTUMN HOLIDAYS OF A COUNTRY PARSON. Crown 8vo., 3s. 6d.

COMMONPLACE PHILOSOPHER. Crown 8vo., 3s 6d.

CRITICAL ESSAYS OF A COUNTRY PARSON. Crown 8vo., 3s. 6d.

EAST COAST DAYS AND MEMORIES. Crown 8vo., 3s. 6d

Boyd ('A. K. H. B.').—Works by A. K. H. BOYD, D.D.—*continued.*

LANDSCAPES, CHURCHES AND MORALITIES. Crown 8vo., 3s. 6d.

LEISURE HOURS IN TOWN. Crown 8vo., 3s. 6d.

LESSONS OF MIDDLE AGE. Cr. 8vo., 3s. 6d.

OUR LITTLE LIFE. Two Series. Cr. 8vo., 3s. 6d. each.

OUR HOMELY COMEDY: AND TRAGEDY. Crown 8vo., 3s. 6d.

RECREATIONS OF A COUNTRY PARSON. Three Series. Cr. 8vo., 3s. 6d. each. First Series. Popular Ed. 8vo., 6d. swd.

Butler.—Works by SAMUEL BUTLER.

EREWHON. Cr. 8vo., 5s.

THE FAIR HAVEN. A Work in Defence of the Miraculous Element in our Lord's Ministry. Cr. 8vo., 7s. 6d.

LIFE AND HABIT. An Essay after a Completer View of Evolution. Cr. 8vo., 7s. 6d

EVOLUTION, OLD AND NEW. Cr. 8vo., 10s. 6d.

ALPS AND SANCTUARIES OF PIEDMONT AND CANTON TICINO. Pt. 4to., 10s. 6d.

LUCK, OR CUNNING, AS THE MAIN MEANS OF ORGANIC MODIFICATION? Cr. 8vo., 7s. 6d.

EX VOTO. An Account of the Sacro Monte or New Jerusalem at Varallo-Sesioa. Crown 8vo., 10s. 6d.

Miscellaneous and Critical Works—*continued*.

Francis.—JUNIUS REVEALED By his surviving Grandson, H. R. FRANCIS. 8vo., 6s.

Halliwell-Phillipps.—A CALENDAR OF THE HALLIWELL - PHILLIPPS COLLECTION OF SHAKESPEAREAN RARITIES. Enlarged by ERNEST E. BAKER, F.S.A. 8vo., 10s. 6d.

Hodgson. — OUTCAST ESSAYS AND VERSE TRANSLATIONS. By W. SHADWORTH HODGSON. Crown 8vo., 8s. 6d.

Hullah.—Works by JOHN HULLAH.
COURSE OF LECTURES ON THE HISTORY OF MODERN MUSIC. 8vo., 8s. 6d.

COURSE OF LECTURES ON THE TRANSITION PERIOD OF MUSICAL HISTORY. 8vo., 10s. 6d.

Jefferies.—Works by RICHARD JEFFERIES.
FIELD AND HEDGEROW : last Essays. With Portrait. Crown 8vo., 3s. 6d.
THE STORY OF MY HEART : my Autobiography. Crown 8vo., 3s. 6d.
RED DEER. With 17 Illustrations. Crown 8vo., 3s. 6d.
THE TOILERS OF THE FIELD. Crown 8vo., 3s. 6d.
WOOD MAGIC: a Fable. Crown 8vo., 3s. 6d.

Johnson.—THE PATENTEE'S MANUAL: a Treatise on the Law and Practice of Letters Patent. By J. & J. H. JOHNSON, Patent Agents, &c. 8vo., 10s. 6d.

Lang.—Works by ANDREW LANG.
LETTERS TO DEAD AUTHORS. Fcp. 8vo., 2s. 6d. net.
BOOKS AND BOOKMEN. With 19 Illustrations. Fcp. 8vo., 2s. 6d. net.
OLD FRIENDS. Fcp. 8vo., 2s. 6d. net.
LETTERS ON LITERATURE. Fcp. 8vo., 2s. 6d. net.

Macfarren.—LECTURES ON HARMONY. By Sir GEO. A. MACFARREN. 8vo., 12s.

Max Müller.—Works by F. MAX MÜLLER.
HIBBERT LECTURES ON THE ORIGIN AND GROWTH OF RELIGION, as illustrated by the Religions of India. Crown 8vo., 7s. 6d.
INTRODUCTION TO THE SCIENCE OF RELIGION : Four Lectures delivered at the Royal Institution. Cr. 8vo., 3s. 6d.
[*continued*.
NATURAL RELIGION. The Gifford Lectures, 1890. Cr. 8vo., 10s. 6d.

Max Müller.—Works by F. MAX MÜLLER.—*continued*.
PHYSICAL RELIGION. The Gifford Lectures, 1890. Cr. 8vo., 10s. 6d.
ANTHROPOLOGICAL RELIGION. The Gifford Lectures, 1891. Cr. 8vo., 10s. 6d.
THEOSOPHY OR PSYCHOLOGICAL RELIGION. The Gifford Lectures, 1892. Cr. 8vo., 10s. 6d.
INDIA : WHAT CAN IT TEACH US ? Cr. 8vo., 3s. 6d.

Mendelssohn.—THE LETTERS OF FELIX MENDELSSOHN. Translated by Lady WALLACE. 2 vols. Cr. 8vo., 10s.

Milner.—COUNTRY PLEASURES: the Chronicle of a Year chiefly in a Garden. By GEORGE MILNER. Cr. 8vo., 3s. 6d.

Proctor.—Works by RICHARD A. PROCTOR.
STRENGTH AND HAPPINESS. With 9 Illustrations. Crown 8vo., 5s.
STRENGTH : How to get Strong and keep Strong, with Chapters on Rowing and Swimming, Fat, Age, and the Waist. With 9 Illus. Cr. 8vo, 2s.

Richardson.—NATIONAL HEALTH. A Review of the Works of Sir Edwin Chadwick, K.C.B. By Sir B. W. RICHARDSON, M.D. Cr., 4s. 6d.

Roget. — A HISTORY OF THE 'OLD WATER-COLOUR SOCIETY' (now the Royal Society of Painters in Water-Colours). By JOHN LEWIS ROGET. 2 vols. Royal 8vo., 42s.

Rossetti.—A SHADOW OF DANTE : being an Essay towards studying Himself, his World, and his Pilgrimage. By MARIA FRANCESCA ROSSETTI. With Illustrations and design on cover by DANTE GABRIEL ROSSETTI. Cr. 8vo., 10s. 6d.

Southey. — CORRESPONDENCE WITH CAROLINE BOWLES. By ROBERT SOUTHEY. Edited by E. DOWDEN. 8vo., 14s.

Wallaschek.—PRIMITIVE MUSIC : an Inquiry into the Origin and Development of Music, Songs, Instruments, Dances, and Pantomimes of Savage Races. By RICHARD WALLASCHEK. With Musical Examples. 8vo., 12s. 6d.

West.—WILLS, AND HOW NOT TO MAKE THEM. With a Selection of Leading Cases. By B. B. WEST, Author of 'Half-Hours with the Millionaires'. Fcp. 8vo., 2s. 6d.

www.ingramcontent.com/pod-product-compliance
Lightning Source LLC
Chambersburg PA
CBHW021114270326
41929CB00009B/872